Out of the Strange Silence
The Challenge of Being Christian in the 21st Century

Brad Thiessen, Editor

Mark D. Baker ◆ Rick Bartlett
Raymond O. Bystrom ◆ Chris William Erdman
Delores Friesen ◆ Timothy J. Geddert
Pierre Gilbert ◆ Bruce L. Guenther
Jim Holm ◆ Jon M. Isaak
Valerie Rempel ◆ Jim Westgate

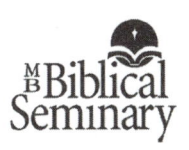

MB Biblical Seminary

Kindred Productions

Kindred Productions is the publishing arm for the Mennonite Brethren Churches. Kindred publishes, promotes and markets print and mixed media resources that help shape our Christian faith and discipleship from the Mennonite Brethren perspective.

Out of the Strange Silence
Copyright © 2005 by Mennonite Brethren Biblical Seminary: Fresno, California; Langley, British Columbia; Winnipeg, Manitoba.

All rights reserved. With the exception of brief excerpts for reviews, no part of this publicatioin may be reproduced, stored in a retrieval system or transmitted, in whole or in part, in any form by any means, electronic, mechanical, photocopying, recording, or otherwise without written permission of MB Biblical Seminary.

Unless otherwise indicated, all Scripture quotations are taken from the Holy Bible: New International Version (North American Edition), copyright © 1973, 1978, 1984 by International Bible Society. Used by permission of Zondervan.

Published simultaneously by Kindred Productions, Winnipeg MB R3M 3Z6 and Kindred Productions, Hillsboro KS 67063

Cover design and illustration by Jeremy Balzer
Printed in Canada by Friesens

National Library of Canada Cataloguing in Publication

   Out of the strange silence : the challenge of being Christian in the 21st century / Brad Thiessen, editor ; Mark D. Baker ... [et al.].

Essays written by the faculty members of the Mennonite Brethren Biblical Seminary on the occasion of its 50th anniversary.
ISBN 1-894791-05-3

1. Christianity. 2. Christian life. 3. Christian leadership. 4. Church and the world. I. Baker, Mark D. (Mark David), 1957- II. Thiessen, Brad, 1969- III. Mennonite Brethren Biblical Seminary (Fresno, Calif.)

BR481.O89 2005   270.8'3   C2005-904446-2

International Standard Book Number: 1-894791-05-3

Out of the Strange Silence

Then, suddenly, out of the strange silence and strange motion there came a tremendous roar. The Eagle Rock on the south wall, about a half a mile up the Valley, gave way and I saw it falling in thousands of ... great boulders.

... As soon as those rock avalanches fell, the streams began to sing new songs ... by what at first sight seemed pure confounded confusion and ruin, the landscapes were enriched ...

— John Muir, *The Earthquake*

Table of Contents

9   **Introduction**
Brad Thiessen

Reading Scripture Anew

19   **Hearing God's Word Together**
Timothy J. Geddert

29   **Embracing a Wider Cross: Contextualizing the Atonement**
Mark D. Baker

49   **God Talk and an Invitation to Biblical Imagination**
Jon M. Isaak

Living the Christian Life

75   **Doing What Jesus Did: A Discipleship Strategy that Really Works**
Jim Holm

85   **To Be, Not Do: Hearing God's Call on Our Lives**
Valerie Rempel

95   **Inviting Jesus into our Midst: The Challenge of Reconciliation and Mutual Accountability**
Timothy J. Geddert

Church Leadership in a New Era

111 Entering the Wreckage: Rescripting the Pastoral Vocation
Chris William Erdman

123 The Emotional Challenges of Pastoral Ministry
Raymond O. Bystrom

139 An Artistic Toolbox for Next Generation Leaders
Rick Bartlett

The Church's Place in the World

151 The Challenge of Being a Community Church in a Commuter Society
Jim Westgate

169 The Challenge of Dual Citizenship
Pierre Gilbert

185 Rediscovering the Value of History and Tradition
Bruce L. Guenther

201 Islands of Hope in the Midst of Despair
Delores Friesen

219 About the Contributors

Introduction:
The Wild Beauty-Making Business

Brad Thiessen

John Muir, one of the early American naturalists, risked his life countless times in his desire to learn more about nature and how it pointed to God. His accounts of adventures from California's Yosemite region to the glaciers of Alaska were so amazing that some doubted their truthfulness. He told of hair-raising face-to-face encounters with rattlesnakes and a grizzly. He wrote of an early visit to Yosemite, when he edged out onto a three-inch-wide ledge, water rushing over him, to peer down the length of a thousand-foot waterfall. In the midst of a fierce windstorm, he climbed to the top of a Douglas Fir to experience the power of the wind.

During a winter spent caretaking for a hotel in the Yosemite Valley, Muir woke in the middle of the night to find himself in the throes of an earthquake. He writes:

> I ran out of my cabin, both glad and frightened… The shocks were so violent and varied and succeeded one another so closely, that I had to balance myself carefully in walking as if on the deck of a ship among waves, and it seemed impossible that the high cliffs of the Valley could escape being shattered.*

The shocks lasted for several minutes, during which Muir says he "feared that the sheer-fronted Sentinel Rock, towering above my cabin would be shaken down." He continues,

> It was a calm moonlight night, and no sound was heard for the first minute or so, save low, muffled underground, bubbling

Introduction

rumblings, and the whispering and rustling of the agitated trees, as if Nature were holding her breath. Then, suddenly, out of the strange silence and strange motion there came a tremendous roar. The Eagle Rock on the south wall, about a half a mile up the Valley, gave way and I saw it falling in thousands of ... great boulders... making a terribly sublime spectacle – an arc of glowing, passionate fire, fifteen hundred feet span. ... The sound was so tremendously deep and broad and earnest, the whole earth like a living creature seemed to have at last found a voice and to be calling to her sister planets.

Instead of fleeing, Muir ran toward the rock slide and climbed up it to explore, even as the rocks were "slowly settling into their places, chafing, grating against one another, groaning, and whispering." Are these the actions of a sane man?

The following day, Muir learned that the Native Americans who lived in the valley had fled. He found "a few white settlers assembled in front of the old Hutchings Hotel comparing notes and meditating flight to the lowlands." He recalls that "the solemnity on their faces was sublime." He joked with one of them that the earthquake was merely "Mother Earth ... trotting us on her knee to amuse us ... but the well-meant joke seemed irreverent and utterly failed, as if only prayerful terror could rightly belong to the wild beauty-making business."

Muir stayed in the Yosemite Valley – not much of a surprise, given his fearless curiosity – to learn what he could from the aftershocks that followed, not knowing if another quake would come.

Muir reflects on the cataclysm not as massive destruction, but as a re-ordering of nature. "By what at first sight seemed pure confounded confusion and ruins, the landscapes were enriched," he writes. "In this work of beauty, every boulder is prepared and measured and put in its place more thoughtfully than are the stones of temples. ... As soon as these rock avalanches fell, the streams began to sing new songs."

Our Own Yosemite

We humans are, with few exceptions, like those settlers in the Yosemite Valley. Each of us has come to this life looking to build a home that will keep us warm, dry and safe. We've sought a slab of bedrock on which to build, because we don't want our home to wash away. We've sought

The Wild Beauty-Making Business

advice from those with experience in building homes, in the hope of avoiding mistakes. We've cut emotional logs that we hope are straight and airtight, so that our home will hold together. We've built a theological roof over our heads that we hope will protect us from the storm. Then we settle in, try our best to get comfortable, and pray that nothing comes along to disrupt the calm.

But whichever era we live in, we are likely to face some new challenge, some earthquake that threatens our security. Christians and the church in early twenty-first century North America seem to be at a crossroads. As we move deeper into a post-modern age, the footings of our faith tradition seem to be shaken by seismic shifts in the relationship between culture, tradition, Truth, community, relevance and faithfulness. We may feel the earth moving beneath us and wonder what destruction will come out of the strange silence. Are the beliefs and assumptions of twentieth-century North American evangelical Christianity dislodging, tumbling toward us in a faith-crushing rockslide?

In the midst of these upheavals, we can become disoriented. How much damage will the avalanche cause? When the dust has settled, will we emerge intact? The earthquake that Muir calls nature's "wild beauty-making business" can seem to us to be the voice and presence of chaos.

When the tremors have ceased, the challenge for us is to look for the good that has come. In the re-ordering that follows such upheaval, can we hear the new songs that the streams are singing? Are we able to see how God is active in our particular place and time, discern what hard lessons are being offered through our experiences?

The challenges we face in our particular culture and era demand a response. We have the option of attempting to flee the area, and that may indeed seem sensible. It may be possible to avoid troubling questions that are posed by our culture and our times, and retreat to the assumptions, pastimes and diversions that keep us comfortable. But fleeing to the safety of the known has its own risks, because earthquakes are vast and indiscriminate in their destruction; and flight deprives a person of the opportunity to see the good that can come out of the chaos.

Muir's approach points to a second option. He saw the earthquake as an opportunity to learn more about the Yosemite Valley and experience beauty in new forms. To him, the risks were far outweighed by the rewards. If God is indeed active in our world, our churches, and our

Introduction

lives, then the uncertainties of our times are not merely harbingers of destruction and death; they are signs of God's ongoing "wild beauty-making business." Our God is great, and any change brings with it new revelations of God's timeless qualities. Rather than hide from the challenges, we may grow most in our faith and knowledge of God by entering into them boldly.

A Celebration and a Challenge

September 2005 marks the fiftieth anniversary of MB Biblical Seminary. Over that time, successive generations of teachers have inspired and equipped about a thousand graduates for Kingdom ministry. They have been a voice within the Mennonite Brethren denomination and the wider church, in North America and around the globe. The Seminary's current faculty members are heirs of a legacy: their thoughts are in part the product of fifty years of theological education and spiritual formation, of one small part of Christ's body seeking to be faithful to their God, pushing at the boundaries of their faith, stretching themselves to greater openness to God's Spirit.

Two years ago, the Seminary's faculty members decided to mark the anniversary by writing a book. Over the months that followed, the guiding topic for the project took several different forms.

A spontaneous lunchtime discussion among a half-dozen faculty members on the Fresno, California campus brought the issue into focus. *If faculty members are to contribute from the heart,* the reasoning went, *the book's topic must allow each person the freedom to speak from their own passion and expertise.* Out of that lunchtime meeting came the approach to the book: each person would contribute a chapter (or two, if they chose) on what they perceive to be a particular challenge for Christians – individually, as congregations, or as the global Church – as we enter the twenty-first century.

These chapters paint pictures of what the contributors perceive to be the rumbles, the cracked earth, the sliding rock for Christians and the church today. If we think of our faith and our understanding of God as the Yosemite Valley – complex, beautiful, mysterious, and based on a firmament of millions of tons of solid rock – these chapters also invite us to be open to the changes that come to any landform over time.

The book has been divided into four sections to reflect the nature of the challenges: "Reading Scripture Anew," "Living the Christian Life," "Church Leadership in a New Era," and "The Church's Place in the World."

The Wild Beauty-Making Business

Tim Geddert begins this collection, and his chapter on "Hearing God's Word Together," with a startling statement: "Many Christians believe (or at least they act as though they believe) that there are several books far more important than the Bible. Unfortunately, we do not know exactly what is written in these books..." Using the example of Christians' varied views on divorce and remarriage, he challenges us to re-assess not our beliefs themselves, but the way at which we arrive at them. Then he describes an alternative approach to reading scripture together: not as an answer book, but as a means of encountering God's will. Is this a message we are ready to hear?

In "Embracing a Wider Cross: Contextualizing the Atonement," Mark Baker examines how our narrow understanding of Christ's death and resurrection limits the power of Christ's atonement message for many in our society and other cultures. He offers four real-life examples of how the scriptures' rich Atonement imagery can provide life-giving new understandings for Christians and the society to which we witness.

Who is this God we love and serve? How can we see and embrace the relevance of the God of the Bible in our worldview? How do the biblical images for God, like shepherd, warrior, king, judge, mother, father, etc., function today? In "God Talk and an Invitation to Biblical Imagination," Jon Isaak seeks to "re-animate the biblical invitation to imagination so that God's people today can see these ancient biblical images in new ways and be drawn once again by their invitation to encounter the one who is Alpha and Omega."

The second section, on living the Christian life, begins with Seminary president Jim Holm holding out a vision of the people of God discovering natural obedience, doing what Jesus did through ongoing discipleship, based on a deepening relationship with the Father. In "Doing What Jesus Did: A Discipleship Strategy that Really Works," he writes, "The tried and true way of discipleship, the way that has been practiced by followers of the Lord for two thousand years, is to do what Jesus did. That way is worth rediscovering in our own day."

Life in a post-modern age has, according to Valerie Rempel, caused many to call into question the nature of vocational calling. This "disease," rooted in distrust of institutions and absolutes, has created low expectations for the future. Does God really have a plan for our lives? In "To Be, Not Do: Hearing God's Call on Our Lives," Valerie, a church historian, examines the question through the lenses of the Old Testa-

Introduction

ment, Jesus and the Apostle Paul, and reformers Martin Luther and John Calvin. Her conclusion, that calling ultimately lies outside of vocation, impacts not just what work we choose, but how we view our life as a whole – a message that is applicable for all people in all vocations in all eras and situations.

In "Inviting Jesus into our Midst: The Challenge of Reconciliation and Mutual Accountability," Tim Geddert points to how Western society's movement from a nominally Christian to a pluralistic worldview has made ethical considerations more varied and cloudy than before. In the midst of this loss of absolutes, how do we become the kind of reconciled and responsible community Jesus intends? Through an examination of Matthew 18, Tim offers provocative insights into the nature of Jesus' command to treat the person who sins against you "as a gentile or a tax collector." His answer points away from the need for rigid standards and toward a church that, like Jesus, never stops trying to win that person back into fellowship. "In such a community," he writes, "Jesus is present 'in our midst.'"

The third section deals with elements of church leadership in a new era. In his chapter "Entering the Wreckage: Rescripting the Pastoral Vocation," Chris Erdman points to the collapse of Western Christendom and with it, the crisis of pastoral ministry. He holds out that if pastors are willing to embrace the twin activities of suspicion and recovery, "God is at work to birth enormously potent missional energy, converting our exhaustion, and rebirthing us for ministry among tired and terribly compromised congregations."

"It may be more difficult to be a pastor today than ever before." Opening with these words, Raymond Bystrom addresses "The Emotional Challenges of Pastoral Ministry." Based on research and personal experience, Bystrom treats ten challenges pastors face based on the nature of the pastoral role and ten challenges they face based on the nature of the pastor's personality, including a brief action plan for dealing with each challenge. He encourages pastors to discuss these emotional challenges with their church board or leadership team, asking them to think of additional actions the congregation might take to support their pastoral staff.

In "An Artistic Toolbox for Next Generation Leaders," Rick Bartlett asks, "How will we 'do church' in ten or twenty years?" As we move beyond the modern era, what qualities will young people need in order to become leaders in the emerging culture? Through an examination of various thinkers on the topic of youth leadership and emerging culture, Rick outlines the tools that will be essential for young people to be "artistic" leaders in an unknown future, and the church's role in developing these new leaders.

The fourth and final section of the book looks at the Church's place in the world. As churches increasingly move toward being commuter-based rather than invested in their local population, the result is "a major spiritual, physical and missional disconnect from the community." The result is that "those in the neighborhood often become cynical about the church and its ability to show the love of Christ in a tangible way." In "The Challenge of being a Community Church in a Commuter Society," Jim Westgate analyses how this happened and offers insight into how congregations can re-invest into a local community that may not represent who the congregation is today.

Christians today are deeply divided on what constitutes appropriate political involvement and what represents a Christian stance on the multitude of issues our society faces. Pierre Gilbert points out in his chapter "The Challenge of Dual Citizenship" that "while all Christians, regardless of religious or political persuasions, will subscribe to the necessity to do good around them, they will not necessarily agree on what constitutes the good, the degree of political activism they should engage in, and the methods that should be used." Our differences of opinions are rooted, to a great extent, in how we understand the relationship between the Kingdom of God and the kingdoms of this world. Although Christians are citizens of the Kingdom of God, they are also called to be fully engaged in the world in which they live. Pierre reflects on the paradox of the Christian's "dual-citizenship" by examining various passages in Micah, Jeremiah, and the book of Romans. He then points to sociologist Fernand Dumont's paradigm of the three levels of human interaction with the world as a model to frame how Christians can manage their status as citizens of the Kingdom and the call to fully participate in the society in which they live.

In "Rediscovering the Value of History and Tradition," Bruce Guenther takes a hard look at how the "heresy of contemporaneity" prompts Protestants to ignore the lessons and the legacy of tradition. He challenges us, first, to know and engage with our historical roots in how we read scripture, stating "it is not a question of whether a particular

Introduction

tradition or culture shapes our reading of the text, it is only a question of identifying which tradition!" Second, he challenges us to acknowledge our historical continuity within the history of the Church, to "see that the Holy Spirit has indeed been active throughout history in other denominations." Third, he challenges evangelical-Anabaptists, such as the Mennonite Brethren denomination of which MB Biblical Seminary is a part, to assess more carefully their understanding of what defines Anabaptism.

Delores Friesen takes on one of the greatest challenges to the world and the Church: the HIV/AIDS epidemic. She looks at how HIV/AIDS affects Christians and others, and how the church can and should be an island of hope. She begins "Islands of Hope in the Midst of Despair" with a story of a young man's struggle with AIDS and eventual death from the disease, and how his parents' congregation dealt with the experience. She then uncovers some of the global effects of HIV/AIDS, and four misconceptions about the disease. As she points to steps Christians can take, she writes, "This pandemic does not have just one solution. It will require 'masses of solutions.'"

The chapters in this book are together a challenge to reassess some of the bedrock on which you, and all of us as a family of faith, have based our beliefs and our practices. What does it mean to be Christian in twenty-first century North America, when many of our assumptions are being tested, and our methods are found to be less effective than in the past?

The writers of this collection hope that as we feel the earth shake beneath our feet, await the oncoming landslide, or survey the re-ordering of the valley floor, we will experience not wanton destruction and chaos but a re-ordering of nature, and that we, like Muir, will hear the streams sing new songs.

---

* All quotations and references regarding John Muir are from "The Earthquake" in *The Wild Muir: Twenty-two of John Muir's Greatest Adventures,* Lee Stetson, ed. (1994: Yosemite Association, Yosemite National Park).

Reading Scripture Anew

Hearing God's Word Together

Timothy J. Geddert

Many Christians believe (or at least they act as though they believe) that there are several books far more important than the Bible. Unfortunately, we do not know *exactly* what is written in these books – in fact we have never seen them! But we know they exist. They must exist, for they are quoted in a book that we *do* have.

So where are these books? They are in God's own heavenly library, no doubt on a bookshelf next to books like *The Lamb's Book of Life* and the scroll written on both sides, which John was privileged to see. The rest of us have never seen any of the books on God's bookshelf. But they are quoted in tiny excerpts all over the Bible. But before I talk about those excerpts, let's talk about the books themselves.

One of these books is a theology text book: *The Complete Truth About Everything Divine*. I suspect this book has pride of place on the shelf. But it is not a theology book like ours. Oh, it deals with some of the same topics: God, the persons of the Trinity, humanity, sin and salvation, the church and eschatology. But in our books on theology, each statement is carefully defended by various proof texts taken from somewhere in scripture. God's book tells the full story, reveals everything there is to know about God and everything divine. If only we could read God's book, we could check the accuracy of our theology books. Some day! By the way, there are no quotations from scripture in God's theology book. In fact, it is the other way around. There are quotations from God's theology book all over the Bible!

A second book in God's library is *The Complete Book of History*. In it we have full and comprehensive records of everything that *really* happened. Moreover, it covers all of "history" – not only human history, not

Reading Scripture Anew

only the history of the universe, but the history even of things divine. We would learn, if we could examine its contents, about the creation of the angels, the fall of Satan, the origins of the physical universe, the sequence and time-frames involved in the fashioning of the earth and the introduction of plant, animal and human life on this planet. We would learn all there is to know about the period before the flood, about the patriarchs, the origins of the nation of Israel, the conquest, the monarchy, the exile. Of course, we know a little about all this because we have the Bible. But if we could read God's history book, we would be able to fill in the gaps, know the whole story, find answers to all our controversial questions.

Of course, the "real historical Jesus" would be pictured perfectly and completely — no more need to compare and harmonize the Gospel accounts, certainly not to speculate what might lie behind them. From God's book we could learn so much more about the early church. We could settle questions about the authorship of books like Hebrews, the dating of books like Galatians, indeed the correct translation of some obscure Greek words that are found in scripture. We would know what sort of veils were worn in Corinth, whether and why people were baptizing for the dead, and just what motivated Paul to tell women to be silent in the churches. Imagine what an advantage we would have, if we could interpret scripture in the light of a perfect knowledge of history. But alas, God's complete book of history is hidden from our eyes. When we get to heaven, we'll ask God! (Or if God is busy with someone else's questions, we will look up the answer in the book!)

A third book on the divine bookshelf is a book of ethics, perhaps entitled *What is Really Right and What is Really Wrong*. I want to spend a bit more time discussing this one. Now if we had an opportunity to examine this book, we would find somewhere within its pages the Ten Commandments, for even before these laws appeared on the pages of scripture, they appeared on tablets of stone, and even before God wrote them in stone, God had written them in the comprehensive heavenly book of ethics. I am sure that somewhere within God's book of ethics we would find the commands to love God and neighbor, perhaps even word for word as these "Greatest Commands" appear either in Leviticus or in one of the Gospel records. (I am not quite sure whether we usually imagine God's books to be written in Hebrew, in Greek, or in English. Perhaps, somewhat like the miracle of tongues at Pentecost, they would appear to be written in the language preference of every person who looked into them.)

But this third book would have other very important entries as well, entries that are not exactly quoted within the pages of the Bible, or if so, only in tiny snippets. In God's book would no doubt be a page on which is explained precisely what God believes about divorce and remarriage: Are both always wrong, or perhaps only remarriage? Are there any grounds that can justify divorce (and if so, what are they)? Can a divorced and remarried person be a church leader? In short, God's book would clearly and concisely answer all the questions we debate as we try to understand scripture.

No doubt God's ethics book would have a page entitled, "Alcohol and whether it is okay to drink it." What a help it would be if we could just once read that page. Those who approve of alcohol only for medicinal purposes, Christian agencies which permit their workers to drink only in situations where it would be socially awkward to refuse, those who gladly open a bottle of champagne in special occasions, and Bavarian Christians who enjoy beer every day . . . all would finally be on the same page! Would some be horrified to realize how often they had sinned? Would others be dismayed at what they had missed out on? Who knows? We all have our opinions, but of course we cannot know for sure, since none of us have been given even a glimpse at that page in God's ethical answer book.

No doubt a lot of Christians would be in for quite a shock, were they granted the privilege of reading those pages in God's book that speak of sexual ethics, or of appropriate and forbidden financial investments, or of violence and nonviolence. In fact, I suspect that if God were to open up this book of ethics and let Christians of all ages and cultures examine its contents, then with every page turned we would hear cries of dismay from some and a loud "I told you so!" from others . . . though I strongly suspect that this exultant cry would not come from the same people each time.

Well, if some readers suspect I am being just a bit facetious, so be it. Yet sometimes when we speak tongue-in-cheek, there is still something there to chew on! In fact, indulge me if I continue to spin out the divine bookshelf idea a bit further.

I think Christians would have varying answers if we asked whether they would expect to find a copy of the *Bible* on God's bookshelf. If there were a copy of it there, it would of course be God's original copy, the one God dictated book by book over many centuries. Others might well doubt that a copy of the Bible is on God's shelf, suspecting rather that God simply spoke extemporaneously when dictating to the prophets and apostles. The "original autographs" on earth would then constitute the first ever *written* copy of God's infallible book.

But whether or not there is a heavenly copy of the Bible on God's bookshelf, the *contents* of the Bible would be there . . . for here is the upshot of all this. Many people imagine that the Bible consists of nothing more nor less than tiny snippets taken from all those other books. That is in fact why we quote Bible verses as our proof texts, when we reconstruct from all the scattered references in the Bible what God's Word *really* says.

If God had so desired, we would have been given access to the heavenly books, the ones that give complete and final answers to our questions of theology, history and ethics. But these are closed to us. Instead, God quoted from them . . . little bits here, little bits there . . . and left it to us to reconstruct what must be in them. But we have direct access only to the Bible. It is the greatest book *we have*, though it quotes from books greater still. In fact, on earth, the Bible is the one book with divine authority, for it is the only one God dictated – indeed, the only one that contains direct quotations from God's heavenly books.

The big problem: If we want to find answers to the questions that plague us, we need to figure out how all the pieces fit together. If only God had quoted full pages from those divine books! If only we could be sure how to get all the pieces back together the right way! It sometimes feels like we are trying to reconstruct pages that have been through a shredder. It's tough and we are often frustrated, but then God's ways have always been mysterious. Fortunately, we have exhaustive concordances, and diligent scholars, study conferences, and seminary courses. We never give up hope that we will get the puzzle pieces together correctly and thereby find out indirectly what is really written in God's books.

As facetious as all this may sound, I am convinced that all this is not far off from what many Christians actually believe and actually do! Take, for example, one of the topics I alluded to above, divorce and remarriage. We are all aware that there are many views as to what the Bible *really* teaches:

MB Biblical Seminary

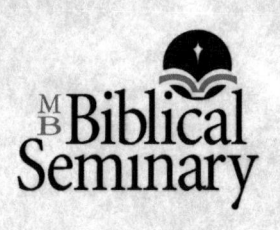

September 2006

Thank you for being such a faithful supporter of the mission of MB Biblical Seminary during the past year. I am enclosing with this note a special thank you gift that is being sent to friends like you. On the occasion of the seminary's 50th anniversary, our faculty members wrote a book which tries to identify some of the major issues facing the MB church at the beginning of the twenty-first century. I invite you to share in the thinking of our faculty.

Thank you for being a partner in fulfilling the mission of the seminary.

Jim Holm
President

- divorce and remarriage are always wrong;
- divorce is wrong except in the cases of adultery or abandonment, and remarriage after a divorce is always wrong unless the divorced partner has died;
- remarriage is wrong unless the preceding divorce was justified on the basis of one of the two "grounds for divorce" recognized by scripture;
- divorce and remarriage are acceptable if and only if thereby a great evil is averted;
- etc.

Now, of course, these cannot all be correct; indeed the defenders of each view argue that their view is the correct one; everyone else has gotten it wrong! Put another way, each claims their view corresponds to what is written on the appropriate page of God's ethics book, and that the other views result from putting the scattered pieces together wrongly. So our beliefs vary widely. But the *method behind* each of the views is pretty much the same. We get out a concordance and look up every reference in scripture where the word "divorce" appears. All the texts are then laid out on the table (usually without very much of the context still attached to the relevant verses). And now begins the arduous task of seeing how the pieces fit together. After all, we need to reconstruct the page that God cut up into little pieces and scattered all over the Bible. And obviously God's original page made good sense, represented a coherent, and of course the correct, view. So the pieces we have found must fit harmoniously together, somehow. Correctly interpreted, Matthew 5:31,32, including the so-called "exception clause," must harmonize with the correct interpretation of Mark 10:11,12, where all exceptions seem to be excluded. Moreover, Matthew 19:3-9 and Luke 16:18 somehow have to say the same thing as well, not to mention Romans 7:1-3, 1 Cor. 7:8-16 and (depending on our view of the Old Testament's continuing relevance) Deuteronomy 24:1-4. Why do people come up with varying views on what the Bible teaches? Because they fit the pieces together differently — because they twist and bend the pieces into varying shapes in order to get them to fit together at all — because they can't quite agree on exactly which texts should be included in the reconstructed picture.

Reading Scripture Anew

It is like putting together a jigsaw puzzle – only harder. When we put a jigsaw puzzle together, we sometimes make mistakes along the way. But we eventually correct them. If a piece is turned the wrong direction or attached in the wrong place, we eventually get stuck, and are unable to finish the reconstruction. We discover our mistake eventually and move on. When the picture is complete, we know that each piece is in the right place and that the resulting picture is the one the manufacturers intended. Here is where "reconstructing God's page" is tougher. As with jigsaw puzzles, we need to find the pieces that fit together. Only here the pieces do not fit together quite as neatly. In fact the pieces fit (sort of) in a variety of ways. Various pictures emerge, depending on which way a piece is turned and to which pieces it is attached. And there is no picture on the puzzle box for us to use as a reference. In the end we find a way to make the pieces fit, and we see which picture emerges. If only we could be sure it looks like the one in God's heavenly book! We are quite sure it does, but our critics also think theirs is the correct reconstruction. We can't both be right.

Does anyone really believe that this jigsaw method (we could also call it the "concordance method") is a helpful and reliable way of discovering anything important, anything true? Just imagine if my children would practice it on me. How might that look?

Well, we sometimes have chocolates or other sweets in the house. But the children are not allowed to help themselves at will. There have to be some controls. Now suppose I actually were a consistent parent, and that I had guidelines, reasonable guidelines, which determined whether or not it was an appropriate time for the children to help themselves to a candy. But suppose I refused the kids direct access to what those guidelines were (perhaps they were written clearly in my journal, which I kept secret from them). Moreover, what if the children desperately wanted to know my *real* guidelines, but all I would say to them was, "You've heard me talk about this before; you should know what I believe!" I would pretty much be forcing them to use the jigsaw puzzle method.

They would try to recall every time I had ever made a comment about candies. Then they would take all my statements and lay them out on the table (without remembering the original contexts, note well). Then they would look for the hidden harmony behind all the statements, by trying to get them all to fit together. Their recall might not be perfect, but since they would disagree on my true guidelines, each of the children would help the others remember statements of mine that the others were forgetting. Once the pieces were there on the table, spread out like pieces of a jigsaw puzzle, they would try to make them all fit together. They would write their own reconstructed version of what's really written in Dad's hidden journal.

Truth is, our children do more of that than we know what to do with! Like the time Benjamin came to me and said, "Yesterday you let Kristina have a candy when she finished playing piano. I just played the piano, so I'm going to go get a candy, okay?" The trouble is, yesterday it was 4:00 pm and now it is ten minutes before supper. Moreover, Kristina diligently practiced for her lesson, whereas Benjamin pounded on the keys for a few minutes and doesn't even take piano lessons!

Does anyone seriously believe that this method helps anyone learn anything important, let alone discover God's guidance when we have serious questions?

So What is the Alternative?

God does not have a bookshelf. In heaven there is no theology book, no *Complete Book of Everything Divine*. Instead, there is God. The goal of Bible study is not to find, with the help of a concordance, ten verses that prove that God is omnipotent, another ten proving God is omniscient, and so on. The goal of Bible study is to catch glimpses of God! Some pages will reveal a radiant smiling artist, some a tear-filled father with outstretched arms, some a benevolent king, perhaps with a child on his lap, some a concerned parent, a mighty warrior, or a gentle loving shepherd. As we read and relive the stories of scripture (leaving each text in its context), we learn to know this God. And we learn to approach God appropriately, depending upon our circumstances and our needs.

In heaven there is no complete book of history. Indeed, history is not complete! God is still making history, along with us. But God has a goal and God is faithful. And on the pages of scripture we read stories of God's past faithfulness, so that we can learn to trust God for the future. We catch glimpses of God intervening in human affairs (or better worded, helping humans discover that living is a divine affair). And then we are reassured that God will not abandon us, whatever we face. Scripture offers us something far more important than historical facts: it reveals that God makes all life meaningful, whatever happens to us – whatever happened in the past, whatever will happen in the future.

Reading Scripture Anew

In heaven there is no once-for-all answer book for every ethical question. Rather there is a holy God! And God's holiness is not measured by rules that prescribe what is allowed and forbidden. Rather God is "set apart" . . . a God unlike all other gods. The other gods we worship are legalistic gods, or capricious gods, or indulging gods. We worship them because we want the security of easy answers, or the freedom to do as we please, or vending machines to give us our hearts' desires. The holy God warns us against those things that will hurt us, calls us to do that which builds up others, continues to love us when we fail to understand or fail to follow, and molds us to be holy ourselves.

We cannot completely do without theology books, and history books, and ethics books. But let us never presume that our books somehow correspond exactly with books on a heavenly bookshelf. And let's never let our books become infallible guides for how to read scripture. Let's let only God be that! And let's remember that even though we have an infallible guide, we are not infallible followers. We catch only glimpses of the God who appears on scripture's pages. We hear only echoes of the God who guides our reading of scripture. Sometimes we see only faint signposts on the road of life, showing us which way to turn. And so we need each other.

We need each other as we read scripture together. We need each other so that we can see more in each story than any one of us can see alone. We need each other so that others can remind us of other biblical stories that we would rather suppress in order to focus on our personal favorites (the ones that clearly support our preferred opinions). We need each other in order that our diverse experiences of God can help us appreciate the diverse accounts in scripture. We need each other to guard us against too quickly harmonizing everything (and in the process making scripture say what we want to hear).

In case all this has been too theoretical – in case a concrete example is needed to show what I think all this means for us when we gather around scripture – I return to the example of divorce and remarriage.

The Bible does not provide us with tiny snippets from a "divorce-remarriage" page in God's eternal ethics book. Rather the Bible gives us, before all else, portraits of Jesus. If we used the concordance method, Mark 2:23-28 would never enter a discussion on divorce and remarriage. After all the word "divorce" does not appear in that text. But Mark 2:23-28 and many other Gospel texts teach us that Jesus places humans and their needs above all human rules, even above some biblical rules. And so that text has everything to do with the question, for it tells us that no matter what rules we construct from or discern in scripture, there may well be situations where the unique needs of the affected individuals must take precedence.

Using the concordance method, we would set Deuteronomy 24:1-4 alongside Mark 10:2-12 and then try to harmonize them, never noticing that in Mark 10 Jesus tells the Pharisees that Deuteronomy 24 is the wrong text in which to find an answer to their question! And the right text to which Jesus directs them (Gen. 2:24) would not even be among our jigsaw pieces, for the word "divorce" does not appear in that text.

The concordance method would regularly lead us to make two texts say the same thing, when in fact they often quite deliberately say opposite things. We should not expect them to say the same thing, if they provide answers to different questions asked by different people in different situations!

As I have studied the "divorce texts" in scripture, I have become convinced that their diversity is not a problem to be solved, but a blessing to be discovered. Every biblical text is part of God's inspired Word. But not every text contains the right answer to whatever question we might happen to be asking. When we carefully observe how each text provides glimpses of God's will for the specific situations they were intended to address, we gain a heart of wisdom, so that we can discern God's responses to the situations we face. If we ignore the contexts and simply try to read the words off the page, we hear God's will far less clearly.

Some people fear the open-endedness that results when we abandon the "one answer fits all" approach. I have a much greater fear of an exaggerated longing for clear and simple answers. In fact if our primary method is to gather verses with a concordance and force them to fit like a jigsaw puzzle, the danger looms large that we will find clever strategies for making the Bible say what we want it to say, and then devise subtle (or not so subtle) ways of imposing our will on others.

"God said it! I believe it! That settles it!" That sounds so pious and safe and conservative. But please don't try it at home! Rather let us be shaped together by the Word of God as we read it together, as we allow it to shape our view of God and the world, as we are drawn into the stories, as we catch glimpses of God along the way, as we trust the

Spirit to guide our reflections, as we model our lives after the heart of Jesus. We so much want once-for-all clear and permanent answers to all our questions. But we are far better off with a Living Word. That is, no doubt, why God gave us that instead of what some people might have preferred.

Embracing a Wider Cross: Contextualizing the Atonement

Mark D. Baker

A seminary education generally shapes students gradually: skills develop through observation and practice, information is added piece by piece or story by story, and character is slowly sculpted. There are moments, however, when a single book, discussion, experience or lecture causes immediate and radical change. Reading Gustaf Aulén's book *Christus Victor* provided one of those transformational moments during my seminary education.

Before reading Aulén, I had not thought deeply about the meaning and significance of Christ's death. I had little need to – its meaning was clear and obvious. For many years I had understood and explained to others how Jesus' dying on the cross provided atonement, the possibility of restored relationship with God: through his suffering, Jesus took on the punishment for our sin that God demanded and we deserved. Once this demand for punishment was satisfied, God could justly pardon us. I articulated this view of the atonement long before I knew its name: penal satisfaction theory.

Aulén, however, advocated a different explanation of the atonement. He emphasized that our salvation comes through Christ's triumph over sin, death and the powers of evil. Aulén's book radically changed my perspective not because he led me to switch my explanation of the atonement for his, but because his book opened up to me the reality that there is more than one way of understanding how the cross and resurrection provide our salvation. I discovered that what I had assumed was the one and only way of explaining the atonement, the theory of penal satisfaction, was in fact relatively new – for the first thousand years of Christianity the Church had not thought of the cross as a payment that appeased God's wrath, but as a victory over the devil.

Reading his book brought me to a totally new place. There opened before me a door I had not known existed. Stepping through that door produced new thoughts and convictions that led to further study and eventually led me to write a book with Joel Green, *Recovering the Scandal of the Cross: Atonement in New Testament and Contemporary Contexts*. In the book we argue that contemporary Christians would do well to follow the example of the biblical writers and first missionaries. Rather than relying on a single explanation of the atonement, we should be open to using a variety of images and metaphors to proclaim the saving significance of the cross and resurrection.

Transformation Through the Cross: Stories from Differing Contexts

The four stories that follow display some of the problems caused by using just one explanation of the atonement, one that describes the cross as satisfying God's demand for punishment. They also point to the life-changing potential of imitating scripture and using a full range of atonement images.

A Japanese pastor asked Norman Kraus, a Mennonite missionary, "Why did Jesus have to die?" The pastor immediately clarified that he knew the answer – that Jesus had to die to pay the penalty that God required for our sins – but that he did not find the explanation satisfying. Kraus pondered the question over the course of several months. He concluded that the traditional penal satisfaction explanation of the atonement was intelligible in a guilt-based society such as ours, which understand wrongs as an infraction against a legal or moral code. This guilt could be remedied through punishment that would relieve guilt. However, that same explanation would be foreign and unintelligible in a shame-based society like Japan, where both the wrong committed and the remedy are understood and felt in more relational ways. The wrongdoer is ridiculed or removed and hence feels alienation and shame, not guilt. When Kraus set aside the penal satisfaction model and read with new eyes, he found rich biblical material, including specific references to shame, that allowed him to proclaim to the Japanese how the cross and resurrection of Jesus Christ provides freedom from the burden of shame and restores their relationship with God. By opening up to more than one biblical explanation of the atonement, we can talk of Jesus bearing our shame and healing our alienation, in an ultimate sense, through the cross and resurrection. This has great evangelistic potential and pastoral significance not only in "shame-based" cultures, but also in North America where people can be burdened by both guilt and shame.

A woman grew up in a troubled home in which her relationship with her father was almost exclusively one of fear. That experience made it easy for her to imagine her heavenly Father as a strict disciplinarian as well. Her church's teaching on the cross exacerbated the problem. She drifted away from the church because, in her words, "Any God that demanded the death of his son in order to forgive is a God I want nothing to do with." Recently, however, a pastor lent her *Recovering the Scandal of the Cross*. Reading it was life-giving and transformational. She encountered alternative explanations of the atonement that "blew away her categories." Her relationship with God has developed into something deep, rich and beautiful.

When I left behind the need to have one theory that captured the full significance of the cross, a wonderful thing happened: I was free to use presentations of the saving significance of the cross and resurrection that I would have previously rejected as being incomplete. The reality is that any image or explanation is incomplete, which is one of the reasons we find multiple images of atonement in the Bible. For instance, we can look at Jesus' life and death and ask, "What does Jesus' vulnerably entering into our human situation, his gracious forgiving attitude, his willingness to suffer for the sake of others and his refusal to seek revenge reveal to us about the character of God?" Although that question falls short of communicating a full understanding of the atonement, it could have significant transformational impact for someone like the woman described in the preceding paragraph, and contribute to her salvation. The revelatory nature of the cross is part of its saving power.

Jon Isaak, a MB Biblical Seminary professor, recently taught in the Congo for two weeks. He perceived that students experienced a disconnect between the theology they received from the West and their daily life, including their experiences of the role of evil as an active power. Jon led his students through the same door Gustaf Aulén opened to me, and together they read texts of salvation in new ways. For example, Jon observes, "Colossians 2:15 describes Jesus' death in ways that are rarely utilized in western theology, with its preference for personal forgiveness. Instead, this text describes Jesus' death as that which 'disarmed the rulers and authorities and made a public example of them, triumphing over them in it."[1] The cross is central in Christianity and it should not surprise us that once these students saw the connection between the cross and their daily lives they also began to see greater connections between other theological themes and their lived reality.

John Shorack, a missionary with InnerChange in Venezuela, lived with a disconnect as well, between the cross and its implications for the Church's ministry in the world. His understanding of the atonement presented the cross as a legal transaction that declares us righteous without changing us. In his context, this understanding renders the cross powerless to inspire or instruct and in his words, "leaves the Church with weak converts who experience a measure of joy and relief at receiving forgiveness from their sins." Reading *Recovering the Scandal of the Cross* enabled him to develop a theology of the atonement that is integrally related to his church's living out the way of the cross in a poor neighborhood. He is now working with Venezuelan church leaders to exchange their former theory of atonement for images that empower them and give a compelling vision of a life-reorienting relationship with the God who forgives them.

But the Bible Says...

I hope that reading these stories awakens within you the desire to look beyond penal satisfaction theory as the only explanation of the atonement, so you can begin to explore the variety of ways we can understand and communicate God's saving work. I can also imagine that the examples leave you with many questions. Even if, from the above stories, you can sense the benefit of using different images of atonement, it may be that when you read the Bible you do not see alternatives, but only penal satisfaction. You may ask, "How can you critique penal satisfaction when the Bible so clearly teaches it?" I cannot in one chapter explore in detail even the most prominent biblical texts on this topic, nor hope to answer all the questions you might have. I will, however, make a few comments that can help those with questions imagine the possibility that there are other ways of reading the biblical texts that to their eyes so clearly teach that Jesus died on the cross to appease God the Father so that God could forgive us.

A first step in imagining this possibility might be recognizing that for centuries Christians did not see penal satisfaction in the Bible at all, and Orthodox Christians still read their Bibles without seeing it. Frederica Mathews-Green, writing from an Orthodox perspective, states that with a few exceptions Christian writers before Anselm believed that God did in fact freely forgive us like the father in the Prodigal Son. She asks:

> Would Christians really have misunderstood their salvation for a thousand years? Did the people Paul wrote his letters to have no idea what he was talking about? Did the early martyrs die without understanding the Cross that saved them? . . . Before Anselm (1033-1109), the problem salvation addresses is seen as located in us. We are infected by death as a result of Adam's fall. This infection will cause us to be spiritually sick and to commit sin. ... Christ offers a rescue. ... With Anselm, the problem of salvation is between us and God (we have a debt we can't pay). After Anselm it is even sometimes formulated as *within* God (His wrath won't be quenched until the debt is paid).[2]

She observes that "when we speak of Christ paying with his blood we don't necessarily have to imagine a two-sided transaction." She gives a contemporary example. If a policeman rescued some hostages, but was wounded in the process, we might say, "he paid with his blood." "But that doesn't mean the kidnappers were left gloating over a vial of blood."[3]

A glance at history and a glance through Orthodox lenses invites us to imagine other possibilities as we look at texts that appear to "clearly" communicate penal satisfaction. Looking at the broader biblical text and observing texts in tension with penal satisfaction may be a helpful next step in imagining other readings of "penal satisfaction texts." Raymund Schwager points out a few of these points of tension:

> According to the doctrine of infinite satisfaction, one is indeed fully justified in speaking of a transfer of Christ's merits to all repentant sinners. But this overlooks that it is not just the punishment for sins but the sins themselves that were transferred to the holy one. Yet it is precisely this process that the New Testament writings stress so clearly. Furthermore, the image of God that stood behind the long-accepted satisfaction theory

can hardly be brought into harmony with the father to whom Jesus repeatedly referred. The parables of the prodigal son (Luke 15:11-32) and the merciless creditor (Matt 18:23-35) make it clear that God forgives without demanding satisfaction and payment in return. He demands only that we forgive others as unconditionally as we are granted unconditional mercy. ... The Gospel of Matthew goes so far as to put the parable of the merciless creditor in direct connection with Jesus' command to his disciples to forgive without limit. ... If Jesus demands of human beings a limitless forgiveness, then the Father whom he makes known must be even more willing to do so.[4]

Although Paul has written a number of the texts which many would point to as "clearly" describing salvation through penal satisfaction, we can also find texts from his writings that are in tension with penal satisfaction. Some clearly portray *Christus Victor* imagery (I Cor. 2:6-8; Col. 2:15), and others communicate ideas in direct tension with the logic of penal satisfaction. For instance, note the direction of the reconciling work in this verse: "All this is from God, who reconciled us to himself through Christ" (II Cor. 5:18). In contrast, penal satisfaction describes the cross's action as directed towards God and changing something that allows God to be reconciled to us. William Placher observes,

> It is worth noting that focusing on God's need to be reconciled to us gets things backwards, from the New Testament standpoint. For Paul, it is we who need to be reconciled to God, not the other way around. God's love endures; it is our sin that has broken our relationship with God; it is we who like sheep have gone astray. The barriers that have to be broken down in reconciliation were built from our side.[5]

The tension between these biblical passages and penal satisfaction can buttress the possibility that there may be other ways of reading those texts that "clearly" teach penal satisfaction. Even, however, if one wants to imagine other readings it is often quite difficult to do so if one has always read them as texts describing penal satisfaction.

For example, a student in a Christology class who was both engaged by and sympathetic to our book, *Recovering the Scandal of the Cross,* stated,

"I want to agree with what you are saying, but I was reading Romans and there it is plain and simple, 'the wages of sin is death' (6:23). It's penal satisfaction. How can you say the cross is not a penalty for our sins that God demands?" The student could imagine no other possibility.

There are, however, other ways of reading this verse. First of all, there are options regarding who we picture as the paymaster, the one making the payment of death. Penal satisfaction pictures God delivering this payment. One could just as easily picture Satan as paying out death. Or we could also imagine sin itself paying the wage of death. The latter two provide images of atonement quite different than penal satisfaction. Secondly, we can picture the payment taking place in different ways. Penal satisfaction would tend to view it as a punishment given out by a judge (God) in response to a sinful life. We can also, however, read this as saying that a sinful life causes death. It is what sin pays – what it leads to. Sin gives death, and God's gift is life. In this latter picture death is an integrated consequence of the sinful life itself. Our sin leads to death. Jesus enters into our world and lives in a way that causes him to suffer the ultimate consequence of sin – death, rejection – not because God demanded that penalty in order to be appeased, but because that is what our alienation causes, leads to. But the gift of God, the response of God, is life, forgiveness.

As a final exercise in imagining other readings of a text that "clearly" indicates penal satisfaction, I will briefly look at two verses from a section of Romans 3 on which we could easily spend chapters exploring the reasoning for various readings.

> Being justified freely by his grace through the redemption that is in Christ Jesus: Whom God hath set forth to be a propitiation through faith in his blood, to declare his righteousness. . . (Rom. 3:24-25 KJV).

> They are justified by his grace as a gift, through the redemption which is in Christ Jesus, who God put forward as an expiation by his blood, to be received by faith. This was to show God's righteousness. . . (Rom. 3:24-25 RSV).

> . . . justified freely by his grace through the redemption that came by Christ Jesus. God presented him as a sacrifice of atone-

ment, through faith in his blood. He did this to demonstrate his justice. . . (Rom. 3:24-25 NIV).

They are now justified by his grace as a gift, through the redemption that is in Christ Jesus, who God put forward as a sacrifice of atonement by his blood, effective through faith. He did this to show his righteousness. . . (Rom. 3:24-25 NRSV).

For many, to read these lines is to hear a statement of the basic tenets of penal satisfaction. If one reads the phrase "sacrifice of atonement" through the lens of penal satisfaction (or with the King James Version's "propitiation" echoing in your mind) it would appear this clearly teaches that the cross brings salvation through penal satisfaction. Are there other ways to understand "sacrifice of atonement?" Clearly the translators of the Revised Standard Version thought so because they chose the word "expiation" rather than "propitiation" or "sacrifice of atonement."

The Greek word *hilastērion* can be translated as: mercy seat (or place of atonement in the holy of holies), propitiation (atonement through an offering of appeasement that turns away divine wrath), or expiation (atonement through the covering over or obliterating of sin). Heated debate has taken place over the translation of this word. The NIV and NRSV have done well to use "sacrifice of atonement" and thus allow for interpretation as either propitiation or expiation. I will not attempt to even summarize the debate, let alone resolve it.[6] I bring up the debate, and the various translations, to highlight that to read this verse as describing Jesus paying the penalty of our sins and appeasing God's wrath is a possible reading, but not the only possible reading. One can also easily read this in the direction pointed to above in relation to the II Corinthians text: the cross as an action aimed not at satisfying God's need to punish, but at breaking down a barrier on the human side that prevents relationship with God.

Of course I have only addressed one word in these verses, and one might quickly point to the phrase about this atoning act being a demonstration of God's justice or righteousness, and claim that is the key to showing us how to translate and interpret *hilastērion*. Here again, however, we can read the text in different ways. From the perspective of penal satisfaction, God demonstrates justice or righteousness by carrying out the punishment humans deserved, which then allows God to pardon our sins while still satisfying a standard of justice which demands punishment. But one can argue that such a reading places the transformative significance of Christ's death in the wrong place. What is required is not a transformation within God's heart toward sinners; rather, justice comes through a transformation of their sinful existence before God. And to present those two options is not to even bring up the issue of how we are interpreting the word "justice." Through the lens of a Western legal system one is just because one meets the standard of the law. But a Hebraic understanding of justice is more relational: one is just because one keeps one's covenants and commitments to others.[7] So we could say that God is considered just not because of meeting a standard which says a penalty is required, but because God is faithful to the covenantal promise to provide salvation to Israel and through Israel, to the world.

As the last few sentences demonstrate, our interpretations of biblical texts on the atonement are dependent on and intertwined with our understanding of a number of other biblical and theological concepts such as sin, judgment, mercy, justice and salvation, to name a few—all the more reason why in a few pages I cannot offer an adequate argument for or against any particular approach to the atonement. Hopefully, however, I have said enough to open up the possibility of the Bible presenting other approaches to the atonement than penal satisfaction. For a more complete discussion I refer readers to our book *Recovering the Scandal of the Cross*.

Following the New Testament Model

One could read this chapter as being missiologically driven. The four stories at the beginning of the chapter communicate both the necessity and potential of contextualizing the message of the cross and resurrection. In reality, however, the chapter is biblically driven. To proclaim the saving significance of the cross and resurrection using a variety of images, and adapting those images to different contexts, is not a twenty-first century missiological innovation. Rather it is something we learn from the theologian/missionaries in the New Testament.

In their struggle to make sense of Jesus' crucifixion, the New Testament writers drew on the language and thought patterns of Israel's religion and on life experiences within the larger Greco-Roman world. Within the pages of the New Testament, the saving significance of the death of Jesus is represented chiefly (though not exclusively) via five constellations of images. Each is borrowed from a significant sphere of public life in ancient Palestine and the larger Greco-Roman world: the court of law (e.g., justification), commercial dealings (e.g., redemption), personal relationships (whether among individuals or groups—e.g., reconciliation), worship (e.g., sacrifice), and the battleground (e.g., triumph over evil).

Why are so many images enlisted in the atonement theology of the New Testament? First, because language for the atonement is metaphorical,[8] and given the nature of metaphor, it is unthinkable that one soteriological model could express all of the truth. Hence, even if Christians have always spoken with one voice in their affirmation of Jesus as our Savior, this affirmation has been understood in a variety of ways already in the New Testament, and certainly since.

A second reason for this plurality is pastoral. The language in which one construes the efficacy of Jesus' death is dependent in part on the needs one hopes to address. "Very different models and categories are used to describe the 'lost' condition of the human race prior to Christ. ... Different descriptions of the human situation inevitably lead to different explanations of how this has been altered by the work of Christ."[9] If people are lost, they need to be found. If they are oppressed by hostile powers, they need to be delivered. If they exist in a state of enmity, they need to be reconciled. And so on.

Third, a plurality of metaphors is used to draw out the salvific significance of Jesus' death and resurrection because of wider cultural considerations. If the message of salvation is to be grasped in ever-expanding cultural circles, then that message must be articulated in culture-specific ways.

Thus a central and fundamental guideline we learn from the New Testament authors is the importance of using a variety of images to proclaim the scandal of the cross, and that different contexts will require different metaphors. If we wish to be faithful to scripture, we too must continuously seek out metaphors, new and old, that speak effectively and specifically to our various worlds. Yet, if we follow in the path of the New Testament writers, the metaphors we deploy will be at home, but never too comfortable, in our settings. Those writers sought, and we seek, not only to be understood by but also to shape people and social systems around us. Moreover, we will not eschew earlier models or the reality to which they point, but will carry on our constructive work fully in conversation with, and under the guidance of, the scriptures of Israel and the Church, and of apostolic testimony.

Contextualizing the Atonement for Today: An Example[10]

Presentations of the atonement that portray the cross in terms of the penal satisfaction theory do connect with some people. As the stories at the beginning of the chapter portray, however, they do not connect with others; they fail to communicate the full breadth of the saving significance of the cross and resurrection and they potentially distort people's concept of God. Therefore to widely and successfully proclaim the full message of the cross we must develop new images and metaphors for the diverse contexts in which we minister in the twenty-first century.

I end this chapter with one example of my efforts to do what I challenged you to do in the previous paragraph. What follows is a parable to the junior high Sunday school class at College Community Church (Mennonite Brethren) in Fresno, California. Through the parable I sought to communicate the relationship between Jesus' life, the atoning work of the cross, and the saving significance of the cross in a way that connects with as well as challenges the world of the students in the class. The parable:

> On the central California coast was a town that had no public beach. The twists and turns of the rocky coastline hid a number of sandy coves, but all of them were completely surrounded by private estates and had no public access.
>
> A few years ago, an older man who owned one of these estates began feeling sorry for the local young people who had to travel to the next town up the coast to swim, surf, or play on a beach. He decided to invite them to enjoy his beach. At all the local schools the man put up posters announcing that he was opening up his beach, and telling the youth they would find a clearly marked access path near his driveway on 342 Ocean Drive.
>
> The man did not, however, simply open up the path. He thought carefully about helping young people have as good a time as possible on the beach. He gathered up some old boogie boards, surfboards and wetsuits from his garage, and even bought some used ones from a surf shop in a nearby town. He could remember how frustrated he had been as a

teenager when he could only stay in the cold water a little while because he didn't have a wetsuit like many others did. He had a local carpenter build a shed to store the equipment in and even put a few volleyballs and nets in it as well.

The owner welcomed all of the town's youth to use the beach, and stated this plainly on the sign at the top of the path to the beach. Although the welcome was unrestricted he did limit some activities. He wanted to enhance everyone's beach experience and knew that too many people on a side in volleyball, or too many surfers trying to catch one wave, made it worse for everyone. So he posted a sign on the beach that designated one side of the beach for boogie boarding and swimming and the other side for surfing; the sign stated that no more than ten people at a time should surf (and if more wanted to they should work out a rotation system that would let all get a chance); it also stated that no more than nine players should be on each side in volleyball; the sign encouraged everyone to remember to wear sun screen; and finally, the sign invited the youth to drop by and visit the owner as they left the beach. Many began using the beach and some did stop by, sit with him on his deck , have a coke and talk for awhile.

Although the man was too old to do much more than take morning and evening walks on the beach, he loved sitting out on the deck and watching others have fun on his beach. As the months and seasons passed, however, he became confused and concerned. Young people rarely stopped by to visit and he observed that although most of those who did come to the beach would stay for hours, others would leave very soon after arriving. It also seemed there were less and less youth showing up as time went by. So the owner invited his grandson David, a teenager who lived in a different state, to come and spend some time in the town so that he could invite other youth to come to the beach and encourage them to swim, surf and play volleyball.

David spent his first day not at the beach, but around the town, inviting the youth he encountered to come hang out at the beach. Their responses confused him. Some mumbled, "Maybe," while others shuffled their feet, turned their eyes away and said something like, "Nah, I'm not into going to the beach anymore." Most surprising was when someone bluntly said, "No way, too many rules at that beach." David remarked in disbelief, "What do you mean? There are only a few guidelines on the sign." The teenager explained, "Well, it's not your grandfather's sign that's the problem; it's what the beach clique say the sign means, and the rules they have added. I mean, it used to be that, because of the rule about only nine people being on a side at a time, whenever more than eighteen people wanted to play volleyball, we would set up another net. But now they say only the best eighteen people can play. Period."

Someone else added, "Yeah, and instead of taking turns surfing, they say that only people with new wetsuits can surf. That's how they make sure they can go surfing as much as they want." A younger girl jumped in. "Whenever we use the old wetsuits your grandfather put in the shed, they make fun of us and tell us not to come back unless we get nicer ones. They say, 'We don't want to be seen on the same beach as people in those ugly suits.'" Another boy spoke bitterly. "Sometimes they're mean like that, but other times they act real stuck up, and say things like, 'The sign says to wear sun screen and you don't have shades on. You better go home or you might hurt your eyes.' But if you do wear shades that they don't think are cool, they make fun of you and say they don't want you around if you're going to look so stupid."

Finally an older Hispanic teenager added, "They even have a rule that says that only people who speak good English can be there. When I pointed to the sign which says everyone is welcome, they said, 'But the sign is in English and the owner speaks English; what the sign really means is all youth who speak English good can use the beach.'"

David had heard enough. Clearly one group of young people at the beach were making up rules to exclude those not in their group and insulting and embarrassing everybody else. "Who are these people," he asked, "this group that's making all the rules?" The teenagers around him told him to go to the beach and see for himself.

The next day David went to the beach to spend time with the people there. At first he thought the kids he had talked with the day before had been exaggerating. Although the young people on the beach were not overly friendly, they didn't seem so mean. In fact, when he told them he was the owner's grandson, they said very nice things about his grandfather and told David how much they appreciated his grandfather letting them use the beach.

David enjoyed surfing with a few others and then joined a small group that was playing volleyball. Everything was going fine until a teenage boy, about his age, came over and asked if he could join the game. A girl sneered and said, "You know you aren't good enough.

There's a lot more than eighteen people better than you, and only nine can play on a side."

The boy pointed at David, "How come you're letting him play? He's not part of your group." A boy from the other side of the net said, "But he's a good player like us; and even if you were better, I wouldn't want to be seen on the same volleyball court as you with such stupid shades. And where'd you get that swimsuit – from the nerd rack at Wal-mart?" Suddenly David wondered how these people would have treated him if he wasn't a good player, or if he hadn't been wearing the new wetsuit his grandfather had given him for Christmas. He no longer doubted the complaints he had heard the day before.

That evening David told his grandfather all about what he had heard in town and what had happened at the beach. It saddened David to see his grandfather's pained expression as he listened to the report. David told his grandfather that when he had talked to the boy that had been put down and denied the chance to play volleyball, the boy had angrily said, "Tell your grandfather that he should teach those kids a lesson by kicking them off the beach like they've done to so many of us."

David's grandfather sighed. "I understand why some of the youth in town would love the feeling of revenge if I banned the clique from the beach. But kicking them off the beach would destroy the spirit of the beach. Actually I guess we could say it would leave things the way they are right now, only with a different group excluded. No, David, we don't need to punish this group. If they don't change, sooner or later they'll find themselves hurt by the same rules and pressures to be cool that they are using against others right now. They will find themselves suffering humiliation and exclusion just as they put down and exclude others." David interrupted. "How would that happen unless you go down and kick them off the beach yourself?"

His grandfather responded, "Maybe if you think of it the opposite way it will help. If everyone on the beach accepted others and included them in their games, no one would have to worry about not fitting in or being disrespected. But this clique has drawn lines between insiders and outsiders, between good volleyball players and bad volleyball players, those who are cool and those who are not. Once those lines are drawn, even those who drew them have to make sure they stay on the right side of the lines. Even now some of them are suffering because of their own rules. Tonight a few are probably worrying that if more volleyball

Embracing a Wider Cross

players as good as you show up, they'll be kicked out of the game. Others know that if they don't have enough money to get new wetsuits, sunglasses, and bathing suits every year, they might be ridiculed. And all of them have to wonder if people like them for who they really are, or only for their clothes and abilities. So we don't need to add to their punishment. If they stick to their rules, sooner or later those rules will kick them off the beach."

His grandfather paused for a moment and then said, "What we should do is warn them and try to show them a different way of living. I want you to go back to town tomorrow and invite the youth that have been excluded to come with you back to the beach. The popular kids won't include them, but you can set up your own volleyball net, and swim and surf with the ones who have been excluded. Of course there will likely be a confrontation. But it is important that in both your words and deeds you live out the fundamental rule of the beach: that it is open for everyone to use and share, and that even includes the clique who wants to keep it for themselves. Don't try to take their surf boards away or anything like that. Instead, warn them about what I've just said."

When David showed up the next day with some people, all of whom had been insulted and shunned by the "in-group" for one reason or another, he noticed that the beach clique looked at him differently than they had the day before. When he set up a volleyball net and started playing with the people he had invited, the clique started insulting not just David's new friends, but David himself.

Every day that week David brought some of the excluded youth with him to the beach and to visit with his grandfather. Although he focused on helping them feel as welcome as possible, not on upsetting the clique, inevitably every day there was a conflict—either because the clique didn't want to let the others go surfing, or just because their insults and threats were so strong that people would leave. Each time this happened, David would say firmly that the beach was for everyone and then warn the clique that they would be much better off if they stopped shunning and insulting others; stopping was the only way to avoid eventually being excluded and insulted themselves.

The popular kids became more and more upset with David because with him on the beach, their rules, threats and scornful statements did not have the power they used to have. They wanted to chase him off

Reading Scripture Anew

the beach, but they feared that if they insulted him too directly all the people he had been bringing might get upset and chase them off the beach.

The people in the clique came up with a plan. Over a couple of days they began including in their games and group some of those they had previously excluded. Then they did a lot of gossiping about David, about how he was ruining the beach for everyone.

Then one afternoon the clique started an argument with David over having two volleyball courts set up. They began yelling, "David must go! David must go!" They pointed, and yelled, kicked sand and threw the volleyball at him. Gradually those who had been playing on the other court with David melted away. Some of them even started yelling at David as well. One member of the clique picked up a rock and threw it at David's feet, yelling, "Get out of here, and don't come back!" Someone else threw a bottle that hit him. More rocks and bottles started flying, and one hit David on the side of the head and knocked him out. Most people hurriedly left the beach; others swaggered away sneering, "Bet he won't be causing trouble on the beach anymore."

After the clique and almost everyone else had left, a few of the young people cautiously walked over and kneeled down beside David, and then carried him up the path to his Grandfather's house. He had recovered consciousness by the time they got to the door, but he was moaning and unable to stand without support. His grandfather opened the door, gasped and cried out, "What happened?" But before they had a chance to answer he was already telling them to put David in the car. As he rushed David to a hospital, one of the young people recounted what had happened. In the emergency room the grandfather sat beside David's bed with tears streaming down his face. David needed stitches, many bandages, and a cast for a broken arm, and he had to stay in the hospital for a few days.

While in the hospital David and his grandfather talked a lot about what had happened and how they should respond. His grandfather wrote a short letter to the youth of the town which he later posted on the signs on the beach and at the start of the path leading to it. He wrote:

To those who hurt my grandson,
You have made a tragic mistake and have done a horrible thing.
You have insulted, hurt and kicked off the beach the one person

who had the most right to be there, someone from my family and hence an owner of the beach. As I desired, he sought to help everyone feel welcome and have a good time. Just as he already told you, your rules and insults did indeed lead to pain and exclusion, but it was David, not you, who suffered that pain and David, rather than you, who was excluded. It can end here. There does not have to be any more exclusion. Anyone in town would agree that you deserve to be arrested and permanently kicked off the beach. But that is not my desire. I forgive you, and David forgives you. We will not press charges. My hunch is that hidden under all your cockiness, posing and disrespecting others is not the confidence you display, but insecurity and fear. Our forgiveness gives you an opportunity to start over. I invite you to trust that my desire for the beach to be a place of welcome and inclusion is better for you, and a better way to lessen your insecurities and fears, than doing things that include some but embarrass and exclude others. I want nothing more than for my beach to be a place where all feel welcomed and accepted, and that includes each of you.

David's injuries kept him from going down to the beach in the few days left before he had to return to his home. He did, however, limp downtown to seek out some of his friends. Since some of them had actually joined the group in chasing David off the beach, and the rest had not stood up for him, they expected David to either ignore them or angrily demand to know why they had turned on him or not helped him. But David surprised them.

David greeted them warmly and invited them to join him for a frappucino, his treat. As they sat around a table, he repeated what his grandfather had said in the note: what the clique, and those who had joined it, had done was a horrible thing. But David and his grandfather were forgiving them. All of them could be confident that his grandfather would always let them go to the beach; there was no reason to fear him. And they could seek his forgiveness if they committed other wrongs on the beach in the future.

Most of them apologized to David in one way or another, and one girl who had fallen under the influence of the clique when its members started including her, and who had energetically joined them in throwing things at David, sadly asked for forgiveness. She said, "I got sucked into it. I was out of control; it was like there was this power urging me on." David agreed and said that power would have grown even stronger if he had responded in the same way back, seeking revenge by insulting, accusing and trying to exclude those who had shamed and hurt him.

David went on to explain that he hoped this whole experience would lead the clique to stop insulting and excluding others, but he guessed that many members of the clique would keep doing their cliquish thing. David invited his friends, however, to think of him having already suffered in their place the worst sort of insulting and excluding they could experience. He said, "It did not crush me for good. See, I am here again, being accepted by you and sharing drinks and friendship with you right now. You can try to learn to shrug off their insults like I am. You don't have to let that clique's insults and rules determine what you do or how you feel. Go back and enjoy the beach!"

From that day on the beach was a different place. The ugly scene of chasing David off the beach, followed by the forgiving note from David's grandfather, seemed to shake up and transform some of the members of the clique, and they became more relaxed about what they wore to the beach or how good they were in volleyball. They also stopped making fun of others, and more frequently spent time visiting with David's grandfather. As David predicted, however, some of them did not change. They continued to insult and laugh at others, but if they would have been honest enough to admit it, they were even more insecure than they had been before, in part because their words did not seem to have the same power that they used to.

But other youths came and put on the old wetsuits from the storage shed or got out a volleyball net, and they seemed unaffected by the same insults that had kept them away before. Surprisingly, those without expensive shades or new swimsuits, and some of those who spoke with an accent, did not simply ignore the insults, but from time to time actually invited those insulting them to join in a game, or catch a wave together.

NOTES

1. Jon Isaak, "Found in Translation," *In Touch* (March 2004), 6-7.

2. Frederica Mathews-Green, "The Meaning of Christ's Suffering," *Books & Culture* 10, no.2 (March/April 2004), 29.

3. Mathews-Green, "The Meaning of Christ's Suffering," 28. We make similar points in regard to "ransom" in *Recovering the Scandal of the Cross*, and develop the argument using biblical texts; see 38-43, 93-94, 100-02.

4. Raymund Schwager, *Must There Be Scapegoats?: Violence and Redemption in the Bible* (New York: Crossroad, 2000), 206-07.

5. William Placher, "Christ Takes Our Place: Rethinking Atonement," *Interpretation* 53, no. 1 (1999), 16.

6. For an excellent short summary of the arguments for the various translations and the theological ramifications of those readings see: Judith M. Gundry-Volf, "Expiation, Propitiation, Mercy Seat," in *Dictionary of Paul and His Letters*, Edited by Gerald F. Hawthorne, Ralph P. Martin, and Daniel G. Reid (Downers Grove, IL: InterVarsity, 1993), 279-84.

7. For a short description of these differing concepts of justice see: "Justification" by Richard B. Hays in the *Anchor Bible Dictionary* vol. III, ed. David N. Freedman, (New York: Doubleday, 1992), 1129-1133. For a longer discussion see: James D. G. Dunn and Alan M. Suggate, *The Justice of God: A Fresh Look at the Old Doctrine of Justification by Faith* (Grand Rapids, MI: Eerdmans, 1993).

8. See, though, the concreteness of the concept of "reconciliation" as a description of the new relationship between God and humanity that follows from the cross of Christ (I. Howard Marshall, "The Meaning of 'Reconciliation'," in *Jesus the Saviour: Studies in New Testament Theology* [Downers Grove, IL: InterVarsity, 1990], 258-74).

9. C.M. Tuckett, "Atonement in the NT," in *Anchor Bible Dictionary*, 1:518-22 (518).

10. This presentation of the atonement will be published in a forthcoming collection of contextualized presentations of the atonement that I am editing. It is tentatively titled *Proclaiming the Scandal of the Cross* (Baker Books).

God-Talk and an Invitation to Biblical Imagination[1]

Jon M. Isaak

Imagination is a quality that we praise in our youngsters. And yet as we age, our imagination often gets less exercise and is less valued. It may even be held with some suspicion. By contrast, the biblical writers use much imagination and many provocative images as they give witness to their encounter with God. This should not be surprising, because as G.B. Caird used to say, whenever people come face-to-face with the one who is Alpha and Omega, that encounter can only be adequately viewed through the lens of metaphor and image.[2] Using what they knew something about, the biblical writers described what they were convinced was true, but did not fully grasp. Grasped instead by the Spirit of God, they used their own words – metaphors, images, and word pictures – to give witness to God's activity among them.

Unfortunately, there is a tendency in our western world to reduce the impact of the biblical writers' God-talk imagery and its power to transform. Of course, no one starts out trying to drain the power of these metaphors. Nevertheless, the effort to simplify, manage, and organize biblical God-talk imagery in tight theological system tends to domesticate them and dull their transformative impact.

I remain convinced that the metaphors used by the biblical writers to represent God, like sovereign, judge, father, etc., do have power to shape God's people in the twenty-first century. In this chapter my goal is to re-animate the biblical invitation to imagination so that God's people today can see these ancient biblical images in new ways and be drawn once again by their invitation to encounter the one who is Alpha and Omega.[3]

Reading Scripture Anew

Before the case for God-talk and biblical imagination can be made, the question of framework needs to be addressed. Is there an alternative to the western systematic theological frame, with its long history of reductionism and domestication as noted above? Yes, indeed! Biblical theology, differently than systematic theology, sets out another framework from which to hear the call to biblical imagination issued by the God-talk imagery in the Bible.

The key to biblical theology lies in discerning how the diversity of images as well as the diversity of theologies represented by each writer sings together in multi-part harmony. The Christian Bible, which includes the Hebrew Bible or Old Testament and the New Testament, functions like a symphonic orchestra or mass choir. If we attend to each writer's voice, a resonance space is created by the symphonic effect of multiple voices. In this space, the harmonizing tension between the voices enables successive generations of God's people to be shaped by the same theological vision that first moved these writers to give witness to God's activity in the world. Unlike some systematic theologies, the aim is not to force all the voices to sing in unison, even though this may seem at first to be simpler and more straightforward. Instead, while the tensions between the biblical voices may sound disturbing and even dissonant, the confession God's people have made from the start is that authentic life is only really discovered when we resonate with the way God's people have always heard, experienced, and participated in the life of God. Working with a framework of biblical theology, I invite you to join me in reviewing how the biblical writers describe God through metaphor, image, and word picture.

Starting with the Hebrew Bible, we see that these ancient writers did the same thing that the New Testament writers after them would do – use what they knew something about to describe that which they knew to be true, but did not fully grasp. Moved by their experience of the self-involving God, these ancient writers used the only language adequate for this experience, namely metaphor (e.g., shepherd, Ps 23:1; warrior, Exod 15:3; fortress, Jer 16:19; mother, Ps 131:2; king, Ps 95:3). It is perhaps surprising, but instructive, to note that the biblical writers show no interest in speculating on the origins or the inner workings of God in metaphysical or philosophical terms. Instead, they choose to concentrate on identifying the living God as the one who is before all (Gen 1:1) and who discloses the very self of God to humanity in the historical process

God Talk and an Invitation to Biblical Imagination

(in patriarchal families, Gen 12-50; in deliverance from Egypt, Exod 3-15; in covenantal and legal systems, Exod 19-40; in sacrificial systems, Lev 1-7; and in monarchy, 1 Sam 8-12).

So, how then do the New Testament writers themselves talk about God? One noteworthy observation is that the proper name of the Hebrew God, YHWH, is absent from the New Testament. It is likely that a severe reading of Exodus 20:7 ("You shall not take the name of the LORD in vain")[4] caused the Hebrew people to eventually abandon the pronunciation of YHWH long before the Christian movement began. Instead, the Hebrews identified their God as the Lord and even read Adonai (which means Lord) every time the Tetragrammaton (YHWH) appeared in the text.

A further observation is that the early Christians used the term Lord, the term referring to God, in reference to Jesus. The explanation for this development is rooted in the early Christian experience of Jesus, which caused major dissonance for the first disciples. How could they understand Jesus' crucifixion and his resurrection, given their inherited Jewish religious symbols for how God works in the world? Their experience of the resurrected Jesus flew in the face of their reading of Torah ("anyone hung on a tree is under God's curse," Deut 21:22-23). Yet, they were convinced that God had vindicated the crucified Jesus and that God had raised Jesus from the dead, indicating that the new age was dawning (1 Cor 10:11). For God to be involved with such an event in the first place took some reconfiguration. How is God dealing with evil here in this horrific event? How is God being faithful to the covenant promises to Israel through all this? These questions sent the early Christians back to the Torah. In the old text they found new ways to understand their experience. Texts like Psalm 110:1, Psalm 118:22, Zechariah 9:9, and the Servant Songs of Isaiah (42, 49, 50, 53, 61) were heard for the first time as messianic texts.[5] In the interplay between text and experience, mediated by interpretation, the confession of a crucified and risen Messiah resulted in a new articulation of language used to talk about God.

In this way, the early Jesus movement introduced yet another shift in Jewish theism. Like their Hebrew ancestors before them, who had abandoned belief in many gods (polytheism, Gen 31:19-35; 35:2-4), then belief in one god among many (henotheism, Exod 20:1-7; Deut 32:8-9), finally by the end of the Exile to understand YHWH as the only God (monotheism, Isa 40), the early Christians came to recognize most clearly "the glory of God in the face of Jesus" (2 Cor 4:6). Based on their experience of the resurrection, the signs and wonders that animated their times of worship, and their conviction that the risen Lord was among them as they gathered for prayer, they used the familiar patterns within Judaism to give expression to their new experience. They worshiped God's agent, Messiah Jesus, as though he was God. To not do so would be to reject God, for God was surely behind all that they had experienced.[6] Their re-reading of Torah helped them to see that God was indeed faithful to the covenant promises and that the dominion of evil was actually being broken – death could not keep Jesus in its grip. This mutation within Jewish monotheism was not surprising. Since the Master of the Universe was most clearly present and represented in the life, death, and resurrection of Jesus of Nazareth (who else could possibly be responsible for such a life?), it was not a great leap to expand the language of Lord associated with YHWH (in the Old Testament) to include also Messiah Jesus (in the New Testament).

So, what do the New Testament writers actually say about the God whom they have come to know in Jesus? What God-talk images do they use? How can these images be re-animated by solid biblical imagination so that God's people can continue to be shaped by these ancient metaphors even in the twenty-first century? We begin our quest by exploring seven such images used by the New Testament writers to give expression to their conception of God.[7]

God is One

This is the most basic Judeo-Christian confession – God is one – inclusive, exclusive, unique, primary, and transcendent. Furthermore, the early Christian confessions, that God is one and that Jesus is Lord, were never seen as contradictory or in conflict with one another. Instead, they were heard together as the proclamation of God's salvation for the world. For example, Paul uses God's "oneness" to ground his argument that the gentiles are now to be included in God's global shalom project whose goal is the salvation of "all Israel," as in representatives from all tribes and nations (Rom 3:29-31; 11:25-26).

The early Christians confessed, without apparent difficulty, "one God" and "one Lord" (1 Cor 8:6), since they were convinced that in Jesus' life, death, and resurrection, God had chosen to be fully disclosed in these last days. Their experience of the risen Lord in corporate worship (signs, wonders, healing, life, etc.) convinced them that Jesus was the Christ, God's agent for the world's salvation. They never thought of themselves as talking about two gods (or three, for that matter).

Within the Hebrew tradition, the Spirit was known among God's people as the "Spirit of God" or the "Spirit of YHWH." However, after the resurrection, when Jesus was recognized in the worship experience as Lord of the church, it was natural that this experience of God's power was identified as the "Spirit of the Lord." In Romans 8:9, Paul uses "Spirit of God" and "Spirit of Christ" to identify the rule of the "Spirit" in which believers now participate. Notice the unified expression of God's gracious reconciling presence and the seamless identity shared by all three. The same is true in 1 Corinthians 12:4-6 where Paul explains that diverse spiritual gifts are held together by the reality of "the same Spirit ... the same Lord ... the same God who activates all of them in everyone."

Later, fourth-century Greek theologians tried to conceptualize this relation in terms of essence or substance and spoke of "three persons" or "three masks." However, such rationalizations have tended to introduce more problems than they solve. Is God like ice, water, and vapor? Is God evolving from one stage to the next? By contrast, the New Testament writers give no evidence of ever imagining God to have three parts, or evolving from one form to another. How then is the relationship between the "persons" of the Trinity to be conceptualized? Are their roles different? Does the Son satisfy the Father's wrath by paying the penalty for sin? Such abstractions in some Trinitarian thinking have compromised the unity and oneness of God's "being-in-relation."

The doctrine of the Trinity that eventually emerged is an attempt to recognize the multiplex character of God's "being-in-relation," without suggesting three individual deities. This continues to be difficult for western "either/or" thinking. However, instead of focusing on "substance" or "personalities," there is more promise in describing the Trinity in terms of relationship or as a community-of-being. Thus, the basic Trinitarian confession remains: God, as revealed in Jesus, is fully personal within God's own mode of existence (i.e., relational and therefore necessarily plural) and God, as creator, wills to give God's very self to the creatures of the world in loving relationship.[8] In this way, there is dynamic and relational unity within God's being.

The corollary that accompanies the confession that God is one is that there are also lesser enemy powers (1 Cor 10:19-22). However, unlike the capricious and competitive dualism within the pantheon of gods familiar to Israel's pagan neighbors, these enemy powers are not in a dualistic conflict with God,[9] since God is the All Powerful One (Deut 32:8-9; Ps 8:5-6). Still, Paul reminds the early Christians that they should not kid themselves – evil's death-dealing ways have become increasingly sophisticated during these "last days," especially after being exposed at the cross (Rom 6:4, 12). Evil ought not to be trivialized, even as it is being brought under the "heel of God's reign" (Rom 16:20; 1 Cor 6:3) through its own self-destruction. Evil cannot be killed, nor will it just roll over and give up.

In the twenty-first century, to confess that God is one is to confess the unity of God's will and purpose. God's desire is to complete creation and bring the global shalom project to fulfillment on God's own terms. No doubt such a confession will be dismissed in our pluralistic western world as intolerant, totalizing, and politically incorrect. However, to these detractors we can say that such a confession need not equate God's "oneness" with the absolute correctness of a particular religious system – even Christianity! All religious systems are human constructs and each one must answer to God for its construction and its behavior (1 Cor 3:13). I believe that an open, but centered, confession of God's oneness has enormous potential for promoting healthy God-talk in our time with family, friends, colleagues, acquaintances, and strangers.

The Creator as the Giver of Life

The affirmation that God is the one who makes the dead alive (Ezek 37:3-6) and the specifically Christian identification of God as the one who raised Jesus from the dead (1 Cor 15:3-4) reaffirm the more general concept of God as the giver of all life. God does not deal in death. Death is the wage of sin (Rom 6:23). In contrast, God's goal is to give life (John 10:10).

God spares no expense to undo the dominion of sin, evil, and death, as is made clear by God's own self-giving love offered at Calvary. At the cross, we see both the lengths to which Satan will go to eliminate all challengers to evil's death-dealing ways and the lengths to which God will go to make sure that death does not have the last word and that life prevails. Unbeknownst to Satan, the divine purpose is forwarded in the very act of resisting it (1 Cor 2:8; Col 2:15). From the divine perspective, God's purpose to establish life is described as being "destined before the foundation of the world" (1 Pet 1:20).

God's life-giving mission will one day come to completion for all those who choose to join God (Heb 9:27-28). Just exactly how the end will happen (whether in historical time, in post-mortem, or in some other way) is not spelled out in the biblical witness. What is certain is the victory and the shape of the final transformation of creation, but even this is depicted in metaphor and image. John's Revelation portrays God's final shalom as a place where all the nations are represented creatively engaged in God's work of glory, without tears, sin or death – only light and life (Rev 21:22-22:7).

How effective or practical is such a hope in the twenty-first century? Can it capture the imagination of this generation? What happens to a people claiming Jesus as its norm? They could end up killed like he was or misunderstood as aiding evil by their refusal to use violence to stop evil. Yet, the victory of the Lamb at the cross sets in motion both the end of evil and the goal for creation. Now, during these last days, when God is exercising great patience, God's people are expected to live out of the resources of what is yet to be completed. This is not about being passive, but about being active in our resistance to evil in all its forms, while knowing all along that evil too must be free to be evil and carry on hell-bent toward separation from God and destruction. Such freedom is characteristic of God's kind of agape love as seen from the beginning in Israel's own creation mythology. God did not create evil, but allowed people to rebel against God's way, giving evil the allegiance it needed to become the dominating superpower that it has become. This schema is a direct contradiction to the pagan creation mythology of Israel's neighbors, which is rooted in violence, deception, and chaos.[10] For Israel, God is before the chaos (Gen 1:1-2). So, it makes sense for God's people to hold up Jesus' life and ministry of non-violent resistance to evil as normative, not necessarily because it "works," but because it is rooted in creation and anticipates the triumph of the Lamb that was slain.[11]

Of course, this kind of "gracious divine patience" is not the complete answer to evil. Just as the doctrine of creation affirms that God made humanity free and the doctrine of redemption says that sin's freedom led the God-filled man, Jesus, to the cross, so also "the doctrine of hell lets sin free, finally and irrevocably, to choose separation from God."[12] At the final judgment, the old age, dominated by evil, achieves its goal as it is finally left to itself along with all that is loyal to it. Having chosen to have nothing to do with God's life, it excludes itself from "the new heaven and new earth," the consummation of God's creation which began in Christ.

In the meantime, Christian communities live empowered by Christ's Spirit to invite one and all to abandon their rebellion against God and choose life. In addition, the Christian community shaped by the norm of Jesus fully embraces the mandate to give witness to the powers of evil, inviting them also to abandon their death-dealing ways. This is how God continues to "re-order" the ruling authorities (Rom 13:1). Thus, even the Christian's responsibility for helping to defeat evil is based on the refusal to meet evil on its own terms. Why? To crush the evil adversary is to be vanquished by evil, because it means accepting evil's standards.[13] Again, this is not a doctrine of passivity or acquiescence to unproven affirmations. No. It is to live out of the same trust in God that Jesus pioneered and perfected (Heb 12:2). Jesus was convinced that going to the cross was right in itself, even though its "rightness" in terms of ultimate effect was not yet apparent.[14]

In the same way, the church's social and political engagements in the world must be indirect. The church is not like the soap that cleans, but more like the orange tomato ring that remains after washing a load of spaghetti-stained dishes — evidence of grime absorption. This is one of Paul's images for the church (1 Cor 4:13). Like the cross, which unmasked evil's ancient death-dealing ways (Col 2:15), evil is undone indirectly, as the resurrection confirms Jesus' way to be indeed God's way. Thus, God makes the victory over death accessible to all who are baptized into the risen Lord and who now refuse to play according to the old way of death within the domination system. What is the domination system? "It is characterized by unjust economic relations, oppressive political relations, biased race relations, patriarchal gender relations, hierarchical power relations, and the use of violence to maintain them all."[15]

While the powers will not be able to hear our critique fully, because they are guided by self-preservation and self-interest, this does not release the church from its obligation to stand up and unmask the powers through indirect action (i.e., exposing, sensitizing, testifying, and creating alternative systems). Paul understands that direct action against evil will not work. So, in the present, he says, it is better to be wronged, than to do wrong (1 Cor 6:7) and ultimately, "to overcome evil with good" (Rom 12:21). Furthermore, in contemporary terms, the church's indirect engagement with society will rule out using suicide bombings, lynching of homosexuals, bombing of abortion clinics, keeping a gun under the pillow, and using violence to achieve even justifiable ends.

And so we in the twenty-first century need not lose hope, but with resolve, join God's mission in the "now time," inviting all to abandon their rebellion against God and to choose life – there is so much more to life than death! The way of Jesus remains the only way to deal with and undo the power of evil and break the cycle of violence. I am convinced that such a vision for God as the real life-giver is capable of capturing the imagination of today's generation, just as it did those of previous generations (Gen 12:1-4; John 6:68).

God as the Sovereign Ruler

The New Testament writers specifically assert God's sovereignty with reference to Jesus' life. In the resurrection and exaltation of Jesus, God proved to be the one who overcomes the mighty and exalts the humble. The cross was not some accident or mistake; nor was it orchestrated to change God's mind about humanity. It was a willful act of aggression on the part of Satan, the evil one. However, God, the sovereign and knower of all things, was able to absorb even this horrific event and use it to undo evil's power over our world. Ironically, the act that Satan intended to use for Jesus' destruction turned out to be the cause of Satan's own self-destruction. Unlike John Milton's view in *Paradise Lost*,[16] the biblical narrative is more interested to show that Satan's ouster and fall from grace occurred at the cross, not the result of a pre-cosmic rebellion before the dawn of time; Jesus' ministry is about reversing Adam's failure (Rom 5:12-21; Phil 2:5-11) and undoing Satan's grip in order to take creation to its intended goal.[17]

Satan's cover was blown at that first Easter. It was the scandal that rocked the world, as Jesus said, "I watched Satan fall from heaven like a flash of lightening" (Luke 10:18). Never again would evil's ploys be masked and hidden in the same way, for they are being rendered inoperative (1 Cor 2:6). From now on anyone associating with Jesus' way would also be free of evil's grip, empowered to actually see the evil one and say "No!" Of course, this would not eliminate death, disease, and destruction just yet. In fact, Jesus predicted these would intensify (Matt 10:34-36; Luke 12:51-53), as we are in the last days of Satan's defrocked rule. Nevertheless, Satan's ultimate power over humanity is broken, because death no longer has the last word – Jesus is alive!

And so the confession that God is sovereign means that God will eventually overcome all opposition. Yet this affirmation is never read as fatalism or as depreciation of human freedom or of creation's responsibility. Neither is God's sovereignty thought of as some kind of game where God orchestrates events based on God's foreknowledge of our choices, so that all things always turn out a certain way.

In good non-western fashion, both the sovereignty of God and human freedom are affirmed without an attempt to resolve at any particular moment the tension between them.[18] The tension provides the space within which the faithful have always found life and authentic existence. Why pray to God, if all is pre-programmed? Conversely, why pray to God, if it is all up to me? Instead, the faithful find strength in prayer because both God's sovereignty and human freedom are affirmed at the same time, even though many westerners would see these as contradictory affirmations.

Often people try to take sides in the old Calvin vs. Arminius debate.[19] Calvin highlighted God's determination of events, while Arminius highlighted human responsibility in shaping these same events. This is not an "either/or" situation – we do not need to choose between Calvin and Arminius! The biblical writers, without embarrassment, were able to hold both God's sovereignty and human free will together. They did not see these two views as contradictory or incompatible. Without difficulty they could affirm that Pharaoh "hardened his heart" (Exod 9:34) and that "the LORD hardened the heart of Pharaoh" (Exod 9:12).

The point is that Calvin and Arminius made God's sovereignty and human free will a riddle to be solved one way or another, whereas they both need to be allowed to stand side by side. The Bible does not view God's foreknowledge as reducing or eliminating human freedom and responsibility. God has given us freedom to respond. God knows us as free creatures. Both the purposes for humanity and God's plan for their accomplishment are designed according to that knowledge.[20]

We who live in the twenty-first century are invited to develop our "both/and" biblical imagination further in order to resonate with the

God Talk and an Invitation to Biblical Imagination

biblical witness to a God who is ultimately in control, willing good for the entire universe. This is not to be confused with domination or fatalism or malicious coercion; God's kind of "control" is participatory. God created the universe without violent means (unlike pagan creation mythology), cares for it, governs it, and works for its good in the long run, also without violent means (unlike some contemporary theological systems, such as the one seen in Lahaye & Jenkins's *Left Behind* series[21]). While God has all the power potential, God chooses to invite humanity's participation in completing God's goal for creation (i.e., shalom). Human freedom and responsibility are built in and respected. I think the twenty-first century God-seeker will find such an articulation of God's control provocative, attractive, and worth exploring.

God as the Righteous Judge

The two aspects that the New Testament writers affirm about God's judgments are that God is impartial (Rom 3:9-20) and that God does and will set things right (Rom 11:25-36; Rev 20:11-15). For the early Christians their experience of the salvation of the gentiles was seen as evidence that God is impartial and that God is demonstrating righteousness in the world by including them within God's newly reconfigured people.

Still, we need to make a critical observation about God's judgment. Unlike most human types of judgment, God's judgments are not about vindictive punishment, nor motivated by resentment or retaliation.[22] Certainly, the biblical writers do use "vengeance" images (Exod 32:12; Deut 29:28; 2 Kgs 22:13; Col 3:6). However, even the biblical writers realize that this anthropomorphic imagery cannot be pushed too far, because they also stress that God's vengeance is different from human vengeance (Isa 55:8-9; Deut 32:35; Rom 12:17-19). By definition, human vengeance is based on the withdrawal of previous good will or a change in attitude toward the one causing harm. God's kind of vengeance is not about withdrawal, as God does not leave the table (Jer 3), but is based on the public righting of wrong. The attitude God has toward creation and the purpose God has for creation cannot change – that would be a "self-contradiction of God's essential goodness."[23]

Therefore, the judgment of God appears to be more about honoring the free choices that people make. God does not want our harm (God's antecedent will arising from God's nature is for life); however, when human beings choose to deny their identity or choose to remove themselves from God, that choice is granted (God's consequent will arising from the acts of human beings). Like the father of the prodigal in Luke 15, it is as if God says, "If you reject your true self, if you leave your true home, your suffering will be very profound, because away from my love you cannot live."[24]

However, that is not the end of the story. God's respect for human choice is coupled with the father's indefatigable longing for the restoration of his relationship with his child. The father never gives up on his son; he continues to watch and wait for his son. While he would never force his son to receive his love, neither would he abandon the son. Instead, the father "outwaits" the son! So it is with God's judgment; it is not about God handing out punishments, but about a discernment process where we come to know who we were created to be as God's beloved children. This may be a painful experience and it may take a long time, because the choices we make have real and lasting consequences. However, God's judgments can be counted on to bring the righting of wrong and the restoration of relationship.

So, what about the New Testament images of the final judgment? The New Testament writers use four images to describe the final judgment.[25] Each of them has strengths and weaknesses. In other words, each image illuminates some aspect of the final judgment, but if pushed too hard or taken exclusively, proves less helpful and even distracting. Let's review each one.

Literal eternal punishment (Matt 25:1-46) describes a scenario where those who die without acknowledging God are punished eternally in hell. Here the image of Gehenna (the smoldering garbage dump outside Jerusalem) is taken literally and the word "eternal" is taken chronologically as everlasting. The strength of this image is that it certainly provides a vivid picture of the serious consequences of ongoing rebellion against God and continued allegiance to the death-dealing ways of sin. However, a punitive hell does not deal satisfactorily with God's goodness. If evil continues to be punished in hell, then evil still exists and will never be eradicated. Can God be happy with a scenario where most of the world burns in eternal punishment? This is not a very successful rescue plan. Furthermore, how can that which undergoes destruction, never be destroyed?

Annihilation of evil (2 Pet 3:3-15) is the scenario that posits Jesus' return in a different fashion from the way he lived and ministered in

God Talk and an Invitation to Biblical Imagination

Galilee. Here, instead of unmasking the powers of evil by challenging them at Golgotha as the suffering servant, Jesus returns to take direct action – he bombs the enemy to nothingness. In fact, all of creation is destroyed and the righteous ones are rescued to repopulate the new heaven and earth. The strength of this image is that it too provides a powerful reminder of the fact that evil will be defeated in the end. However, in this scenario, the Creator sustains staggering losses as most of creation is destroyed. How effective is this rescue operation? According to Genesis 8:21, God promised never to destroy the world again. Furthermore, this solution also gives evil the last word, since in the end it is the destructive power of death that wipes out creation.

Conditional immortality (Rev 21:1-22:7) imagines a scenario where heaven is seen as the ultimate stage in life's journey. Heaven provides the highest potential for realizing the fullness of God's presence. This view takes the Hebrew idea of embodiment seriously, as only those acknowledging the rule of God will have their souls embodied. All the rest remain dead because, having removed themselves from the love of the father, they cannot live. Without access to the Tree of Life, sinful humanity simply dies and stays dead – they perish. Hell is the self-chosen state or "the second death." The strength of this image is that it takes seriously the consequential nature of human choices. However, this scenario too has problems. Again God's salvation plan seems impotent and ultimately limited by human beings. God seems weak and not very loving, like a parent who says to the child, "Go ahead, play in the traffic. I warned you, but if you insist, go ahead and get yourself killed."

Creation completion (Col 1:9-20) describes yet another scenario where Christ's victory over sin, evil, and death is for all creation. In Christ, all things are reconciled to God the father. In the end, love does overcome evil and all is perfected. God's invitational love is indefatigable and ultimately triumphant. Paul is convinced that one day "all Israel" will be saved (Rom 11:25), meaning presumably representatives from all the nations (Gen 12:1-3). However, this scenario should not be confused with universalism, which holds that all ways, whether good or evil, eventually lead to God without any need to abandon rebellion against the creator. Rather, the picture is one where God never withdraws the offer of life (Luke 15). In this scenario, unbelievers who enter death experience the shock and pain of entering a lighted room, accustomed as they are to living in darkness. Those who persist in refusing to embrace the light will only experience more pain, not less, in hell. However, God is able to outwait "even the vilest offender" who turns at last to abandon the ways of death, darkness, and destruction so that "at the name of Jesus every knee should bend" (Phil 2:10). The strength of this image is that it tries to balance God's sovereignty with human freedom and to imagine judgment as clarification, illumination, and discernment – not as vindictive punishment. However, this scenario too has problems. It raises questions about the nature of the church's mission and the imperatives of Christian discipleship.

All four of these scenarios regarding the final judgment emerge from the multiple voices of the New Testament writers. Should they be reduced to one? Should some be ruled out? Unlike the images of God that we have explored so far, these four images of judgment are not complementary – any one image effectively eliminates the other three. While one image is likely nearer "the truth" than the others (I lean toward the fourth), to eliminate any would be to claim more than we can or should. Still, there are three things that ought to be said which can significantly shape biblical imagination in the twenty-first century regarding God's judgment.

First, however we imagine the concept of judgment, it must be shaped by the self-disclosure of God in Jesus. It is theologically inconsistent to say that God will abandon God's character of agape love at some point in the future. Likewise, it is equally inconsistent to imagine that God could "wink" at evil, as if it did not matter.

Furthermore, however we imagine God's judgment, it must not let human co-operation or human freedom be trivialized, manipulated, or eliminated. Both double predestination and universalism trample on the fundamental characteristic of God and the humanity created in God's image, namely, freedom.

Finally, however we imagine the final judgment, it must keep the Church's mandate clearly focused on God's mission to invite all creation and every individual to authentic life and to unalienated relationship. God's mission is not about providing "hellfire insurance," but about the tremendous opportunities to experience authentic living from now on. The gospel invitation is to come along now and begin to experience authentic living – if one persists in rebellion, it will only get more difficult to come along. There is much to miss, even now, not to mention having to put up with the consequences of choosing alienation from God.[26]

God as the Faithful One

God keeps promises. God does not divorce (Hos 2:19). For Paul this characteristic of God is what guides his whole argument in Romans. The inclusion of the gentiles and the eventual salvation of all God's children are predicated on the conviction that God is faithful. Romans 9-11 gives witness to Paul's attempt to reconcile his experience of God's Spirit now among the gentiles with what he knows to be true as a good Jew. Paul is convinced that God is faithful to the promise of election; "the gifts and the calling of God are irrevocable" (11:29).

Yet, how can Paul explain the fact that his brothers and sisters in Judaism are not responding to Jesus as Messiah? Is God playing fair? Is God taking back the gift of election from the Jews? God's reputation is on the line! If God has actually given up on the Jews, then what assurance is there that God will not cast anyone aside in preference for yet another people? This idea is unthinkable and Paul backs away from it, asserting rather that the Jewish rejection must be a "temporary" reality. He calls this a "hardening" that has the redemptive purpose of giving access to the gentiles so that ultimately "all Israel will be saved" (11:26) as promised long ago (Gen 12:1-3).

In good Semitic form, the biblical writers often express as a "purpose" what is foreseen as a "result."[27] In Mark 4:12 we read of the apparently harsh statement where Jesus chooses to say everything in parables to those on the "outside," so that they may not understand. Their misunderstanding appears to be Jesus' purpose. The parallel passage in Matthew 13:13 has Jesus speaking to the "outsiders" in parables because they do not understand. Matthew then inserts a citation from Isaiah 6:9-10 probably to show that the rejection experienced by Isaiah is also now being experienced by Jesus – so, here, the "outsider's" misunderstanding is a result of their rejection. Thus, Matthew chooses to express the people's misunderstanding as a "result" of rejection, whereas Mark expresses the same thing as Jesus' "purpose."

What is going on here? This is another example of the dual causation so typical of the ancient near-eastern worldview.[28] Joseph can say to his brothers without any problem, "even though you intended to do harm to me, God intended it for good" (Gen 50:20). For the biblical writers everything can be explained as God's faithful purpose and at the same time the same experience can be explained as a result of human choices, since humanity is responsible for its own outcomes. The biblical writers do not seem to be bothered by this tension (who is to blame? is it a purpose or is it a result?) as much as westerners are. They in their ancient near-eastern way can affirm both to be true at the same time. The bottom line is that in everything, God is absolutely faithful to God's people-gathering purpose and promise.

There is no better illustration of God's faithfulness than the faithfulness of Jesus (Rom 3:21-26). This is the core of the Good News that early Christians proclaimed: namely, their experience of Jesus' faithful life, which led to his death and resurrection (1 Cor 15:3-4). They experienced Jesus not only as the one who, on God's behalf, re-called Israel to be and to do what had always been intended for God's people (to be "a light to the nations," Isa 49:6), but also as the one who actualized the potential for being truly human, like no one else had. Jesus fulfilled adamic humanity (Rom 5:12-21) and thereby became the primary source and paradigm for the new humanity, "the last Adam" (1 Cor 15:45) and the "firstborn of all creation" (Col 1:15).

Thus, Jesus embodied the climax and culmination of what it means to be human. As we are identified with Jesus (i.e., "baptized into Christ," Gal 3:27), we too can finally access the truth of who we are as God's beloved. In this way, the imprint of God's image that we all share is liberated to emerge and flourish as God had always intended. Jesus' faithful life and ministry is not about solving God's problem, but about taking creation that final step forward to being what we were intended to be in the first place. Jesus' faithful life has its origin in the unchanging purpose and love of God (John 1:1-5). In this way, later theologians described Jesus as fully divine and fully human, in that Jesus revealed fully the character of God and completed fully God's goal for humanity. Framed in this way, I believe the image of God's faithfulness has enormous potential for embrace in the twenty-first century where fragmentation and unfaithfulness are so common.

God as the Forgiving and Merciful One

The heart of God is agape love, which is purposeful, tough, consequential, and unrelenting. It is not that God has two faces, a loving one and a judging one, as if God needs to choose which job to do each day: "Shall I love the world today or shall I punish it?" Neither should the mercy and love of God be confused with indulgent love. Instead, it is a tough love – a love that aims at transformation, growth, and reconciliation.

God Talk and an Invitation to Biblical Imagination

God does not condemn people (John 3:16-17). God does not punish people, as if to pay them back for their rebellion. God does, however, allow people to experience the full consequences of their choices (Rom 1:18-31) because God's mercy is pure and non-coercive.

So, what about the biblical images of "wrath" in the Old and New Testaments? As we have seen with so much of the language and imagery of the Bible, these images often say more about the limitations of our human linguistic expression than about the heart of God. A careful distinction needs to be made here.[29] God's wrath is not an emotional outburst of revenge or of punishment designed to stop sinners from sinning, but rather it is the impersonal process that attaches to sinners the consequences of their error. These death-dealing and destructive consequences are not fundamentally part of God's life-giving purpose for humanity as described above. This is likely what Paul means when he says, "Beloved, never avenge yourselves, but leave room for the wrath of God" (Rom 12:19). Now, does this mean God "winks at evil"? No, the face of God is set uncompromisingly against evil and God will do all that it takes to make things right. God does personally resist evil – after all, God is called a "warrior" (Exod 15:3). However, God does not use violence or coercion to overcome evil. Instead, God's ultimate "weapon" is the persuasive power of self-giving love (Rom 12:9-21). The cross is the clearest expression of God's kind of wrath and it is called the "wrath of the Lamb" (Rev 6:16-17).

The New Testament writers are clear that Jesus' ministry had everything to do with the demonstration of the love of God. Yet, they do not try to explain the mechanism by which the death and resurrection of Jesus became effective for our salvation. Was God's anger satisfied by Jesus' death? Were the evil powers tricked or "paid off"? Was it something else? Instead, the New Testament writers prefer to use metaphors drawn from worlds they knew something about (courtroom, commerce, worship, relationships, battleground) in order to talk about something they did not fully understand, but were convinced was true: namely, that Jesus is alive.[30] Death could not hold him down. The new age has dawned. The powers of the old age no longer have jurisdiction over those associated with the risen Lord (1 Cor 2:6).

Typically, Western Christians have pictured the Redemption Drama as an interchange between two players – God and Jesus – with the cross providing the means of exchange (payment for sin) that allows humanity back into God's presence. While this schema may address one of the biblical metaphors (i.e., the courtroom), how well does it integrate the others? What does it say about God, Jesus, humanity, and sin? Does it not introduce other problems?

Consider how inserting a third player – the Power of Sin – changes the schema. Actually, such a schema taps into a view that is more ancient than the Western two-player model. The early Christians regularly conceptualized the redemption drama as involving three players, namely, God, the Power of Evil, and Jesus. The three-player redemption drama also explains the courtroom metaphor, although differently. Now it is Satan who is judged by God and found to have illegitimately overstepped jurisdiction by killing Jesus. Since Jesus never gave primary allegiance to Satan as all the rest of us have at some point, Satan could not keep Jesus in evil's death-grip. Furthermore, all who associate themselves with Jesus now have a share in the victory over death.

I suggest that it is precisely here where the invitation to biblical imagination can be heard the loudest in our twenty-first century Western world. By embracing a three-player redemption model we are enabled to re-read old texts of salvation in ways that challenge our western preoccupation with minimizing spiritual powers, promoting personal autonomy, and fixating on guilt and punishment. For example, in Colossians 2:15, Paul describes Jesus' death in ways that are rarely utilized in western theology with its preference for personal forgiveness and the two-player redemption. Instead, with graphic three-player vividness, Jesus' death is characterized as that which "disarmed the rulers and authorities and made a public example of them, triumphing over them in it." As western thought is being reshaped in the twenty-first century, we are invited to hear our non-western global brothers and sisters explain the great biblical themes of salvation in ways that may be new for us, but are really as ancient as the biblical writers themselves.

God as the Father

The New Testament writers also use the parental image of "father" to describe God, because Jesus himself called God his father – the one who faithfully saves and cares for his children (Mark 8:38; 11:25; 13:32; 14:36). This metaphor is rooted in the patriarchal household system where families are identified and characterized by the leading father figure. Paul says that believers can now cry out to abba, father (Rom 8:15; Gal 4:6), because of their adoption into the "family" of God. The image is associated with liberation from past bondage in the family of darkness. It means leaving our rebellion behind and accepting at last our true identity as God's beloved. Such adoption underlines the assertion that membership in God's family is not based on DNA, ethnicity, wealth, gender, etc. Instead, it involves leaving "old family" loyalties in order to be baptized into this "new family" (Mark 3:31-35). In this case, water is thicker than blood. The Christian community is a family of brothers, sisters, and mothers, that is, all those who have left one dominion for another, the reign of God where there is but one father: God (Mark 10:29-30; 13:32; Matt 23:9).

Unfortunately, some have used the masculine imagery for God to justify the suppression of women in the church and in society. This is a direct reversal of the way the early Christians understood the gospel message. Paul is well known for inviting women (such Lydia in Acts 16:11-15, and others in Romans 16:1-16) to join God's mission, which also included exploring the new way of being male and female within the new humanity that Jesus embodied (Gal 3:28; 1 Cor 11:11). However, these initial advances in being truly human were reversed within a generation after Paul's ministry, only to be perpetuated through the following centuries. Male church leaders have often exploited Paul's temporary and situational restriction of women from their share in church leadership (1 Cor 14:34-35; 1 Tim 2:11-12), as if it were timeless and universal. Such views adversely affect our image of God and of women and can lead to idolatry. To think of God exclusively in terms of masculine gender turns God into an idol. Ontologically, we must define God as "beyond gender," just as we recognize God as personal, but "beyond personality."[31]

Today, in many communities, "man" no longer includes both men and women, nor do masculine pronouns like "him" include both genders. So then, which pronoun would be appropriate for God, who is beyond gender? An obvious solution to this linguistic problem in English has not yet appeared. However, I believe it is vital that we continue to search for ways to re-contextualize the metaphor of God as father in such a way that it can continue to stir the imagination of today's generation without losing the intimacy and the respect that this parental image conveys. Let the search continue.

Reading Scripture Anew

I am convinced that these seven New Testament God-talk images, when played together, can create a profoundly moving invitation for any generation or any culture to re-imagine its participation in the life of God. By singing along, the church of the twenty-first century joins "the cloud of witnesses" (Heb 12:1-2) from previous generations in continuing to be shaped within the multi-voice biblical choir – all giving witness to God's people-gathering activity that aims to bring global transformation and thus to complete God's work of creation.

NOTES

1. This chapter is an adaptation of my New Testament Theology lecture for the week when the students at Mennonite Brethren Biblical Seminary and I explore the New Testament writers' reflections on the topic of "God." The New Testament Theology class meets for fourteen weeks. The first seven weeks are devoted to exploring the various "theologies" of the New Testament writers. The second seven weeks are dedicated to discerning contributions to various topics that emerge from a "discussion among the New Testament writers," in an effort to sketch the space within which the contemporary church does its own ongoing theological reflection, construction, and appropriation.

    David Ewert (1975-1981), John E. Toews (1982-1995), Timothy J. Geddert (1996-), and I (2002-) have taught New Testament Theology at M.B. Biblical Seminary. The course is part two of a two-part Biblical Theology course launched in 1967 that has become one of the centerpieces of the seminary curriculum. See Elmer A. Martens, "Realizing the Vision [of M.B. Biblical Seminary]: through Biblical Theology" in *The Seminary Story: Twenty Years of Education in Ministry*, ed. A.J. Klassen (Fresno, Calif.: Mennonite Brethren Biblical Seminary, 1975), 35-40. Elmer A. Martens began teaching the Old Testament Theology course in 1969 and continues to do so. All four men were my teachers during my seminary studies (1990-1994). This chapter is dedicated to my teachers, David Ewert, Timothy J. Geddert, Elmer A. Martens, and John E. Toews, who are now also my friends.

2. George B. Caird, *The Language and Imagery of the Bible. With New Introduction by N.T. Wright* (Grand Rapids, Mich.: Eerdmans, 1980, 1997), 271.

3. See also Edward A. Das and Frank J. Matera, eds. *The Forgotten God: Perspectives in Biblical Theology* (Louisville, KY: Westminster John Knox Press, 2002); Jerome H. Neyrey, *Render to God: New Testament Understandings of the Divine* (Minneapolis: Fortress Press, 2004); Neil Richardson, *God in the New Testament* (Peterborough, U.K.: Epworth Press, 1999); Marianne Meye Thompson, *The Promise of the Father: Jesus and God in the New Testament* (Louisville, KY: Westminster John Knox Press, 2000).

4. All scriptures are taken from the New Revised Standard Version.

5. Luke T. Johnson, *The Writings of the New Testament: An Interpretation,* Revised Edition (Minneapolis: Fortress Press, 1986, 1999), 147.

6. Larry W. Hurtado, *One God, One Lord: Early Christian Devotion and Ancient Jewish Monotheism*, Second Edition (Edinburgh: T & T Clark, 1988, 1998), 122.

7. These seven images are drawn from a New Testament Theology lecture that John E. Toews gave at the seminary on April 14, 1993.

8. C. Norman Kraus, *God our Savior: Theology in a Christological Mode* (Scottdale, PA: Herald Press, 1991), 93.

9. Paul G. Hiebert, "Spiritual Warfare and Worldviews." *Direction* 29 (Fall 2000), 114-124.

10. See *Creation Epic* (Akkadian). Trans. by E.A. Speiser. Pages 31-39 in vol. 1 of *The Ancient Near East: An Anthology of Texts and Pictures*. Edited by J.B. Pritchard (Princeton, NJ: Princeton University Press, 1958).

11. John H. Yoder, *The Original Revolution: Essays on Christian Pacifism* (Scottdale, PA.: Herald Press, 1971), 61.

12. Yoder, *The Original Revolution*, 62.

13. Yoder, *The Original Revolution*, 63.

14. Yoder, *The Original Revolution*, 63.

15. Walter Wink, *The Powers that Be: Theology for a New Millennium* (New York: Doubleday, 1998), 39.

16. John Milton, *Paradise Lost*. First published 1674. (New York: Penguin, 2003).

17. George B. Caird, *New Testament Theology*. Compiled and edited by L.D. Hurst (Oxford: Clarendon Press, 1994), 97.

18. Caird, *The Language and Imagery of the Bible* , 117-121.

19. See Gregory A. Boyd, *Is God to Blame? Moving Beyond Pat Answers to the Problem of Evil* (Downers Grove, IL: InterVarsity Press, 2003); Clark H. Pinnock, *Most Moved Mover: A Theology of God's Openness* (Grand Rapids, MI: Baker Academic Press, 2001); John Piper et al., eds., *Beyond the Bounds: Open Theism and the Undermining of Biblical Christianity* (Wheaton, IL: Crossway Books, 2003); John Sanders, *The God who Risks: A Theology of Providence* (Downers Grove, IL: InterVarsity Press, 1998).

20. Kraus, 84; see also Timothy J. Geddert, "Working Together for Good (Romans 8:28)," *Mennonite Brethren Herald*, June 23, 2000; Pierre Gilbert, "Human Free Will and Divine Determinism: Pharaoh, a Case Study," *Direction* 30 (Spring 2001), 76-87.

21. Timothy Lahaye and Jerry Jenkins. *Left Behind* Series (Carol Stream, IL: Tyndale House Publishers, 1995-2004).

22. Kraus, *God our Savior,* 210.

23. Kraus, *God our Savior,* 210; see 2 Tim 2:11-13.

24. See Henri Nouwen, *The Return of the Prodigal Son: A Story of Homecoming* (New York: Continuum, 1992).

25. Kraus, *God our Savior*, 212-215.

26. See Clive S. Lewis, *The Great Divorce*. 1st published 1946. (New York: Harper SanFrancisco, 2001).

27. David Ewert, *How to Understand the Bible* (Scottdale, PA.: Herald Press, 2000), 167.

28. Caird, *The Language and Imagery of the Bible*, 203.

29. Caird, *New Testament Theology*, 87.

30. Joel Green and Mark Baker, *Recovering the Scandal of the Cross: Atonement in New Testament & Contemporary Contexts* (Downers Grove, IL: InterVarsity Press, 2000), 97.

31. Kraus, *God our Savior*, 96.

Living the Christian Life

Doing What Jesus Did: A Discipleship Strategy That Really Works

Jim Holm

Discipleship has been one of the key words of the vocabulary of the church in the last fifty years. Churches have formed discipleship committees, chosen pastors of discipleship, purchased materials to help discipleship happen, conducted clinics, attended seminars, and read from the abundance of books written on the topic. As congregations have crafted mission statements, the word *discipleship* has figured prominently in their thinking. In fact, it would be nearly impossible to worship in an evangelical church for any length of time without hearing a sermon or a lesson urging one to follow Jesus, to be a disciple.

For those in the Anabaptist tradition, discipleship receives, if anything, an even stronger emphasis. One might even say that the Anabaptists co-opted the word to describe their own history. It was Hans Denck, the mystical Anabaptist of the sixteenth century, who coined one of the most famous discipleship sayings: "No one may truly know Christ except one who follows him in life."[1]

So much has been written and spoken on the subject of discipleship that the reader might well wonder if another chapter in another book is worth the time and effort to write and to read. After all, there are so many models of discipleship out there – seeker sensitive models, purpose driven models, natural church development models, small group models, church renewal models, and so on – that it would seem the field has been plowed pretty deeply already. However, sometimes a return to some basic principles may be helpful; asking some basic questions may clear the air and refocus one's thinking. This chapter attempts to do that.

Living the Christian Life

A no doubt apocryphal story tells of Vince Lombardi, the legendary coach of the Green Bay Packers football team. Lombardi coached Green Bay during the years when that football team was the pride of the National Football League. The story says that the Packers traveled down to Chicago to play the doormat of the league, the Chicago Bears. It should have been a whitewash for the Pack, but the Bears were loaded for – well, bear. Chicago swatted Green Bay all over the field with such energy that the game was over long before the final gun sounded. On the trip back to Green Bay, Coach Lombardi was livid. He announced that his team would hold a practice the moment they returned home. The players sighed and grumbled. They were tired and demoralized and wanted nothing more than a hot shower and a soft mattress. They knew, however, never to argue with Coach Lombardi. When they arrived in Green Bay, he had the lights turned on over the practice field and gathered his team on the sidelines. "Men," he announced, "we got whipped today, so tonight we are going back to the basics." Holding up a ball in his right hand, Lombardi said, "Men, this is a football."

That's pretty basic. Imagine telling a group of professional football players, "This is a football." That's like telling a librarian, "This is a book," or telling a mother of twins, "This is a diaper." Some things are basic. However, it could be that returning to basics might give some fresh insights that could help channel our thinking into new directions. That's what we might try to do with the word *discipleship*.

Many think that discipleship began with the challenge of Jesus to his followers to go and make disciples (Mat 28:19). The idea, however, can be found in the Old Testament. In fact, Jesus may have picked the charge which he gave to his followers right from the pages of the scriptures he knew. Consider, for example, Isaiah 49. This chapter is one of the Servant Songs of Isaiah, in which God charges his Servant with the responsibility of ministry to and among God's people. For many followers of Jesus, the Servant Songs are messianic. Consider the first six verses of Isaiah 49. The passage begins with a statement by the Servant, indicating that the Lord called him before he was born, and declared him to be the Servant. In verse 4, however, the Servant speaks of his frustration with his mission. "I have labored to no purpose," he says, "I have spent my strength in vain and for nothing." The Lord now speaks to his servant, in verse 6. "It is too small a thing for you to be my servant to restore the tribes of Jacob and bring back those of Israel I have kept." Frankly, it would seem like bringing the tribes of Jacob back to the Lord would be an assignment that would occupy the Servant for a lifetime. God says, however, "That is too small a thing." So the Lord gives a larger assignment: "I will also make you a light for the Gentiles (or the nations) that you may bring my salvation to the ends of the earth." The mission God has for his Servant is not only to restore the tribes of Jacob, but to bring light to all the nations, to bring salvation to the ends of the earth.

Jesus likely would have been familiar with that scripture, no doubt knowing it very well. In fact, words so similar to Isaiah's are used by our Lord in his Great Commission in Matthew 28 that one could conclude that Christ had the Isaiah text in mind. In Matthew, Jesus is quoted as saying, "Go and make disciples *of all nations*,"[2] the same word that the Servant had been given. If the Isaiah passage is messianic, and since Jesus is the Messiah, then it seems likely that he intentionally took the passage from the Old Testament which contained the commission given to him, and passed it along to his followers. *Your commandment*, he said, *is to complete what the Servant started. Your commandment is discipleship, to make disciples.*

In the remainder of Matthew 28 (verses 19 & 20), Jesus elaborated on what he meant by making disciples. Essentially, his message had two parts. First, he said, you are to baptize people into the Trinitarian community. That is the meaning of the phrase, "baptize them in the name of the Father and the Son and the Holy Spirit." The Father, the Son and the Spirit live in the purest community imaginable. There is no greater harmony than that between the persons of the godhead. So Jesus tells his followers that the same kind of community is to be formed in the church. The second part of his mandate could not be put more plainly: "Teach them (that is, these baptized people, these disciples) to obey *everything I have commanded you*."[3] There is the discipleship statement of Jesus. "Teach followers to obey everything I have commanded you."

This is a time when churches write mission statements, when they work diligently at their vision. Churches speak of the purposes for which they exist, and they have catchy, clever statements that can be illustrated with banners and fancy posters. I wonder, however, if you have ever heard of a church that said its mission was simply *to teach people to obey everything that Jesus commanded*. In the midst of all the hoopla about mission statements, has any church ever adopted this simple motto, "We will teach our people to obey everything Jesus commanded"?

Imagine trying to obey everything Jesus commanded. Some people would respond immediately by declaring, "That's impossible. We should make an attempt at it, certainly, but we also need to recognize in advance that we will all fall short of the mark, and that we will never obey everything Jesus commanded."

That response prompts these questions: Do we take Jesus seriously or not? Was he speaking in hyperbole to make a point? Was he kidding? Or did he mean it when he said that his followers should teach people to obey *everything* he commanded? Furthermore, if he issued that commandment, and he took it seriously, did he think there was a way in which it could be done? If he was serious, and if there is a way to implement what he commanded, that would be the foundation of a discipleship ministry. That would be a discipleship strategy that really works.

What if we as followers of Jesus pledged ourselves to carry out this mandate, to learn to obey everything that Jesus commanded? What if, beyond that, we committed ourselves to lead our churches in doing the same thing? What if we said that it would be possible for our church, your church, to be known as a place where the commandments of Jesus were all obeyed, and where it was expected of people who fellowshipped with that congregation that they would learn to obey the commands of Jesus?

Some might say, "Slow down a minute. That's legalism." Their argument might run something like this: "If I make a list of all the commandments of Jesus, and if I begin to keep a chart on how obedient I am to those commandments, I will simply move into legalism. I will become a Pharisee. I will have my list of commandments, and at the end of every day I will check my performance against that list. I will have some good days, when my score is excellent, and some days when I don't even break par, when my whole life seems like a double-bogie. Beyond that, in addition to being legalistic about my own life, I will begin to compare myself with others. That is really pharisaical. I will watch you, to see how good you are doing when it comes to the commandments. I will want to know if you are a success, what your score is. Eventually, it will not matter to me so much if I keep all of the commandments, so long as I am ahead of you." That may be the legalistic argument.

We need to stop right there and learn something about Jesus. Jesus did not intend to make his followers into legalists or Pharisees. In fact, one of the key words that should characterize the lifestyle of a follower

Doing What Jesus Did

of Jesus should be the word *naturally*. I submit to you that it was natural for Jesus to live the way he lived, that he didn't have to work hard to live his life. I'm not suggesting that his life was easy, or that he didn't face any hardships. I am suggesting that he responded to those hardships naturally, without forcing himself or keeping score of how well he was doing. An example from the life of Christ might illustrate this point. When Jesus was being nailed to the cross, he spoke to his Father, but those around him heard what he said: "Father, forgive them, for they do not know what they are doing" (Luke 23:34). Reflect on those words for a moment. Was it natural for Jesus to speak like that, even when being persecuted, or did he force himself, through gritted teeth, to ask his Father to forgive those people who were attempting to murder him? I suggest to you that it was perfectly natural for Jesus to speak words of forgiveness – that for him to say anything else would have been unnatural. I suggest to you, further, that Jesus intended for his followers to live the same kind of natural life. What else could our Lord have meant when he told his disciples to take his yoke upon them and learn from him, and when he assured them that his yoke was easy and his burden was light? (Matt 11:28-30).

Suppose that you are tracking with me this far. Suppose that you agree that Jesus meant to be taken literally, that he wasn't training legalists, and that he felt it was possible for his followers to obey all of his commandments and to do so *naturally*. Suppose further that you wanted to live that kind of natural discipleship, where obedience to the commands of Christ was as natural as breathing, and suppose you wanted others to do the same. What would you do?

Actually, it is not complicated, though it isn't accidental. Discipleship is not only possible, it is intended; but it isn't a haphazard or accidental process. Jesus himself, along with the writers of the New Testament, both show us and tell us how it can happen, how discipleship really works. Let's begin with Jesus himself. Our Lord said that his followers would be able to obey all the commandments by doing two things. He said that the words of Moses and all the messages of the prophets could be summed up in two commandments (Matt 22:36-40). The first commandment said, "Love the Lord your God with all your heart and with all your soul and with all your strength and with all your mind" (Luke 10:27). To paraphrase, *Love God and put everything you have into it. Don't leave anything out. Love him with all you've got.* The second commandment, Jesus said, was similar to the first: "Love your neighbor as you love yourself" – or to say it another way, *love your neighbor and put everything you have into it.*

It turns out that obeying all the commands of Jesus isn't that complicated. He said that all of his commands boil down to two, and that if those two are obeyed, everything else he said would be obeyed also. The next steps are the important ones, for this is where the understanding and the practice of discipleship breaks down. Up to this point we have been working with knowledge, describing what we need to *know* about discipleship. Now we move to the action section, what we will *do* in order to obey the commandments of Jesus as he commanded them. Often the spiritual life falters when it comes to the practice. Our problem frequently is that we know what to do, but we don't do it. So now to the doing.

The first thing to understand is that one can never be like Jesus by trying to be like Jesus. Not only does such trying lead to the legalism mentioned above, it simply doesn't work. If trying to be like Jesus made us that way, all sincere followers of the Lord would be model disciples. Outward conformity does not produce inward change. In the state of California, where I live, every freeway has a whole set of signs by the side of the road. These signs are written in very plain English and they say, "Speed Limit" and then they show a number. The signs are not difficult to understand. In fact, I imagine that even a person who understood no English would be able to figure out the meaning of the signs. However, if you were to watch the driving patterns of the people who use the freeway, you might think that all Californians are illiterate, because they exceed the number on those signs regularly. The State of California is not dumb, however. They have a whole fleet of black and white cars with red lights on top that drive back and forth on those freeways. Here is the amazing thing: when the black and white car is on the freeway, all the other drivers are able to understand the signs, and those drivers follow those signs precisely.

Why is that? It is because the police officer in the black and white car is able to enforce conformity to the law because he carries the power of the authority of the state. But he cannot change people from the inside so that they want to obey the law naturally. That is why, as soon as the police car leaves the freeway, the drivers go back to the same speed they were traveling before. The same is true of the commandments of

Jesus. We can't obey them by trying to obey them. All that produces is outward conformity. Instead, we need a change on the inside, so that obedience to Jesus comes naturally.

So how does natural obedience come about? How do we do what Jesus commanded – naturally? The answer is that we become disciples the same way Jesus did, by doing the things Jesus did. We look at the life of Jesus, and ask what made him have such an intimate relationship with his Father; we ask how he naturally loved his neighbor as himself. Then we set our minds to begin to do the things that Jesus did that allowed the Father to work in his life on earth. We assume that if the kinds of things Jesus did made him into the kind of person he was, then if we do the things that Jesus did we might see the same kind of person develop in us. We observe what Jesus did and we determine to practice doing what he did until it becomes natural for us.

Apply these principles to the two commandments which Jesus gave, those commandments which he said fulfill all the Law and the Prophets. How did Jesus obey the first commandment, to love God with all his heart, soul, mind and strength? As we read in the Gospels, we notice that Jesus did several things that probably deepened his relationship with his heavenly Father. For example, we find recorded nearly a half dozen times in the Gospels that Jesus went off alone to be with God for extended periods of solitude and prayer. In Mark 1:35 we find that Jesus rose up very early in the morning, before the sun came up, and went off to a solitary place, where he prayed. In Mark 6:45-46, we note that Jesus sent his disciples across the Lake of Galilee in a boat, while he went up on a mountainside to pray. In Luke 6:12, the Gospel writer records that the Lord went out to a mountainside to pray, and that he spent the whole night in prayer. Jesus, though he was the Son of God and shared the divine nature, found it necessary for his spiritual health to spend extended times of quietness alone with God in prayer. It seems reasonable that in these quiet times he cultivated the love for his Father that fulfilled the first commandment. During those quiet times, Jesus no doubt received direction in prayer, came to a deeper understanding of the Father's will, and entered into a more intimate fellowship with the Father.

If that is what Jesus did, and if he is the model of discipleship, then it makes sense that if we seek the Father as he did, we too will find a life of deeper intimacy with God, learn of God's priorities for our time, and sense his will. Yet extended time alone with God is something that many of us almost never have. Perhaps we could learn from Jesus about loving God with everything we have.

Perhaps another example will help to make this clearer. We know from scripture that Jesus both taught about and practiced the discipline of fasting. Near the beginning of his public ministry, he fasted for forty days in the wilderness. In his teaching in the Sermon on the Mount, he talked of fasting as if it was a regular part of the life of a disciple. As an observant Jew, Jesus no doubt observed fast days as part of his regular practice. The purpose of fasting is to deny the body the nourishment from food that it craves so that the soul can be nourished by God. When Jesus' disciples came to him (John 4) at the well in Samaria and asked him to eat the food that they had brought, Jesus declared to them that he had food they knew nothing about (verse 32). Our Lord did not mean that he had a sandwich tucked into the folds of his robe. He meant that he found nourishment in doing the will of the One who had sent him. Jesus was nourished from contact with the Father. During his times of fasting, he no doubt fed on the word of God and on the presence of the Father.

Fasting is another one of those things that many of us almost never take time for. When our body craves lunch, we feed it. But if Jesus practiced fasting, and if fasting put him in touch with the Father, perhaps that is something we could do. If it helped Jesus to achieve obedience to the first commandment, perhaps it would help us also.

There are other examples that space does not permit us to consider. For instance, Jesus memorized scripture. We know that he quoted the scriptures regularly, having immersed himself in their truths. The scriptures helped him to understand the will of God in his present situation. Couldn't that work for us also?

Then there is the second commandment. Here, too, we can learn from Jesus how to love our neighbor. For example, we read how he fellowshipped with a small group of disciples, sharing his life intimately with them. So we ask God to help us find a small group of believers with whom we might share our lives. In that sharing we learn not only to love our little group but to be more loving to all people – naturally. Or, to cite another example, we learn that Jesus interceded regularly in prayer for others. So we decide to do the same thing, and in praying we notice that we begin to grow in love for others, even for our enemies.

Doing What Jesus Did

Here is what happens. We decide to do some of the simple things that Jesus did and we do them regularly, always inviting God to form the character of Christ in us. When we do these things, the kinds of things we can do, God begins to work in us in such a way to conform us into disciples, so that the character of Christ flows from us naturally, so that we come to the point where we live our lives the way Christ would live them if he were us.

In short, doing things that Jesus did might be the clearest understanding of discipleship we could ever have. Doing what Jesus did might be better than all the workshops and seminars we could attend, or all the books we could read.

This sounds so simple that many might think it is too easy. But Jesus said his yoke was easy. He didn't mean that there were no problems for those who followed him, but he must have meant that living a life of discipleship was easier than any other kind of life. And why shouldn't it be? If we are living in harmony with our Creator, if we are living as he intended, that ought to be the easiest way to live.

There will always be programs of discipleship, new methods, new materials, even new gimmicks. But the tried and true way of discipleship, the way that has been practiced by followers of the Lord for two thousand years, is to do what Jesus did. That way is worth rediscovering in our own day.

NOTES

1. Quoted in Kenneth Ronald Davis, *Anabaptism and Asceticism: A Study in Intellectual Origins* (Scottdale, PA: Herald Press, 1974), 223.

2. The italics are mine.

3. The italics are mine.

To Be, Not Do: Hearing God's Call on Our Lives

Valerie Rempel

We live in what has often been referred to as a post-modern age, this period of history in which there seem to be significant cultural shifts away from what characterized the modern, industrial age. Those of us who live in the West seem to be caught in a period of instability where we recognize that the old ways of doing things no longer seem to work, and yet the new patterns are not completely established. Paul Lakeland describes this time as the "interplay between the given and the novel." He writes that "consciously or unconsciously, the present moment takes an attitude toward the preceding time. It may improve upon it, abandon it, transform it, castigate it, but it cannot simply repeat it."[1]

This dis-ease with what was arises, in part, out of our growing suspicion that the very things designed to solve human ills have only given us new problems. As a result, there is an increasing distrust of established institutions and patterns of life. Many people find themselves unwilling to commit to any absolute, particularly an absolute that is passed on from a previous generation. In a world that seems increasingly unstable, truth becomes relative, and many people have turned to a search for some kind of authentic experience as a way of giving meaning to their existence. Instead of trusting what has been handed down, many are willing to accept only what they have personally experienced. Out of that grows our culture's increased fascination with drugs, sexual promiscuity, extreme sports and travel, as well as alternative forms of spirituality. Some choose to cushion themselves in artificially created worlds such as the shopping mall, the gambling casino, or even the vacation resort. Basically, we live in a world and a culture that is, as Lakeland rather succinctly puts it, "characterized by cheerful ahistoricality, contented rootlessness, guiltless consumerism, and low expectations of the future."[2]

Given this reality, it is not surprising that so many Christians are concerned about calling. Having been oft-told that God has a plan for our lives, we are left wondering how that plan fits into this world, because in many ways, these are our experiences, too. Many are questioning the institutions of the church, and even the theological traditions that have been passed down. In many places our worship services have become battlefields over the way people experience God's presence and participate in worship. We struggle with changing cultural values regarding marriage and family life. And even as Christians, we worry about our jobs. The traditional loyalty of a company to an employee, or an employee to a company, rarely exists anymore, even for Christians. We live in a society where the average worker will have a succession of jobs over his or her working lifetime. We may well wonder what that means for Christian calling and vocation!

If we are to do biblical and theological reflection on the subject of calling as it relates to work, we need to set some guidelines. To begin with, we need to recognize that at some level our concern about the issue of calling is reflective of privilege. In general, we only worry about meaning if our basic needs are met. In some parts of the world unemployment is rampant and a job, any job, would be welcome. Even in North America, there are many people who struggle to put food on the table and keep a roof overhead. If it takes all my energy to simply live, I am not likely to worry about meaning or a sense of calling in my job. I will be preoccupied with survival.

At the same time, just because this isn't a question for everyone (e.g., it may not be a critical question for my Christian brother or sister living in the third world), does not negate the reality of the problem for many people in North America. This is a question many people in our culture are asking, so we need to take it seriously. At the same time, in whatever way we answer the question of meaning and calling in our work, the basic ideas need to be able to be contextualized for other settings. In other words, what I say about work and calling in North America should have some relevance for work and calling in other, less privileged parts of the world.

Secondly, whatever we say about work and calling needs to be meaningful across a range of jobs and professions, and should not assume that people with so-called ordinary jobs do not find them meaningful. In an article about calling and vocation, a Christian professor wondered if the maintenance man at his university found any meaning in his work, if he felt connected to the mission of the larger institution. I found myself thinking, "He's probably the only one who gets it – the floors were dirty, and now they're clean! We should all be so fortunate as to see that kind of demonstrable progress in our jobs!" Maybe it is the professor trying to teach a church history course to a group of seminary students who has more cause to wonder about the meaning or significance of his or her work. Do we really need to know about medieval monasticism or the great awakenings in order to preach the gospel or minister effectively in the church? My point is this: whatever we say about meaning in work must be applicable for both the maintenance worker and the university professor.

It must also take into account the various ways in which people come to their jobs, and recognize that not everyone is presented with a wide range of choices when it comes it work, or, for that matter, is prone to a great deal of intellectual reflection about personal identity and meaning. For example, while some readers may have chosen their profession in answer to a distinct sense of God's call in their life and as one choice out of many possible occupations, others may have come to their jobs by happenstance. They needed employment, the job was there, it seemed a good fit and they took it. For example, one of my first jobs was summer employment at a retirement and nursing facility in my small hometown. There were people who worked there out of a genuine sense of Christian service, but there were others who worked there because it meant they did not have to commute to a larger city, they had the option of working part-time, or the job did not require a college education. My own employment fell into those categories. The job was in town, I could ride my bicycle to work, and they were willing to employ a rather unskilled teenager whose previous work experience was mostly babysitting. What we say about calling needs to take this reality into consideration. Some people simply have more choices than others, and some people are more inclined to introspection than others. Not everyone worries about whether or not they are "called" to the work they do.

Most importantly, whatever we say about calling should take seriously biblical ideas and themes. We belong to a theological tradition that has tried to take the Bible seriously as normative for faith and life. In doing theological reflection we are bringing our experiences into a kind of conversation with the biblical text and our faith tradition, but this is not something we do just to pass the time. Our theological reflection is done for the Christian community which seeks to be faithful to God. Our understanding of calling and vocation must be rooted in the biblical text and have something to say not only to us as individuals, but to the wider Christian community.

Within the Christian tradition, we often use "calling" to describe our understanding of God's particular will for our lives as it relates to the work we do, especially when that work is church-related. In the Bible, however, the word is most often used in the same way that it is more commonly used today to refer to the way I might call out a greeting to someone I meet. In general, the Bible's use of the word "call" does not seem to have reference to the idea of being called to a particular vocation or leadership role.

Beginning in the Old Testament, what we understand as "call" language is used to refer to God's activity in summoning together a people to participate in God's work in the world. As R. Paul Stevens puts it, "It is a call to salvation, a call to holiness and a call to service."[3] When the Old Testament writers refer to the call of God they are not talking about leadership roles, or particular occupations, but about the call to salvation. God calls a people together, names them, forms them into a new community, and calls them to worship God alone.

In the New Testament this idea of calling continues, but we often see it in the particular, rather than the corporate, as individuals are called to join what is becoming an expanded community of God's people. Jesus "calls" or "invites" people to repent of their sins, to turn to him and to follow him in a life of discipleship that is expressed in one's daily living. Jesus invites people to new life, a life lived as citizens in the Kingdom of God, and we have those marvelous passages in the gospel accounts in which Jesus describes what Kingdom living is like. It is expressed in love for one's neighbor as well as one's enemies, in honest dealings, in caring for the helpless or needy, in sharing one's resources, and so forth. Again, let me stress the invitational nature of Jesus' call. Jesus invites people to come and to follow him – he never compels people to follow.

The Pauline epistles also use "call" language. Here again we see Paul using "call" language primarily in reference to the salvation that is found in Christ and in living the Christian way, though he also refers to being "called" in his own experience of anointing as an apostle of Christ Jesus. Again, what I want to highlight is the invitation to new life. To be called is to be invited into a new relationship with Christ and a reconciled relationship with God the Father. In addition, it is a call to live at peace with other believers and as the family of God. But there is one other kind of usage that is important to note, as well. Paul uses "call" language when advising young Christians about their life situations at the time they first accepted Jesus' invitation to new life. For example, in 1 Corinthians 7, Paul suggests that becoming a Christian does not give someone the right to leave an unbelieving spouse, nor does it mean that one must immediately leave his or her present employment. In a similar fashion, gentiles do not have to become Jews (they do not have to be circumcised), nor do Jews have to repudiate their Jewish heritage, become "uncircumcised." Being called by God is transformational, but that transformation does not give us license to abandon all other commitments. I do not mean to imply that other commitments in any way outweigh our obligation to follow Jesus once we have accepted that invitation. Paul is concerned about the stability and witness of these young churches. When he encourages people to stay in the situation they were in when they heard and responded to God's call, he is reminding them of their obligation to live like Christians even in situations that are less than ideal, such as marriages in which one partner is not a believer, being a bond-servant or slave, etc. True freedom, he points out, is found through Christ.

Even though early Christians did not immediately leave their occupations when they became believers, those who understood their work to be incompatible with the Christian life did eventually change occupations when possible. It remains true that some jobs are difficult for Christians to do, given their reordered lives and the ethics of the Kingdom. It is a sort of divine mystery. To be called by God does not mean that I have to give up my occupation or that I have to take up a particular occupation. At the same time, because the call of God so transforms my life, I may not feel free to continue in an occupation that conflicts with the Kingdom values I am learning to embrace.

Martin Luther and John Calvin, the great 16th century Protestant reformers, significantly shaped the modern understanding of calling and vocation by dignifying ordinary work. As a result, Protestants often warn against the dangers of a Catholic understanding of calling with its stress on the spiritual life over the secular. This is exemplified by an understanding that has viewed monasticism as the highest form of service to God, in contrast to the ordinary work performed by the laity. For many years, we Protestants have tended to talk as if only ministers and missionaries are called by God to Christian service.

Yet one can also find warnings about Protestant views of calling. It seems that in their reaction to the monastic tradition of withdrawal from the world, Luther and Calvin helped to spiritualize ordinary work for the Protestant movement. As a result, Protestants have tended to elevate secular work to the point where calling is frequently confused with a vocation or job.

When this happens, it can be tempting to see some jobs as more "meaningful," which leads to a hierarchy in which we view ministers and missionaries as being the most called, with people in medicine and other caring professions close behind, followed by those in agriculture and business, and ending with lawyers and investment people down near the bottom, just slightly above people who do questionable things for a living.

I do not think the biblical text gives us much encouragement in that direction. All believers are called to service in the church and the world. When we talk about the priesthood of all believers we are acknowledging that all of us are called to minister to each other. It is useful, at this point, to refer to the biblical texts which remind us that the Holy Spirit gifts the church with various ministerial roles with the goal of building up the entire body. Furthermore, Paul reminds us that we cannot distinguish between roles. The foot can't say, for example, "Because I am not a hand, I do not belong to the body" (1 Cor 12:15ff). By implication, if we agree that clergy are not more called than other Christians, I think we have to say that health professionals are not more called than bankers, and so on down the line. We are not going to rate callings or occupations on some sort of sliding scale. What would be the formula for that kind of calculation? At the same time, in our efforts to acknowledge the ministry opportunities in the wider marketplace and to give them value, it is important that we not shift to the view that it is ministers and missionaries who are out of touch with "real" life and "real" people and "real" ministry. I am all for expanding our sense of Christian calling to all areas of life and work, but highly uncomfortable with devaluing the roles of pastors and missionaries to the point where they are viewed as escapees from "real" life and ministry. If that is the case, what am I supposed to do about my job, which is directly related to training people for church ministry and mission? Furthermore, I grew up in a pastor's home and had a front row seat to the parade of human problems and concerns that confront pastors on a weekly basis. There is a great deal of "real" life occurring within our church congregations and in our local communities. Just because these situations are often held in confidence, does not mean that they do not exist.

Understanding all believers as called by God also has implications, I think, for the diversity of jobs available to us. In my context, for example, the Seminary president travels a great deal of the time, but I seldom take note of his schedule. This is not because it does not matter, but because on a day-to-day basis his absence or presence on campus affects me very little. By contrast, I am very aware of when the faculty receptionist is absent. She directs traffic, listens to students and faculty rant and rave about all sorts of subjects, keeps the photocopier going, and helps out at a moment's notice. Who is more valuable to the institution? More called to service? The receptionist is on the front lines, so to speak, and I really notice whether she is there or not, but without the funds raised by the Seminary president, and the work he does with our board of directors and conference leaders, the institution itself would be in jeopardy. If the maintenance staff doesn't take care of the buildings, my teaching is hampered. If I fail to give time and thought to class preparation, I cheat my students of their tuition money. It is a case where, as Paul puts it, the ear can't say "because I am not an eye, I do not belong to the body." What would happen if the whole body were an eye, i.e., a secretary, a fund-raiser, a professor? As the apostle writes in 1 Corinthins 12, "where would the sense of hearing be?" The point I am trying to make is this: our calling to live as children of God and followers of Jesus Christ gets worked out in these daily situations. Bernard Adeney puts it like this: "Whether work is for necessity, for fulfillment, or for vocation, Christians are called to transform their work into a mode of servanthood."[4]

Unfortunately, one common understanding of calling is that God has a particular assignment for each Christian – we simply have to find it. I am troubled by this understanding. I have work that I find meaningful and enjoy. My salary allows me to contribute to Kingdom work, make mortgage payments, and take the occasional vacation, but other workers are not so fortunate. Can I simply assume that minimum wage workers have been assigned to routine, low-paying tasks? What about the seamstress working in a sweatshop somewhere in Asia so that I can buy cheap clothes in California? Is that God-ordained? This view seems to suggest that God has a sort of cosmic work assignment chart, but raises the question of why we should expect to get the most choice and most meaningful assignments. What about someone who does not find satisfaction or deep meaning in their work? Does that mean they are out of God's will (that they have not found their assigned place?) or that they are rebelling against the place they had been assigned? Viewing God's call as simply a matter of finding my assigned place only works if I like the place I think I'm assigned. If every time I get bored, or dissatisfied, receive a difficult employee review or face distasteful work assignments I begin to question whether or not I have missed God's call, I am likely to live with a great deal of uncertainty and self-doubt.

Ultimately, to be called by God is to be given life, and that new life sets in place a transformation of our desires, values, and goals. We belong to God, are a part of God's people, and are challenged to join in the work God is doing in the world. That holds true whether we are employed or unemployed, whether we live in North America or elsewhere, whether we are maintenance workers or university professors. The call of God is first to be, not to do. This addresses, I think, the problem of identity that is so rampant in our culture. In a society that endlessly seeks to answer the question "Who am I?" we are charged to ask, "Whose am I?"[5] The answer, of course, is that I belong to God! Whatever call we feel to a profession is secondary to our call to live as a Christian.

Perhaps this seems too simplistic. I hope not. I think it is vitally important for us to understand ourselves as called. It is important because then we begin to grasp the treasure that we hold, a treasure that is meant to be shared with all people, everywhere. In the same way I have been invited, "called," to become a child of God, I am invited to follow Jesus in the way of the cross, a way of service and of love. That will, I think, impact how I work, and it may even impact where I work as I test my decisions and choices against the ethics of the Bible. But ultimately, it will propel me to live as a Christian on all the days of my life, at work, at home and at play.

Hearing God's Call on Our Lives

Let me close by testing this against the guidelines I set earlier. Does this apply to those of us living in North America as well as to those in other parts of the world? Yes, God calls people from all nations to take on a new identity as the children of God. Does this apply to the maintenance worker as well as the university professor, the employed and the unemployed? Yes, God calls people from all walks of life (just think of the Bible stories: tent-makers, fishermen, tax collectors, prostitutes, soldiers, businesswomen, kings, and slaves), and he calls them all to a new way of living that is reflective of Kingdom values: honesty, integrity, faithfulness, and service. Does it help us answer the question of identity in a world that is searching for meaning? Yes. My primary identity is not formed by my job, but by the decision to accept the invitation to follow Jesus. Christians are called to faithfully proclaim the good news of the Kingdom, to witness to the power of God to change lives, to be ethical in all of their dealings, to offer cups of cold water, to feed the hungry and shelter the destitute. This can be done, should be done, whatever our occupation.

NOTES

1. Paul Lakeland, *Postmodernity: Christian Identity in a Fragmented Age*. Series: Guides to Theological Inquiry, Kathryn Tanner, ed. (Minneapolis: Fortress Press, 1997), 1.

2. Lakeland, *Postmodernity*, xiii.

3. R. Paul Stevens, *The Other Six Days: Vocation, Work, and Ministry in Biblical Perspectives* (Grand Rapids, MI: Eerdmans, 1999), 84-85.

4. Bernard Adeney, "Work: Necessity, Vocation and Strategy," *Radix* (Jan/Feb 1984), 15.

5. I am indebted to Howard Loewen for this important distinction.

Inviting Jesus into our Midst: The Challenge of Reconciliation and Mutual Accountability

Timothy J. Geddert

We live in a pluralistic world. The ethical norms and guidelines that we subscribe to will likely not be shared by most of the people around us, as was once the case. And how do people respond to such ethical questions? Here are some examples:

> *I am responsible to no one but myself. I seek my own ethical guidelines. As long as I don't hurt other people, I can do whatever I personally believe is right.* (This is a typical viewpoint representing the spirit of our individualistic age.)

> *I have the Bible and I have a conscience. I can decide for myself what I believe is right and wrong!* (This is a typical Christian viewpoint in our individualistic age.)

> *I just look for an authority I can trust – my pastor, a Christian writer or a radio preacher – and they tell me what the Bible really says is right or wrong.* (This is a typical evangelical reaction to our society's individualism and to the relativism it often breeds.)

> *You are a mutually accountable fellowship. I will be present with you and help you to seek ethical guidelines as a community. You will bind and loose each other in my name.* (This is how Jesus responds to our individualistic age.)

The reformer, Martin Luther, defined the church as the place where the Word of God is rightly preached and the sacraments of the church are rightly administered. Such a definition of the church provides little motivation to become a responsible community where members are mutually accountable to one another. The radical reformers of the same era defined church quite differently. Church was understood to be the place where people freely commit themselves to become disciples of Jesus and freely commit themselves to their brothers and sisters in a community of accountability. Such an understanding of the church centralizes relationships characterized by mutual responsibility and accountability.

Throughout the centuries the spiritual descendents of these early radical reformers have sought to retain and embody this "community" understanding of church – sometimes with success, sometimes with serious failure. There are many steps separating two extremes: on one side, a heartless legalistic church discipline and on the other side, an attitude of unbounded tolerance, where everyone can do as they please. And I dare say Anabaptist and Mennonite churches, who have tried to follow the radical reformation path, have found themselves at different times and in different places at every point between those extremes.

We have not reached the goal. We have not become church as Jesus intended it to be. But those willing to take courageous steps towards this ideal will experience God's help in becoming what Jesus had in mind.

Matthew 18 provides insights that may help us to become the kind of reconciled responsible community Jesus intends. Nowhere in scripture do we find another speech of Jesus that describes as clearly his ideal for the church. For this reason the early Anabaptist churches considered this chapter of central importance in their understanding of "church." So let's examine the chapter and see which basic convictions, which warnings, which recommendations, and which promises it contains, that might help us on the way.*

Who is the Greatest? (Verses 1-5)

¹At that time the disciples came to Jesus and asked, "Who is the greatest in the kingdom of heaven?" ²He called a child, whom he put among them, ³and said, "Truly I tell you, unless you change and become like children, you will never enter the kingdom of heaven. ⁴Whoever becomes humble like this child is the greatest in the kingdom of heaven. ⁵Whoever welcomes one such child in my name welcomes me."

If we want to be church as Jesus intended it, then everything depends on our approach to God's Kingdom, to church, and to our relationships to each other. The disciples of Jesus were imagining God's Kingdom to be something like this: Jesus would become a powerful political ruler in a reconstituted free Israelite state. And they, his followers, would be at his side, ministers in his government, those who would share his glory and his authority. And it was not enough to hold fast to the conviction that all of them would be great rulers in the new kingdom. They also wanted to know who among them would have the *most* power and prestige. That is the background to the disciples' question: "Who is the greatest in the kingdom of heaven?" (verse 1).

Jesus' reaction? "Careful! With that kind of attitude, you won't even be there with me in God's kingdom!" (Note that Matthew's Gospel often speaks of Kingdom of *Heaven*, but means the same thing as Kingdom of *God*.) It is clear to Jesus that the time is ripe for another object lesson. He takes a child, small, helpless, neither presumptuous nor audacious, without rights and without power. He places the child in their midst and looks at his followers. No doubt they are somewhat taken aback as Jesus makes his three astonishing claims:

- This is what you must be like!
- One like this child is the greatest in God's kingdom!
- If you want to accept me, then accept people like this child!

Do we want to become the kind of committed fellowship in which Jesus truly makes his presence felt? The way to this goal starts with our attitudes. We do not seek to increase our power and influence; we do not aim to become "great" according to the standards of this world. Rather, with childlike trust, we accept an entirely new kind of greatness, one that is given to us as a gift . . . if only we will humble ourselves and receive it, and thus receive Jesus. We do not seek rights and privileges; rather, we invest what we are and have in the lives of those who are with us on the journey, and who are unable to meet the challenges of the discipleship journey on their own . . . and that is all of us! That is how Jesus' presence becomes real and tangible among us.

Living the Christian Life

Be Careful About Yourself and Your Influence (Verses 6-10)

⁶"If any of you put a stumbling block before one of these little ones who believe in me, it would be better for you if a great millstone were fastened around your neck and you were drowned in the depth of the sea. ⁷Woe to the world because of stumbling blocks! Occasions for stumbling are bound to come, but woe to the one by whom the stumbling block comes!

⁸"If your hand or your foot causes you to stumble, cut it off and throw it away; it is better for you to enter life maimed or lame than to have two hands or two feet and to be thrown into the eternal fire. ⁹And if your eye causes you to stumble, tear it out and throw it away; it is better for you to enter life with one eye than to have two eyes and to be thrown into the hell of fire.

¹⁰"Take care that you do not despise one of these little ones; for, I tell you, in heaven their angels continually see the face of my Father in heaven."

Jesus has just said that children are models for us (verse 3). Now he adds: And we are models for them (verse 6). We observe them and imitate their childlike attitudes. They watch us and see in our actions what is important on the road of discipleship. What a responsibility rests with us! When we are modeling the wrong things, or when they misunderstand our actions and we "put a stumbling block before one of these little ones," then we are to hear Jesus' warning: "It would be better for you if a great millstone were fastened around your neck and you were drowned in the depths of the sea" (verse 6). Jesus often used picture language, made drastic claims and exaggerated to make his point. His goal, of course, is not to make us live terrified that we might qualify for this inescapable drowning (or something so bad this would seem preferable!). Nor should we live anxiously, always insecure whether we might have taken a false step and fearing God's judgment will rain down swiftly. With his hyperbolic statement, Jesus was saying as loudly and clearly as possible: "This is important!"

If we want to make progress in the direction Christ wants to lead us, we will need to pay attention to the consequences of our actions. Only so can we pursue the supremely important goal of helping the "little ones," the vulnerable, the easily-wounded beginners on the road of discipleship. Jesus speaks of the drastic measures we should be willing to take: "Cut off the hand; hack off the foot; tear out the eye!" Again he uses hyperbole. He clearly does not mean it literally; but he does mean it seriously. We are asked to take drastic measures, if necessary, to avoid irresistible temptations ourselves, and to keep from putting stumbling blocks in the way of the "little ones."

Jesus knows how easily each of us can despise others, particularly those whose weakness ends up costing us some of our freedom. So he says, "Do not despise one of these little ones" (verse 10). On the contrary, protect them and help them, just as God does. God even charges the heavenly angels to watch over the little ones, the vulnerable ones.

Most of our Bibles do not contain any verse 11, though it might appear in brackets or in a footnote. The "missing material" was in fact added by a scribe somewhere along the way. But its contents actually fit this context rather well: "For the Son of Man came to save the lost." If God took such serious measures to bring us onto the right path, then we want to make our contribution toward helping others as they walk along this path with us.

Seeking, Finding, Celebrating (Verses 12-14)

Most of us know that Jesus used the parable of the lost sheep to explain to people why he was eating at the same table with tax collectors and "sinners." He was *seeking* these people. And having found them, he was *celebrating* with them. But that explanation is found in Luke 15! We should not read that interpretation into this text. Here the same parable is used for a very different purpose.

Here the Christian community is the sheep herd. We are the vulnerable sheep. All our attempts to flee temptation, to be the right kinds of models for others, to help people along the way, will never produce the perfect community. They cannot, for the community is made up of fallible people. There will be some who will go astray (and here it means they will do something that distances them from the shepherd and his flock). And we will do the same!

The life of a disciple consists of good beginnings, good intentions, some successes, some failures, and many detours along the way. Those on the discipleship road will need to be granted new starts, and they will need to take courageous steps, as they return to the path of discipleship. For that we need each other.

Just as God went after the lost sheep, so we go after each other. Sheep do not always wander so far away that the serious measures recounted next need to be taken. But in Jesus' flock we watch out for each other as the shepherd watches out for us. We want to make sure that we stay together. We are not border patrols keeping the wrong people out, or prison guards keeping people in. And when wrong steps are taken, we neither scold nor punish. Rather we care for each other. We watch out for each other, lovingly and respectfully. We are not out to rob each other of freedom. We honor each other, but we also help each other. We reject the sort of individualism that says everyone is free to do as they please; we know it would be far too dangerous to live that way.

Jesus' parable assumes that we will *notice* if a sheep has wandered away. It assumes that it is important for us to stay together, that we very much want the wandering sheep back again, and even that the *sheep* would certainly want to be back in the fold, if only it could find the way. The parable also assumes we know how to celebrate forgiveness, reconciliation and new beginnings. On all these points we are a long way from the goal. Our ideals for the church, and particularly God's ideals for the church, far outstrip the reality. But Jesus, whom God sent to win us back to the fold, is our model. If God is ready to throw a party when just one is found, we too can celebrate our small victories in these matters.

Like a Gentile and a Tax Collector (Verses 15-17)

We cringe just reading these titles. Some translations even use "pagan" or "heathen" instead of "gentile!" And we know what the people around Jesus thought of tax collectors. Who wants to be called names like that? What Christian congregation has the right to throw around epithets like that for those who do not stay in the fold? If we then read the contents of these three verses we cringe even further. Who is claiming the right to define "sin?" Who has the right to confront another person for his or her behavior? Haven't we learned anything from the legalism and hypocrisy of the past?

Whatever others have done with this passage, I for one do not read this text as a roadmap leading to the exclusion of a sinner from the Christian community. Exactly the opposite is represented here. From beginning to end the goal of the passage is to do everything possible to win back a brother or a sister. In the Bible "sin" means "failing to reach the goal." When our actions and our relationships somehow miss the target, we do everything we can to help each other head for the goal again.

> "If another member of the church sins against you, go and point out the fault when the two of you are alone. If the member listens to you, you have regained that one" (verse 15).

The goal is to recognize the failure and clean it up, without the rest of the community needing to know anything about it. Confidentiality is preserved. The goal is always reconciliation, never to set up the "sinner" as a bad example. No, it gets taken care of privately, if at all possible.

The two words "against you" that are included in the NRSV (above) are in fact missing in many Bible manuscripts. There is uncertainty whether they truly belong to the text. If they belong in the text, the text might actually be talking about a conflict between two people. Maybe each of them thinks the other is at fault. The text would then be saying that when barriers come between two people in the community, we do not simply accept that as a fact of life. Each is responsible to go to the other and seek to clear up the problem. An unreconciled relationship will hurt the individuals involved and the entire community.

Even if the two little words "against you" do not belong to the original text, there is at least the possibility that we are still dealing with only a misunderstanding. Maybe I have a critical attitude toward the other person. So we attempt to clear up the matter between us. Of course it might really be the case that one person has seriously sinned, against me or in some other way. Then, too, I give my best effort to help the person. The attitudes that we have already encountered in this chapter must characterize my approach, if there is to be a chance of true success in winning the person back.

> "But if you are not listened to, take one or two others with you, so that every word may be confirmed by the evidence of two or three witnesses" (verse 16).

The witnesses could play a variety of different roles here. If there has clearly been a serious sin committed, then perhaps they are people who have witnessed what was done. Their role is then to strengthen my attempts to win the person back. "We know what you did, and we are concerned for you!" If we are talking about a conflict in the relationship between two people, then the witnesses are there to observe how I am handling the situation. Am I just trying to justify myself? Am I being fair with the other person? Am I really trying to be helpful? Loving? Forgiving? The witnesses might also be there to help convince the other person that we really do want him or her back again; we all do!

> "If the member refuses to listen to them, tell it to the church, and if the offender refuses to listen even to the church, let such a one be to you as a gentile and a tax collector" (verse 17).

Only in extreme cases, when nothing else has been successful, does the community as a whole get involved. But what kind of "church" are we talking about here? Remember that Jesus is still talking to the twelve disciples. And Matthew is probably thinking of the average sized church of his day, which would be about thirty to forty people who met regularly in a home. In mutually accountable groups of that size the church can effectively act.

What do we do in far larger churches, where many times as many people gather, and where a significant percentage of them do not know (and perhaps do not care about) the person we are trying to win back? It is clear that in such situations "the church" will not be very effective in taking this next step. Thus we need home fellowship groups, leadership teams, perhaps other structures that will help us to act in ways that embody what Jesus had in mind here. Moreover it would be a terrible mistake if we started literally practicing Matthew 18:17 before making significant progress in living out what Jesus has just been teaching about our attitudes to each other in the Christian community (cf. Matt 18:1-16).

The church puts serious effort into winning back the sheep, the person who has wandered away. And when every effort fails? Well then we finally have the right to kick them out of the church, right? No! Just the opposite. We never seek, and are never given, the right to dispense with a fallen member. Rather we take one more step, the most radical step of all, in our ceaseless efforts to gain the person back again. We treat them like a "gentile" and a "tax collector."

Perhaps only I will view the person that way (notice the words "for you" [singular in Greek!]), perhaps the whole church will. Either I or we will now treat this person like a "gentile" and a "tax collector." And what does that mean? It means that if all our attempts so far have failed, we try it the other way around. We no longer view the person as a brother or sister who is going astray; rather we view the person as someone who needs to be won (back) into the fellowship.

We have never given up wanting the person back in our community. But the person's unwillingness to listen to the church has distanced that person from us. (Note carefully that the person is not distanced because of the sin that started the process!) So now we need to treat the person the way Jesus treated tax collectors. (Remember the author of this text, Matthew, was a tax collector himself!) We in no way despise the person, but rather we invite him into our fellowship. We pursue friendship with the person, we exude love and acceptance, as Jesus did. We gladly share meal fellowship with the person. After all, we are doing everything possible to win this person for the community.

It was not the sin that caused the break with the church. It was not because somebody missed the target. Nor are they on the outside because the reconciliation did not work. What's more, the church did not cut off the person from the community. Rather the person removed himself or herself by not listening to the church, by withdrawing from the mutual accountability that defines us. We now accept what the person has chosen to become . . . an outsider to the community. And we hope that the result of their "time out" will be a readiness to come back. We have never given up working towards the reconciliation.

Of course there will be situations in which we need to devise the best possible structures and procedures that can help us carry out what Jesus is teaching here. We are not bound to the literal wording of this text any more than we should literally cut off our hand. Rather this text is communicating to us what is important to Jesus and what kinds of actions foster Christ's ideals among us. The steps that Jesus outlines are designed to emphasize:

- restored and reconciled relationships;
- serious effort to help each other along the discipleship road;
- willingness to receive and to offer correction;
- integrity and as much confidentiality as possible in our efforts to win someone back;
- an unceasing concern and concerted efforts to overcome barriers and restore the wholeness of the community.

To do that we need help (Verses 18-20)

Yes we do! We are not the kind of Christian fellowship that can carry that out successfully. Jesus knew that better than we do. So he promised that we would receive whatever we need in order to practice what he has been teaching. We are invited to take courageous steps in the direction Jesus has shown us, and Jesus promises both his presence and his help. The following verses contain astonishing promises that we may draw on as we follow Jesus' teaching.

> "Truly I tell you, whatever you bind on earth will be bound in heaven, and whatever you loose on earth will be loosed in heaven" (verse 18).

We ask: How in the world are we supposed to practice what Jesus has just taught, when we can't even agree anymore on what constitutes "sin?" Jesus answers: "I will help you to discern which ethical norms you should follow. Church is not merely the place where the word is preached and the sacraments distributed. It is the place where we make ethical decisions, where we think together and decide together what it means to follow Jesus in life."

"Bind" and "loose," the two central terms in this text, were technical terms that were used in Jesus' day to speak in three different ways of legal decisions on ethical matters. A fourth use of the term had to do with "binding" Satan and then "loosing" (setting free) Satan's victims. There are other texts in the Gospels which use the words with this fourth sense (cf. Matt 16:19; Mark 3:27), but it does not seem to fit well into the present texts. The three "ethical meanings" can help us to see what Jesus is getting at here. In first century Judaism people would come to the rabbis and ask them to "bind" or "loose" in any of the following ways:

- Oaths: "I have sworn an oath – bind me or loose me!" What that means is that the oath I have sworn now proves to be a problem. Keeping it would perhaps require me to break a law, but breaking it is itself against the law. Am I bound or loosed? Should I keep it or am I freed from it?
- Ethical decisions: "I would like to do this or that. But I am unsure if the law allows it. Bind me or loose me." That means,

- help me to decide whether my proposed action is prohibited or allowed.
- Forgiveness: "I have done this or that – bind me or loose me." That means, help me to discern whether I have sinned or not, and if so, what I need to do to be fully forgiven.

Jesus is passing this kind of responsibility and authority on to the church! Of course we cannot "bind" and "loose" by simply pushing personal opinions on others or by taking a vote. Just as the Old Testament law was the standard for the rabbis, so the teaching of Jesus and the guidelines we gain from scripture remain binding for us. But it is our responsibility as a Christian community to seek the guidance of Jesus and the scriptures, and to try to understand how they can be applied to the situations we face.

If we, Christ's representatives on earth, can – in Jesus' name and consistent with his teaching – reach a consensus concerning what it means to follow Jesus in our time and place, then heaven will confirm our decisions. That is the promise of Jesus. We find God's support for the divinely-guided decisions that we make together. Jesus in no way promises that we will become infallible, but we will do our best with Jesus' help. If we can remain willing to rethink our decisions, in case we are given new insights, we can freely and confidently live by our present decisions, confident that they represent God's will for us, at least to the best of our ability to discern that now, until God leads us to new insight.

> "Again, truly I tell you, if two of you agree on earth about anything you ask, it will be done for you by my Father in heaven" (verse 19).

If we are serious about becoming the kind of community described in this chapter, we can be sure that our prayer life must improve. It is, after all, completely impossible to truly practice the radical teaching of this chapter in our own strength. What are the two people agreeing in prayer about in this text? Naturally not a new car, or a pay raise, or whatever they might happen to desire at the moment. Jesus is talking about the matters that have been discussed in this chapter. We pray for humility, for integrity, for readiness to be reconciled, for a love that flows towards others (including "tax collectors"), for openness to the insights of others (we need that if we want to bind and loose!), etc. Here the whole is greater than the sum of the parts. We join together in prayer as we seek God's help so that we can practice the attitudes and take the steps outlined in this chapter. And God will hear our prayers.

"For where two or three are gathered in my name, I am there among them" (verse 20).

There it is – the definition of "church" – probably the best one the New Testament has to offer. Church is where two or three are gathered in Jesus' name. Jesus is not describing the main weekly gathering of the church (Sunday worship services). Rather he is describing the very nature of the church itself. It consists of the people who have been gathered, and Jesus among them. God was the one who gathered them together and now they are bound together through their common relationship with Jesus. In the binding fellowship that they have become, Jesus is present in their midst.

These words "among them" (or better "in their midst") remind us of exactly the same words that were used for the child that Jesus placed "among them" (or "in their midst"; cf. verse 2). The words in the original Greek text are exactly the same. Jesus will be present among us not as a ruler, forcing us to do what is right, but as a child, unprotected and dependent on whether we will receive him or not. By receiving each other, we receive Jesus (verse 5), and then the one who is both our model and our Lord will be present "among us," and we will know it.

Immeasurable Forgiveness (Verses 21-35)

This chapter refers to many different attitudes that are crucial in any Christian community. One of them has not yet been explicitly cited, though it has been the assumption of the whole chapter: readiness to forgive. Peter could easily recognize that in what Jesus had just taught. Suddenly he asks, "Lord, if another member of the church sins against me, how often should I forgive? As many as seven times?" (verse 21).

Peter saw forgiveness as a responsibility, and an odious one at that. The parable about forgiveness that Jesus tells ends with a challenge to "forgive from the heart." Those who forgive from the bottom of their heart offer it freely, and gladly, and often. They do not count how many times they have already forgiven.

It is ironic, I think, that we cannot be sure exactly how many times Jesus said Peter should be willing to forgive. In some translations we read, "Not seven times but seventy-seven times." Others read, "Not seven times, but seventy times seven times." That leaves us with a problem. Are we expected by Jesus to forgive 490 times, or would seventy-seven times be sufficient? The original text can be read both ways. The joke is on us if we think it is important to settle this one! The whole point is that nobody's counting. Have I forgiven seventy-seven times already? 490 times? 7,437 times? 16,295 times? We don't know. We don't care. We're not counting. Not if we have begun to recognize our own sinfulness; not if we have begun to learn the attitudes taught in this chapter; not if we have tasted of the immeasurably great forgiveness God has extended to us through pure grace. And if we have tasted of these, then we offer new beginnings to others in the Christian fellowship, not counting how often we have done it before. And then we receive new beginnings just as often from the others.

Those who have tasted of the kind of Christian fellowship Jesus describes in this chapter know that it is worth every effort to pursue this ideal – to become the kind of mutually responsible, forgiving and reconciling community where nobody is just there for the ride. In such a community we participate fully. We do not live for ourselves, we do not hide our weaknesses and our temptations, we do not close our eyes when others are falling way. We bind and loose, we talk openly and honestly with each other and God, and we celebrate when a "lost sheep" is returned to the fold. In such a community Jesus is present "in our midst."

---

* All scripture quotations are taken from the New Revised Standard Version.

Church Leadership
in a New Era

Entering the Wreckage: Rescripting the Pastoral Vocation[1]

Chris William Erdman

The pastors I know, including myself, are exhausted. Leadership is taking a high toll on our marriages, our relationships with our children and friends, our bodies, our beings. We know, more in our bodies than in our brains, that the church is now living in a state of perpetual white-water, and that the certainties and securities of Christendom's stable past are no more. The problem is that we pastors weren't trained for the post-Christendom renegotiation of the church's vocation that is our task today. Christendom afforded the church and its pastors many advantages, but those advantages of power and prestige blinded the church to the many ways the Word of God became compromised to causes subversive and many times antithetical to the reign of God. Still, so terribly enamored with those advantages, we pastors are pressured by anxious church folk and our own anxious selves to keep what we've cherished from slipping through our fingers.

But the collapse of Christendom is a crisis that can no longer be denied. Nor can the church's dislocation from its once privileged position in American culture be expertly managed by highly functioning and competent pastors. We are trained in the skill sets of life within a modern world in which technology and technique provide answers to every problem, but those skills are not helpful now. And our over-reliance on them only proves that the assumptions and practices of the dominant culture have co-opted our imaginations to a way of organizing our lives according to technique rather than the Bible.

But hard work and the competent management of our technological resources won't allow us to continue living in denial; we are standing in the wreckage of our cherished past and unable to engineer the future. Our denial has kept us from grief. And until we learn to grieve we cannot move forward – any pastor who cares for the bereaved knows that. But we haven't identified ourselves as bereaved persons living amid cultural wreckage.

I think the attacks on the World Trade Center and the Pentagon on September 11, 2001 cracked wide our denial and forced us to grieve whether we wanted to or not. This geopolitical crisis and the ensuing global turmoil ended America's naiveté about its life in the world, and begs pastors to do more than serve as chaplains to our nation's collective grief. We are called, as Ricoeur has pointed out, to the twin acts of suspicion (asking hard questions about our past compromises) and recovery (re-entering strange, neglected biblical texts in order to rescript imaginations too long captive to dominant ideologies). This work of suspicion and recovery is precisely the pastoral work the prophet Jeremiah was called to practice in the midst of his nation's wreckage. In and around the decade 598-587 BCE, Jeremiah confronted the pastoral denial and mistaken management strategies of Judah's religious and political leadership.

Current scholarship helps us to see Jeremiah as more than a single, nearly deranged prophet operating on the fringes of Jerusalem society. He was a spokesperson for a political movement within the Jerusalem establishment that dared to view the situation from a very different point of view. With strong ties to the Deuteronomic tradition and the Torah reform movement under Josiah, Jeremiah and the leaders of the movement (which included Baruch and the highly influential and prominent family of Shaphan), critiqued the assumptions of Jerusalem's political and religious establishment textually – that is, from the vantage point of Torah.

The book of Jeremiah, its influence among those living in the wreckage of the Exile, and the birth of new forms of community life exemplified by Ezra in the restoration, testifies that among a society of pastors – who intentionally and regularly enter an alternative reading of our current situation, flying under the radar of the dominant script – God is at work to birth enormously potent missional energy, converting our exhaustion, and rebirthing us for ministry among tired and terribly compromised congregations.

The book of Jeremiah seems to swing rhetorically around two major literary sections, and each section is punctuated by a particular focus.

Death and grief are the major themes giving coherence to chapters 1-25, while hope and new beginnings emerge in chapters 26-52. Several key texts provide prophetic strategies that can help pastors rescript their own ministry tasks in a time of massive social upheaval.

Naming Deadly Compromises: The Pastoral Work of Truth-Telling
Jeremiah 7:27-8:3

Few pastors like conflict. While we expect conflict in pastoral ministry, we don't expect it to be the norm. Most of us avoid it, some of us run from it — few, if any, of us would place the ministry of conflict at the center of our work.

From the beginning of his call to ministry, Jeremiah knew he was not only called into conflict (the world around him was collapsing into political chaos (1:14)); he was also called to provoke it — in fact, by the very act of preaching he would help bring about the collapse of everything his nation held dear (1:10, 19). His ministry of conflict would not only terrify him (1:17), it would endanger his very life (1:19; cf. 26:8).

In contrast, our understanding of ministry today is shaped by the stability and centeredness of the church in Christendom. Our pastoral role was assigned by a culture that, while it was willing to acknowledge the place of religion in its public life, relegated religion to the private values and virtues of its people. Pastors served as priests to society and, apart from a few troublesome fanatics, readily accepted the chaplaincy role assigned to them by those in power. Many of Jeremiah's contemporaries may have envisioned their role in much the same way, seeing their role as supportive of the dominant culture.

Jeremiah imagines the pastoral role very differently: his work is truth-telling, naming the deadly compromises of a people who think that their way of life is blessed by God and therefore is interminable — if the market wavers it will rebound, if enemies should look longingly at its resources its allies will stare them down (7:10).[2]

To these lies, and against this self-assured ideology of security and certainty, Jeremiah dares to utter a vision of death, designed "to pluck up and to pull down, to destroy and to overthrow" (1:10)[3] the practices and symbols of a culture propped up by people who stubbornly refuse to order their lives politically, economically, and religiously according to the Word of God. The Deuteronomic tradition that molds Jeremiah knows that the failure to listen to and obey Yahweh – a failure named four times here in staccato repetition (verses 27-28) – renders only one verdict: death (Deut. 8:19-20). The response is a frenzied, unrestrained wail of grief (verse 29). The land has been defiled, polluted by actions never sanctioned by God, yet practiced by the people. We are left feeling that this people never asked about their practices and had no standard by which to judge them as good or bad – they uncritically carried into their communities the practices of the cultures around them, and are now sacrificing their beloved children to feed the economy and keep the political machine running (verses 30-31).

"*Therefore!*" (verse 31) thunders Jeremiah, speaking the opening words of Yahweh's sentence against Judah. The pastoral task imagined by Jeremiah is a task of naming, drawing conclusions, helping people see connections they couldn't see before. "Topheth," the technology of the nation's idolatry, and "Hinnom," the industrial valley where Judah's God-deaf autonomy belches out its pollution, are renamed so that the people can no longer deny what is going on around them. The way they've ordered their lives, the assumptions and symbols that govern the nation, will kill them. Nothing humanly engineered will stand against Yahweh, who will not allow the evil to continue. This ending will be a "slaughter" – not merely the sacrificing of the weak in the community to maintain the privilege of the strong, but the silencing of all human voices as the mass graves grow too shallow and the vultures feed on human flesh (verses 33-34).

Pastors too easily stop short of the needed work of driving people deep into the consequences of their compromises. A husband locked in a titillating affair, a teenager trapped by an eating disorder can no longer see the truth. The church, too long enamored with the memory of its cultural and political privilege, will not break its allegiance to old systems without massive resistance. And so, the prophet is relentless, piling up imagery to coax his hearers into acknowledging the truth that things cannot continue as they have (8:1-2).

Christendom is no more, and the church, like it or not, must go into exile and there find its true missional identity. But pastors – themselves frightened by the chaos, unclear about what it means for the future, and made anxious by anxious people – those who listen to their sermons, pay their salaries, and cannot help but define the church and its ministry by the standards of the culture around them – will opt to try to hold the center and deny the reality of collapse.

The pastoral work we need today begins here with this first step toward grief, the work of telling the truth by daringly naming our deadly compromises.

Taught to Mourn: The Pastoral Work of Pain-Dwelling
Jeremiah 9:17-22

This hard-nosed work of naming won't build big, successful, "relevant" churches. And that's a problem because we can't imagine church any other way. But it's no secret that doing church like we've done it in the past is extremely difficult for all but a few who are still able to keep the old world going. The work of naming our compromises is aimed at deconstructing all those illusions. The only possible response is grief. People must grieve when their lives fall apart. People must grieve when their cherished symbols are destroyed. People must grieve when their trusted assumptions and confidences are pulled down and ground into the dust. But Americans aren't particularly good at grieving . . . until recently.

It's strange to me that in a nation rocked by the challenge September 11, 2001 brings to all our presumptions of certainty and security, we pastors apparently have so little to offer that differs from the words and actions that fill the media. Our role is tragically reduced to tacking Bible verses onto the larger, more relevant narratives of nationalism and militarism. We feel compelled to do whatever it takes to keep people from coming apart. And by the look of things, our flag-draped sanctuaries, patriotic liturgies, and comforting homilies are helping to keep America going about life as normally as possible. In this sense we're doing everything required of us by the White House. But America doesn't want to go about life as we did before September 11. America knows that our happy certainties and securities lie in shattered ruins, and we can't return to the normalcy we once knew. America as we have known it is no more, and we instinctively know we need to grieve.

But we pastors haven't practiced the grief work necessary to take our people into grief. Instead, instructed by our politicians, we've worked hard to help our people and our nation get back to life as it was. The imaginative redefinition of our lives made possible by the wreckage of September 11 has slipped through our fingers, and our imaginations have been exploited by the political powers of fear, retribution, and national security.

I can't help wonder what might have happened among us had we known how to pick up Jeremiah.

At a point in history not dissimilar from our own, Jeremiah was sent to practice the pastoral work of pain-dwelling for a people whose cherished symbols were destroyed, whose trusted assumptions and confidences were pulled down, and whose lives were falling apart. 598 BCE was a decidedly life-defining moment in the history of Israel. And as much as King Zedekiah tried to manage the nation's crisis in the conventional ways, he could not hold the nation together and could not manipulate his foreign policy to save his skin. A decade of turmoil ended in bitter defeat in 597, and Judah was plunged into exile.

Who is wise enough to make sense of the crisis (7:12)? The politicians and the pundits, for all their lengthy prose, have nothing meaningful to say. The one who pastors God's people in Exile knows that only one form of speech is adequate for the task. This pastor utters the strangeness of poetry in order to teach the broken how to mourn.[1] Poetry subverts our resistance, and through its cadences and imagery insinuates itself in those deep places where it can begin to dismantle our practiced denial of such inexpressible pain and bewilderment.

As opposed to the "wise" whose words are hollow in the face of such chaos, this poem calls out to the skillful mourner who gets to the death-scene first and gets the grieving going (7:29-8:3). These skilled Middle-Eastern women know exactly what to do (9:17-19), for they are the ones who truly know what's going on. Managing technology and wealth, manipulating the media, and providing comforting prayers in the temple are not competencies needed now. Needed now are eyes that weep, hearts that ache, mouths that voice the pain.

The ideology of safety and confidence, and the ideologues so captive to their way of organizing life apart from obedience to Torah, cannot withstand the enacted truth of this dirge-poem. The wise men who think they read the nation's life rightly are outsmarted by the old ladies who are not skilled in domestic policy and foreign diplomacy, but who are the ones who are truly wise. The fools are those whose eyes are dry, trying to hold on to the past and their privileged positions of power in the old order. But the skilled women know that this past is dead and can only be relinquished by grieving and teaching their daughters the words and actions of lament (verse 20).

Pastors can easily be talked out of the painful work of teaching the broken to grieve. Grieving people don't work well. They don't do their jobs, finish homework, make love to their spouses, show up for church meetings. Pastors who, like Jeremiah, teach people to go deep into their pain are threatening to Jerusalem and to Washington, D.C., and they're threatening to church governing boards. In order to keep pastors dwelling in exile from knuckling under, this text piles up more metaphors to make pain-dwelling inescapable. Bodies pile up in the streets, pressing in through windows and doors. Children are cut off from their playmates. Teenagers are cut off from their friends. Even the palace cannot avoid the stench (verse 21). And with eerie echoes of Chapter 8:2-3, "corpses fall like dung" cut down with no one to "gather" them.

Those who imagine their work from within this text will let old ladies lead them.

Old ladies remind pastors of the deep, protracted, messy, and terrifying work necessary to help people dwell in the pain of loss. Those who enter the conditions of exile need pastors who can keep at it for seventy years if necessary. Our compromised lives, ordered not by Torah or by Gospel, are neither broken nor relinquished easily.

Building a Daring Community: The Pastoral Work of Scroll-Keeping
Jeremiah 26:1-24

In 609 BCE, some ten years before the attack that sent shock waves through the nation, it became clear that those who opposed the policies of the Jerusalem establishment might pay for their opposition with their lives. The official position of the palace and the temple refused to acknowledge that their policies and assumptions were contrary to the will of Yahweh and were leading the nation toward ruin.

Pastors must proclaim the word of the Lord in the place where it is often most compromised and, therefore, where it will be most desperately resisted. The house of the Lord is a place of ideological contention, and preaching is the voicing of a claim that subverts the false claims of all its rivals. It seeks and hopes, calling to the hearers to listen and turn from their evil ways (26:3). But if they will not listen, walk in Torah, and obey, then the House they're meeting in will be abandoned and would better serve as a museum or office building with "Shiloh" painted across its door (Psalm 78:60).

When sermons strike at the heart of our compromises, those nurtured in the policies and assumptions of the State recognize the danger of God's counter-word. Priests, prophets, and all the people who heard Jeremiah knew that what he was saying was subversive. They knew that speaking against their great nation, its greatest city, and its national shrine would not be tolerated by the architects of Judah's national life. Jeremiah was liable to end up dead the moment he walked out of the building (verse 8).

This text is about what happens in the parking lot after the Sunday sermon, and it's about pastoral strategies for surviving the rigors of preaching to people who won't relinquish their captivities. It is a drama enacted every time compromises are exposed. Those nearest the seat of power are most resistant, and if they find themselves implicated by the preaching they will do what it takes to get rid of its voice (verse 11).

Preachers are rarely surprised by the reactions of those they know won't like what they are sent to preach. But the reactions that we don't expect are the ones we want to listen to. In the midst of all the brewing trouble caused by Jeremiah's preaching people into the Exile, comes a surprise reaction that is really gospel. People on the outside will often understand what insiders cannot. Here the text makes a dramatic turn. It is some "elders of the land" – people who don't read the newspaper or watch the evening news, people outside the reach of the establishment's propaganda machine – it is political outsiders whose Torah memories are awakened by Jeremiah's Torah preaching (verses 17-19).

There are people still in the land who listen, who walk in Torah, and who heed the prophets (verses 4, 5). The text wants us to know that it's the presence of these people upon whom the future hinges. The fact that Jeremiah wasn't put to death creates a whole new openness to the future that wasn't present in Jeremiah up to this point. There comes a point in pastoral ministry when we're privileged to learn that we're not the sole keeper of the scroll. There are others with us in the work. They may be few, but few is enough.

This is what impresses me about this text. It plants the seeds for what Stulman calls the piety, values, and practices "suitable for the re-imagined community that will emerge from the ruins of exile."[4] It is clear that Jeremiah operated within a community of scroll-keepers. A generation earlier, Shaphan, the secretary to King Josiah, had received from the priest's hand the rediscovered scroll of Torah (2 Kgs 22:8, 10). It may be that the house of Shaphan imagined themselves as keepers of the scroll, and learned ways to nurture a community of faithful adherents that could one day give rise to a prophet like Jeremiah, the community's most forceful and influential proponent against the corruption and compromises of Judah's political and religious elite. It is no surprise then that Ahikam son of Shaphan is the one who at the end of this drama is credited with guarding the life of Jeremiah.[5] The scroll now has a voice, and the community must also guard its interpreters.

The pastoral work of scroll-keeping, building a community around these texts, trusts that after the old order of things is plucked up and pulled down, destroyed and overthrown (Jer 1:10), God will build and plant (1:10) the future on this alternative community that is daring enough to re-imagine the world according to texts very different from those the rest of the world are reading. And while it knows that its life of reading and voicing these texts will not be without risk (this text may name Uriah as the community's first martyr, with eerie parallels to Stephen in the Acts of the Apostles), it also knows the lyrical promise that "the Lord has created a new thing" (Jer 31:22).

Declaring God's Newness: The Pastoral Work of Boundary-Pressing
Jeremiah 31:15-22

Pastors know that they can't help people change by pushing harder in the same direction. Pushing people only increases their resistance. And when people are terminally trapped in destructive or debilitating habits, our approach must be particularly skillful. What matters is not the strength of our ethical urging, but the opening of our imagination. Ricoeur argued that we need what he called "limit experiences:" experiences that press us past the limits of what we currently know, past the defenses of our resistance and into genuine transformation. But before we can have "limit experiences" our imaginations must be opened by "limit expressions" that make the experiences possible. "Limit expressions" are words that imagine newness, and words are the particular tools of the poet.

The Exile seemed impossible to those who let themselves believe that their Jerusalem way of life would never come to an end. But once inside their new captivity of Exile, it seemed just as impossible that they could ever be going home. In order to break through a new resistance that was just as debilitating as the old, the prophet practiced a form of preaching that pressed the boundaries of convention: "limit expressions" spoke Judah into Exile, and "limit expressions" would speak Judah home again.

The rhetoric of this poem presses the boundaries in several ways. First, the poem begins in grief that is immediately reversed by the Lord's strong command to "keep your voice from weeping" (31:16). Second, the description of missing children is reversed by God's announcement that they will return to the land of mother Rachel (verse 16). Third, Judah's stubborn refusal to listen to Torah, walk in Torah, heed the prophets of Torah (26:4-5), and lament its past wickedness (7:30) is reversed by Ephraim's pleading confession (31:18-19). Fourth, the surprising reversal of gender roles signals the unimaginable new things created by Yahweh (verse 22).

This final reversal is particularly important. If the poem draws on creation imagery (Isaiah has a similar phrase in 43:19, but without the explicit language of creation: "I am about to do a new thing") this announcement is astonishing – a use of language packed with missional energy for the birthing of God's new community. In the creation, Adam comes first and his life gives life to Eve (Gen 2:18-23). But in this new creation, the literal rebirthing of a wholly new community, "the Woman is the agent of new life, new hope for a despairing, sorrowing people. [And] in the context of the poem, the Woman is Israel, typified by Rachel who wept for her lost sons and, through a juxtaposition of imagery, by the Virgin/Daughter who is invited to return and, in the grace of God, to rebuild Israel."[6]

This is an astonishing use of metaphor, imagery, and pastoral strategy.[7] There will come a time when pastors will need to be equally daring to call people out of our exile and into the newness of God. When that day comes, we pastors who have used similar strategies for speaking people into exile will revel in a fresh infusion of missional energy that speaks them out of our exile and into the new and hopeful way of life imagined in this text.

In his book *Domination and the Arts of Resistance: Hidden Transcripts*, James C. Scott shows the ways those who live under oppressive systems can exercise enormous power of resistance to the ideological reformulation of their lives according to the symbols and value systems of those who dominate them. The book of Jeremiah and the pastoral strategies practiced by the community that gave it shape suggest that pastoral ministry in post-Christendom, post-September 11 North America understands itself from within the world of those who choose to script their lives as a countercultural presence in a world that does not share its perceptions of the world.

George Lindbeck has said that churches must become "communities that socialize their members into coherent and comprehensive religious outlooks and forms of life," for "the viability of a unified world of the future may well depend on counteracting the acids of modernity."[8] Counteracting the acids of modernity, or those of any other epoch in history, is the pastor's art. Jeremiah knew this well, and bravely carried out his ministry. Similarly, if God is to have a people capable of living evangelically amid the symbols and values, the principalities and powers of those who would dominate us today – co-opting our imaginations to a way of organizing our lives according to the ways of death and not according to God's way of life – then energetic and daring pastoral work in the mode of Jeremiah will be the stuff of such resistance.

God knows all this cannot be performed in isolation. Jeremiah had his scroll keepers, and if we're in luck, we have ours. Alastair MacIntyre, at the close of his celebrated and controversial critique of modern moral philosophy, urges that "What matters at this stage is the construction of local forms of community within which civility and the intellectual and moral life can be sustained through the new dark ages which are already upon us . . . . We are waiting not for a Godot, but for another – doubtless very different – St. Benedict."[9]

I'm wagering that in Jeremiah, and in the religio-political rebels/subversives who gathered with him around old holy texts, we have a school that can gather pastoral leaders in our day to re-imagine their ministries for new, daring acts of faithfulness.

NOTES

1. This chapter was originally published as "Entering the Wreckage: Grief and Hope in Jeremiah, and the Rescripting of the Pastoral Vocation in a Time of Geopolitical Crisis" in *International Review of Mission* April, 2003. Used by permission.

2. Paul Ricoeur remarks about the power of poetry, "My deepest conviction is that poetic language alone restores to us that participation in or belonging to an order of things which precedes our capacity to oppose ourselves to things taken as objects opposed to a subject. Hence the function of poetic discourse is to bring about this emergence of a depth-structure of belonging-to amid the ruins of descriptive discourse." In Lewis S. Mudge, "Paul Ricoeur on Biblical Interpretation," in *Essays on Biblical Interpretation*, ed. Lewis S. Mudge (Philadelphia: Fortress, 1980), 25.

3. All scripture quotations are from the New Revised Standard Version.

4. Louis Stulman, *Order Amid Chaos: Jeremiah as Symbolic Tapestry* (Sheffield: Sheffield Academic Press, 1998), 87.

5. About Ahikam, Holliday writes: "He had been old enough in 622 to serve with his father in the circle of advisors to Josiah (2 Kings 22:12, 14); it is now thirteen years later. It is his brother Gemariah who would be part of the circle of advisors around Jehoiakim when the scroll was burned (36:12, 25), and it will be his son Gedalia to whom the Babylonians will entrust Jeremiah in 587 and whom the Babylonians will appoint to be governor over the province (39:14; 40:7)." William Holladay, *A Commentary on the Book of the Prophet Jeremiah Chapters 26-52* (Philadelphia: Fortress, 1989), 110.

6. Bernhard W. Anderson, "The Lord has Created Something New," *A Prophet to the Nations: Essays in Jeremiah Studies*, ed. Leo G. Perdue and Brian W. Kovacs (Winona Lake, IN: Eisenbrauns, 1984), 380.

7. Walter Brueggemann, *A Commentary on Jeremiah: Exile and Homecoming* (Grand Rapids, MI: Eerdmans, 1998), 286.

8. George Lindbeck, *The Nature of Doctrine: Religion and Theology in a Postliberal Age* (Philadelphia: Westminster, 1984), 127.

9. Alastair MacIntyre, *After Virtue*, second edition (Notre Dame: University of Notre Dame, 1984), 263.

The Emotional Challenges of Pastoral Ministry

Raymond O. Bystrom

It may be more difficult to be a pastor today than ever before. Research indicates that pastors in North America are under extreme stress.[1] One source makes the following claim: "The average pastor is stressed to the point that he or she has at least a 50% chance of a health change as a result."[2] Another study names depression as the second most frequently identified pastoral problem.[3] So what's going on?

There are at least two explanations. One is offered by Gary Harbaugh who says, "Most problems pastors experience ... arise when the pastor forgets he or she is a person."[4] When John Maxwell resigned as pastor of Skyline Wesleyan Church in the mid-90s, he gave the congregation five reasons for his decision. Among his reasons was this one: "This decision is best for me. This week I became forty-eight. Physically I am often tired. I need to go from two jobs to one and 'get my life back.' For too long I have neglected my health, recreation, and personal rest time."[5] Maxwell undoubtedly served his congregation well as a pastor but his statement suggests he did so at the expense of his own needs as a person. Just because pastoring is doing God's work does not mean that everything else will miraculously take care of itself. Harbaugh is right: pastors must remember they are persons.

A second explanation is offered by William Willimon: "Pastors have the most trouble when they forget they are pastors."[6] A special gift from God is available in a wonderful way to those who seek to serve Christ as church leaders. The church needs God-anointed leaders who equip God's people in the style of Ephesians 4. But the pastoral role can be abused. Instances of clergy sexual misconduct are examples of pastors forgetting that they have been called and gifted by God to serve the church, not abuse its members. Clergy sexual misconduct is a violation of God's call and a betrayal of the people's trust.[7] Willimon is right; pastors must remember they are pastors.

In this chapter I want to focus on the human side of pastoral ministry. To be sure, there is a spiritual side to pastoral ministry and I don't want to minimize it. There is a spiritual gift from God that is available for the task and pastors cannot afford to ignore the spiritual disciplines.[8] But there is also a human side to being a pastor. I believe many of the emotional challenges facing today's pastors stem from two different, yet interrelated, sources: the nature of the pastoral role and the nature of the pastor's personality. First, I will describe a few challenges pastors face based on the nature of the pastoral role, providing a brief action plan for addressing each challenge. Next, I will describe some challenges pastors face based on the nature of the pastor's personality, including a brief action plan for dealing with each challenge.

The Nature of the Pastoral Role

1. People Oriented: Pastoring is all about working with people. Pastors are called to serve people but, paradoxically, people are also the problem. There is a vast body of literature on pastoral burn-out that identifies people, not money, as the major source of stress and frustration. For example, in his important study of the causes of forced exits of pastors, Rodney J. Crowell claims the primary reason for forced exits is rampant infighting and conflict within the congregation due to contentious groups or individuals.[9] Clearly, the nature of the pastoral role demands people with exceptional relational skills. Pastoring is people work and people can be difficult.

Action Plan: In the past, pastors were not as well trained for dealing with conflict, difficult persons, and interpersonal communication as are social workers, psychologists, and counselors. Therefore, pastors who lack training in these areas should seek out an appropriate learning center where they can work at strengthening their relational skills, improving their habits of communication, and growing in their ability to manage people.[10]

2. Unstructured Time: By nature pastoring is not a nine-to-five job. Pastors have the sense that they are always on duty. They often get the feeling that their work is never done. One of the advantages of my

The Emotional Challenges of Pastoral Ministry

current job as a teacher is that I know when my day is over. My work has built-in boundaries. When my class is finished and the last student leaves my office, I gather up my papers as well as my laptop computer and head for home. I am no longer on duty. I go home feeling like I've finished my work for the day. I experience closure. Often I work at home in the evening, but it doesn't feel like work. My body knows I'm finished for the day. But pastoral work is different. There is no clearly defined point when pastors are off-duty. They may not be in their offices eight hours a day, but they feel they are always "on call" – and to make matters worse, they never have week-ends off! As a result, pastors are often "eaten up" by their work. They feel like they are always working.

Action Plan: As a pastor, it is very important to understand that the body responds to our perception of the demands being placed upon it. At some point it needs to be sent a message that says the demands of the day are over - it can now relax and start the process of rest and restoration. Since pastoral work, by nature, lacks clear built-in boundaries, pastors must set boundaries to their work and courageously apply them.[11]

3. Multiple Roles: Pastors wear many hats. Once upon a time a typical pastor had five roles to play: teacher, preacher, worship leader, caregiver, and administrator. More recently pastoral work has expanded to fourteen roles.[12] Each role includes a cluster of competencies or skills. For example, the role of preacher requires communication skills, exegetical skills, theological reflection skills, composition skills, homiletical skills, cultural awareness skills – to mention but a few. The average pastor may require as many as seventy skills or competencies to do his job well. Pastors have become jacks-of-all-trades and masters of none. I heard one pastor say, "Brother, you don't know the meaning of variety until you've been a pastor." When pastors get spread too thin, job satisfaction plummets. One of the most damaging aspects of pastoral ministry may very well be the multiplicity of roles.[13] When a person is required to be competent in a multiplicity of roles the prospect of emotional dissonance is extremely high.

Action Plan: Pastors need to define a set of roles to play in the congregation. If this isn't done, they are left wondering who they are and what they are all about. It's particularly important that pastors embrace a cluster of roles that are consistent with their self-image, theological orientation, and the church's social system (that is, all the other leaders must be able to embrace the pastor's defined role set). A problem in any one of these three areas is emotionally devastating. The best approach is to make a short list of one's experiences, strengths, gifts and talents and then make a list of suitable pastoral roles and tasks. There must be a match. If the roles a pastor plays do not allow inner peace, the work will become emotionally draining.[14]

4. Relational Isolation: Pastors are often called to serve congregations far from family and friends, creating wrenching disruptions of relationships. A Canadian study of 198 pastors from eight denominations revealed that "more than half of the pastors (56%) said they felt lonely 'sometimes' to 'always,' and 80% said they experienced a sense of relational isolation 'sometimes' to 'always.'"[15] Another study, conducted by Lyle Larson of the University of Alberta, confirmed the above findings: "So here are human beings with an extra special call to fulfill while still being very human. They are in the limelight. Their families are on review. It's difficult to live this life, which is often very private, very lonely," says Larson.[16] What's going on? How can pastors be lonely when they are surrounded by people week after week? Leadership roles in general tend to bring with them a kind of social isolation. Archibald Hart believes that a major part of the problem for pastors boils down to a role conflict. In his opinion, a pastor cannot be both a pastor and a friend to the same person.[17] It's a role conflict not easily resolved. Maximum professional effectiveness prohibits cultivating deep friendships with persons for whom you are responsible as a pastor.

Action Plan: Since friendship is all about two people meeting one another's needs in a mutual and reciprocal manner, pastors should cultivate deep friendship connections with persons outside the congregation, perhaps with fellow pastors or with people from a previous church. It may very well prove to be the remedy for their relational isolation.

5. Unrealistic Expectations: The walk-on-water syndrome is alive and well in the church.[18] The prestige of the pastor in the larger cultural context may be diminished but people still tend to idealize their pastors and put them on a pedestal. Such high expectations can become a challenge for pastors, especially if they imagine they can live up to these expectations. Pastors are human; they will inevitably fail to live up to all of these unrealistic expectations. Everyone knows when the pastor fails because

The Emotional Challenges of Pastoral Ministry

they have such high-profile roles. The consequence of failing to live up to unrealistic expectations entails loss of self-respect, prestige, and power. "Depression in the minister," says Archibald Hart, "can be a direct result of failing to live up to the expectations the pedestal position creates."[19]

Action Plan: It's impossible to please everyone, and pastors need to learn that important lesson early in their work. They must give themselves permission to be human like the rest of us; they need to be themselves. Also, it's helpful if pastors can weigh personal expectations of themselves against the reality of God's Word and his will for their lives as disciples of Jesus.

6. Inadequate Yardsticks: It's difficult to measure "success" in pastoral ministry. When should a pastor feel good about his or her accomplishments? Every pastor knows intuitively that success in ministry is more than counting bucks, bodies, and buildings. Some pastors try to convince themselves that such data is unimportant. But everyone needs to know how things are going. Unfortunately, pastors lack adequate criteria for assessing their work. The results of pastoring are not as tangible as in other vocations. How do you measure the value of emotional healing in a person's life, or reconciliation between two people who were at war with each other? Over a period of time, the inability to measure accomplishments can lead to feelings of futility, loss, or even depression. Pastors need to feel they are making a difference.

Action Plan: Pastors need to take a long, hard look at God's criteria. The ultimate yardstick is faithfulness. For pastors, it's all about faithfully equipping God's people for ministry where they work, live, and play. If pastors are called to remind the people of God of their true identity, they need to get some honest feedback from key lay leaders on their effectiveness as equippers.

7. Person Centered: In his book *Clergy Self-Care*, Roy Oswald makes an important statement: "Who and what we are as persons is our most effective tool in pastoral ministry."[20] Who we are as persons is immensely important in pastoral ministry. In effect, it is the person who is the computer or the hammer in this business of pastoring. The person of the pastor is the key tool of the trade. The work is deeply personal and there are so many subjective interactions between the pastor and the people. A pastor's personal qualities are essential ingredients of the work.

Action Plan: Pastors need to develop a theology of persons that addresses the matter of identity, or the essence of who they are as persons.[21] Who we are as persons is defined by issues like fidelity to tasks and persons, personal responsibility, acknowledgment of limitations, flexibility of spirit, involvement in caring as well as potentially negative characteristics like self-serving behavior, pursuit of personal advantage, and self-protecting behavior. Pastors need to know who they are as persons.[22]

8. Dwindling Status: Pastors once enjoyed a high social standing but in recent years their public esteem has declined significantly.[23] In part, the low public esteem of pastors is inextricably linked with the church's new role on the margins or periphery of society. As a result, pastors may experience self-doubt and suffer anxiety related to their low status. "Pastors," writes David Fisher, "are in a high demand, low-stroke profession in a culture that does not value their product or work."[24] The dangers that accompany insecurity about identity are manifold. For example, Parker Palmer says, "When we are insecure about our own identities, we create settings that deprive other people of their identities as a way of buttressing our own."[25]

Action Plan: Pastors need to separate their self-image from their role identity. Who we are as persons is not determined by what we do. God wants us to derive our self-image from the truth that we are redeemed children, valued for who we are as persons. Confusing self-image and role identity only prevents God's power from working through us as persons.

9. Consumer Mindsets: The marketplace of society has influenced the way people often think about the nature and purpose of the church.[26] For many, the church is simply a place where certain things happen or, even worse, a vendor of religious goods and services. This understanding of the church effectively means that each church carves out its own niche in the religious marketplace, wins its clientele and makes its own appeal. Church attendees are customers and, if a church doesn't satisfy its customers, they go shopping elsewhere. As a result, relationships in one church are often abandoned for the sake of a better "deal" at another church. Pastors who have watched their members migrate to new "vendors" lose their spiritual passion for ministry. In *Pastors at Risk*, H. B. London and Neil B. Wiseman state: "The loss

The Emotional Challenges of Pastoral Ministry

of relationships in member migration can feed a pastor's vocational depression."[27]

Action Plan: At one level pastors need to accept the reality of the circulation of the saints. It's a given; it goes with the turf of being a pastor in North America in the twenty-first century. At the same time, pastors should resist the tendency to view the church as simply a place where certain things happen, or a vendor of religious goods and services. Instead, embrace the view that the church is a body of people who have been called and sent to represent God's reign in the world.

10. Declining Volunteerism: Too often Christians get involved in a congregation when things are going well, but "jump ship" when the going gets tough. At the best of times, a pastor is fortunate if twenty per cent of the people serve through thick and thin. People are giving less time to church these days. Part of the problem is that in many families both spouses work full-time outside the home, with little time and energy left for church work. Research indicates that as volunteerism declines, pastors tend to shoulder more and more of the burden for ministry in the local congregation. Members who refuse to carry their share of the ministry work-load are a major source of discouragement for pastors.

Action Plan: Pastors need to learn to value the process by which congregational goals are reached as much as the goals themselves. While goals are indeed important, pastors should not undervalue the process of reaching them. Pastors need to strike a balance in emphasis between goals and process. Strongly goal-oriented pastors may experience more frustration in ministry than pastors who are process-oriented.

These, then, are some of the characteristic features of pastoral ministry that have the potential to be problematic for pastors. But there are also aspects of the pastor's personality that can be problematic for pastors.

The Nature of the Pastor's Personality

1. Inability to Partialize Tasks: For some, pastoral ministry is like one big cake they are always munching on week after week. They seem to be unable to partialize their work.[28] If they keep on trying to eat the whole cake of church ministry at once, however, they will eventually

get emotionally sick. For example, if a pastor has the tendency to create impossibly long lists of daily tasks to complete, it may lead to feelings of frustration by the end of the day when the list is not completed. It is important for pastors to be realistic about the amount of work they can accomplish in a single day. Otherwise they will experience feelings of incompleteness on a regular basis.

Action Plan: It is helpful for pastors to learn to break their work down into bite-sized pieces that can be tackled one at a time. Partializing the task is a way of creating boundaries for the daily work of the pastor. For example, Paul Scott Wilson suggests a strategy for partializing the task of sermon preparation. He suggests limiting the preparation of the sermon to an hour or two each day for four or five days. Monday: What the text says. This involves understanding the biblical text (translation plus initial literary and theological readings). Tuesday: What the text means. This involves analysis and explanation of what others have said (study of commentaries, tradition, and theology). Wednesday: What experience says. This involves the discovery of the relevance or application of the text for our time, anticipating the responses of listeners. Thursday: What the preacher says. This involves shaping a sermon that is a response to the biblical text. On Friday, the sermon can be reviewed & learned. If this approach is used, interruptions during the week will feel less disruptive and the week-end will be free for family and friends.[29]

2. Unresolved Sexual Tension: As caregivers, pastors may represent many things to a member of the opposite sex, including father, mother, peer, or even lover. The unmet needs of a person to whom a pastor is extending care may be projected onto the pastor. A pastor may symbolize the fulfillment of another person's unmet needs. Indeed, the more successful the pastor is at loving and caring for people, the more likely the pastor will attract transference. This can become problematic if the pastor also suffers from unresolved sexual tensions. It may lead to sexual misconduct, which is an abuse of power and betrayal of trust. Recent studies reveal the prevalence of this problem. One survey of pastors revealed that 38.6% had had sexual contact with a church member, 12.7% had had sexual intercourse with a church member, and 76.5% claimed that they knew of a minister who had had sexual intercourse with a church member.[30] Another survey of church workers asked if

The Emotional Challenges of Pastoral Ministry

they had ever experienced sexual harassment. Of those surveyed 77% of clergywomen, 20% of the laity, 48% of the students, and 37% of the church staff said, "Yes."[31]

Action Plan: Pastors need to become more aware of the disastrous consequences of clergy sexual misconduct. They also need to be aware of the factors that contribute to sexual misconduct and avoid sexual misconduct at all costs.[32] The Center for the Prevention of Sexual and Domestic Violence is a major resource on clergy misconduct. (Contact the Center at 936 North 34th Street, Ste. 200, Seattle, Washington 98103; phone (206) 634-1903).

3. Messiah Complex: The importance of pastoral ministry must never be denied. The task of attending to the spiritual well-being of the congregation and its people is significant work. But the importance of pastoral work can be exaggerated to the detriment of the pastor. An exaggerated conviction about the importance of the work may be a pastor's way of compensating for the financial and familial sacrifices associated with the task. Or, an inflated belief about the importance of the work may incline the pastor to imagine that his or her role in life is indispensable to humanity and the universe. Since the work is carried out in the service of God, pastors begin to think they are godlike – perfect. Twisted and distorted views of the superiority of the pastoral role can be dangerous, especially if pastors begin to believe their own press. "A tendency toward depression in ministers (when it is not physiological) is directly related to an inability to accept fallibility," writes Archibald Hart.[33]

Action Plan: Healthy pastors focus on what God is able to do with or without them. They learn to focus on what God is doing in the congregation through other people. Also, pastors who are vocationally and spiritually effective do not focus on the idea that pastoral ministry is the greatest of all the vocations. They possess humility about their own contribution and simultaneously stand in awe of what God does through others.

4. Weak Ego Boundaries: Pastors' egos can become so closely identified with the work that they fail to separate their own egos from their work. Who they are and what they do become intertwined. If a pastor's whole existence is determined by his or her work, failure in the workplace is devastating. Also, if pastors' egos are defined solely by their

work, they will have a significant problem when the work is taken away. Retirement can be an especially devastating time for the pastor whose whole identity is wrapped up in his or her work. "If a (pastor's) identity is confined strictly to who he is as 'pastor,'" says Richard Blackmon, "it probably means he needs to establish a clearer boundary between himself as a pastor and himself as a person."[34]

Action Plan: Pastors can do a variety of things to cultivate a higher level of self-definition. There are several ways to establish clear boundaries between "self" as a person and "self" as a pastor. First, they should enlist emotional support from a colleague or friend who can help them separate what's going on in the church from who they are as a person. Also, they can cultivate hobbies or friendships that will broaden their personal identity. It is also helpful to verbalize the kind of pressure they are experiencing at work with selected members of the congregation, asking how to handle the congregants' high expectations.

5. Dislike of Criticism: Our culture has made self-esteem dependent on performance. It follows that any criticism of one's performance can be devastating to one's ego. A pastor's self-esteem is especially vulnerable if it is too dependent upon performance, because so much of what a pastor does is open to the criticism of the congregation. Unless a pastor has the hide of a rhinoceros, he or she is going to be at high risk. Add to the mix the fact that if things are going poorly within the congregational system, the pastor is often the scapegoat for its failures.

Action Plan: One way to deal with criticism is to consciously unhook one's self-esteem from one's performance on the job. Positively speaking, pastors should connect their sense of self-esteem with God's estimate of them as persons.

6. Neglect of Self-Care: All the available data tells us that depression is not only tied to psychology but physiology. There are many physiological causes of depression that can be avoided, or at least controlled. This is especially true of forms of depression that can be linked with fatigue, poor diet, or lack of physical exercise. Pastoral work is sedentary by nature. So it takes conscious planning to make physical exercise an aspect of one's daily routine.

Action Plan: Pastors can do at least four things to care for themselves as persons: Engage in regular physical exercise, honor their Sab-

The Emotional Challenges of Pastoral Ministry

bath (typically it's a Monday), eat healthy food, and make time for spouse and family. It's sheer self-destruction to neglect any of these basics of daily life.

7. Gnostic Tendencies: Gnosticism elevates the spiritual at the expense of the physical. A gnostic attitude among pastors believes the work of the ministry can be accomplished without regard to personal needs. Coupled with this attitude is a tendency for some pastors to deny their humanity. They refuse to accept the fact that they are emotional beings who may (at least once every year!) feel anger. This tendency is only aggravated by lay people who view the pastor as a kind of third sex, neither male nor female. The net effect is that pastors start concealing their humanness, hiding it away, hoping against hope that the truth won't leak out.[35]

Action Plan: Total transparency is not the best solution for fighting off gnostic tendencies. Pastors should not wash their dirty linen in public. Instead they should display the process by which they are growing as Christians. The Gospel's call to become more like Christ involves turning our failures into growth, and our weaknesses into strengths.

8. Narrowly Focused: Pastors rightly encourage the members of their congregation to live well balanced lives. But often they are prone to ignore the distortions in their own lives. Their work can become totally consuming, the singular aim of their lives. Soon they are thinking only about their work, avoiding all other interests, denying themselves hobbies, and losing their sense of balance. Workaholism in the ministry is rampant. "Unfortunately for the minister, this narrow focus also produces a high risk of depression."[36]

Action Plan: There are several practical ways to address this tendency to focus too narrowly on one's work. First, pastors should expand their relationship circle to include people outside the congregation. These outside relationships can help to give the pastor a broader perspective on life. In addition, these relationships can be supportive in times of difficulty. Second, pastors should enlarge their outside activities so they include sporting and cultural events that enrich them as persons.

9. Perfectionist Traits: The perfectionist is not the person who aims to do her very best in each situation. Perfectionists, by definition, have

a built-in system of punishment when they fail to do their best. Perfectionists tend to be compulsive, even obsessive, about their work. They believe they must suffer for not doing things right every time. Given the never-ending nature of pastoral work, the pastor who has perfectionist tendencies is in for a rough ride. For the perfectionist, pastoral ministry can be agonizing. It's bad enough for the conscientious person but it is pure hell for the perfectionist because pastoral work is so comprehensive and limitless.

Action Plan: Pastors who suffer from perfectionist tendencies should seek therapeutic help from a professional. Correcting perfectionist tendencies often requires extended therapy. There are, however, a few simple things that can be done to reduce the devastating nature of this tendency. First, they must give themselves permission to fail. More than one wise counselor claims that failure is the soil of all healthy personal growth. Second, it's helpful to practice a little selective neglect now and again.

10. Prone to Counter-Transference: Transference is a psychoanalytic term for the feelings of the patient towards the analyst.[37] Patients might regard the analyst as if he or she is someone from their past: a mother, a father, a lover. The attitude of the patient toward the analyst may be characterized by feelings of love or hate. These feelings are not focused on the analyst as such but on what the analyst represents to the patient during the analysis. Of course, all of this has implications for pastors and what may happen to them as they seek to care for people of the opposite sex within the congregation. Counter-transference proneness occurs when the unresolved needs of the pastor are transferred by the pastor to the person he or she is serving at the time. For example, if pastors have been deprived of love all of their lives, they may expect people to love them and meet their needs. This can be devastating for such a pastor because people are not going to fulfill such expectations. Also, if a pastor experiences counter-transference in a counseling situation with a person of the opposite sex, it may lead to an abuse of power and a betrayal of trust if not recognized and resisted.

Action Plan: Pastors who are prone to counter-transference should allocate the counselor role to someone less inclined toward counter-transference and perhaps more gifted in this area of ministry. Indeed, they should find someone else to address most, if not all, of the counseling needs of the congregation.

The Emotional Challenges of Pastoral Ministry

These, then, are some of the emotional challenges facing pastors today. Although I have suggested a few things pastors can do to address these challenges, it must be remembered that congregations also bear some responsibility for the emotional well-being of their pastor(s). If you are a pastor, share this chapter with your congregation's leadership team, asking them to think about action steps the church board and congregation might take to help you face these emotional challenges of pastoral ministry.

NOTES

1. Greg Asimakoupoulos, "The Endangered Species," *Leadership* (Winter 1994), 123; Raymond O. Bystrom, "Pressure in the Pulpit," *The Christian Leader* (March, 1994), 4-6; Herbert Freudenberger, *Burnout: The High Cost of High Achievement* (New York: Anchor Press, 1980); Jerry Edelwich and Archie Brodosky, *Burnout-Stages of Disillusionment in the Helping Professions* (Human Sciences Press, 1980); Christine Maslach, "Burn-Out," *Human Behavior* (September 1978), 17-20; Archibald Hart, "Why Ministers Burn-Out," *Coping With Depression in the Ministry and Other Helping Professions* (Nashville, TN: Word, 1984), 113-127; William E. Hume, *Managing Stress in Ministry* (San Francisco: Harper and Row, 1985); Edwin H. Friedman, *Generation to Generation: Family Process in Church and Synagogue* (New York: Guildford, 1985), especially 216-219 on a systems view of burnout.

2. Gary Harbaugh, *Pastor as Person* (Minneapolis, MN: Augsburg, 1984), 9.

3. Louis McBurney, "A Psychiatrist Looks at Troubled Pastors," *Leadership* (Spring 1980), 109, 114.

4. Gary Harbaugh, *Pastor as Person*, 43.

5. John Maxwell, "A Letter of Love to Skyline" (February 26), 1995, 3. (Skyline Wesleyan Church, 1345 Skyline Drive, Lemon Grove, CA 91945).

6. "Why A Pastor Should Not Be A 'Person'," *Theology Today*, Volume 50, No. 4 (January 1994), 580-585.

7. Paul Chaffee, "Preventing Clergy Misconduct," *Accountable Leadership: A Resource Guide for Sustaining Legal, Financial, and Ethical Integrity in Today's Congregations* (San Francisco: Jossey-Bass, 1997), 185-208; Don Posterski, ed., "Clergy Sexual Misconduct: An Abuse of Power," *Context* Volume 3 Issue 2 (May 1993), 1-8; Stanley J. Grenz, "When the Pastor Fails: Sexual Misconduct as a Betrayal of Trust," *Crux* Volume XXXI, No. 2, (June 1995) 23-30.

8. See one or more of the following: Dallas Willard, *The Spirit of the Disciplines* (New York: Harper Collins, 1988); Richard Foster, *Celebration of Discipline* (New York: Harper Collins, 1978); Richard N. Longenecker, ed., *Into God's Presence: Prayer in the New Testament* (Grand Rapids, MI: Eerdmans, 2001); Eugene Peterson, *Working the Angles: The Shape of Pastoral Integrity* (Grand Rapids, MI: Eerdmans, 1987); Eugene Peterson, *Five Smooth Stones for Pastoral Work* (Grand Rapids, MI: Eerdmans, 1980); E. Glenn Hinson, *Spiritual Preparation for Christian Leadership* (Nashville, TN: Upper Room Books, 1999).

9. Rodney J. Crowell, *Musical Pulpits: Clergy and Laypersons Face the Issue of Forced Exits* (San Francisco: Baker, 1992), 57; Menno H. Epp, *The Pastor's Exit* (Win-

nipeg, MB: CMBC, 1984), 28; Marshall Shelley, *Well-Intentioned Dragons: Ministering to Problem People in the Church* (Nashville, TN: Word, 1985); G. Lloyd Rediger, *Clergy Killers: Guidance for Pastors and Congregations Under Attack* (Louisville, KY: Westminister John Knox Press, 1997); Marlin Jeschke, *Discipling in the Church: Recovering a Ministry of the Gospel* (Scottdale, PA Herald Press, 1988).

10. MB Biblical Seminary offers courses in Interpersonal Communication and Basic Institutes of Conflict Mediation and Management (MBBS, 4824 East Butler Avenue, Fresno, CA 93727).

11. A. J. Weaver, "Boundary Issues in Pastoral Care," *Baker Encyclopedia of Psychology & Counseling*, eds. David G. Brenner & Peter C. Hill (Grand Rapids, MI: Baker Books, 1999), 158-159.

12. See David Wells, "The New Disablers," *No Place for Truth* (Grand Rapids, MI: Eerdmans, 1993), 232-233; David Wells, "The D-Minization of the Ministry" *No God But God: Breaking With the Idols of Our Age*, eds. Os Guinness and John Seel. (Chicago: Moody, 1992), 183-184.

13. See Donald P. Smith, *Clergy in the Crossfire: Coping with Role Conflicts in Ministry* (Philadelphia, PA: Westminster Press, 1973),123.

14. See Eugene Peterson's personal struggle to define a set of roles that were consistent with his self-image, theological orientation and the congregation's system: *Under the Unpredictable Plant: An Exploration in Vocational Holiness* (Grand Rapids, MI: Eerdmans, 1992), 34-40; also see Derek Blows, "Limit-Setting" *The New Dictionary of Pastoral Studies*, ed. Wesley Carr (Grand Rapids, MI: Eerdmans, 2002), 201-203.

15. Debra Fieguth, "Loneliness, Isolation Key Issues for Pastors, Survey Reveals," *Christian Week* (November 1, 1994), 5.

16. Doug Koop, "People Who Live in Glass Houses," *Christian Week* (November 1, 1994), 4.

17. Audiotapes by Archibald Hart, *Managing the Emotional Hazards of Minstry: The Minister and Role Conflict* #10 (Pasadena, CA: Fuller Theological Seminary Media Services, Box 115, Pasadena, Ca. 91182, no date).

18. Edward B. Bratcher, *The Walk-On-Water Syndrome: Dealing With the Professional Hazards in Ministry* (Nashville, TN: Word, 1984).

19. Archibald Hart, *Coping With Depression in the Ministry,* 121; Katherine Hancock Ragsdale, *Boundary Wars: Intimacy and Distance in the Healing Relationships* (Cleveland, OH: Pilgrim, 1996).

20. Roy M. Oswald, *Clergy Self-Care: Finding Balance for Effective Ministry* (Herndon, VA: Alban Institute, 1991), x.

21. Parker Palmer, *Let Your Life Speak* (San Francisco: Jossey-Bass, 2000), especially 73-94.

22. See the Profiles of Ministry Program of the Association of Theological Schools, 10 Summit Park Drive, Pittsburgh, PA, 15275. The Profile of Ministry instrument helps pastors recognize those personal characteristics that are most frequently deemed important for ministry.

23. David Wells, "The New Disablers," *No Place for Truth* (Grand Rapids, MI: Eerdmans, 1993), 218-257.

24. David Fisher, *The 21st Century Pastor: A Vision Based On the Ministry of Paul* (Grand Rapids, MI: Zondervan, 1996), 8.

25. Parker Palmer, *Let Your Life Speak*, 86.

26. David Wells, "Clerics Anonymous," *God in the Wasteland* (Grand Rapids, MI: Eerdmans, 1994), 60-87; Philip D. Kenneson & James L. Street, *Selling Out the Church: The Dangers of Church Marketing* (Nashville, TN: Abingdon Press, 1997).

27. H. B. London and Neil B. Wiseman, *Pastors At Risk: Help for Pastors, Hope for Churches* (Colorado Spring, CO: Victor Books, 1993), 37.

28. Archibald Hart, *Coping With Depresssion in the Ministry*, 231.

29. Paul Scott Wilson, *The Practice of Preaching* (Nashville, TN: Abingdon Press, 1995), especially 125-198.

30. Richard Allen Blackmon, Unpublished Ph. D. Dissertation, "The Hazards of the Ministry," (Fuller Theological Seminary, 1984).

31. The Office of Research, General Council on Ministries, The United Methodist Church, *Sexual Harassment in the United Methodist Church* (1990).

32. G. Lloyd Rediger, *Ministry & Sexuality: Cases, Counseling, and Care* (Minneapolis, MN: Fortress, 1990).

33. Archibald Hart, *Coping With Depression in the Ministry*, 20; also see Jay Kessler, *Being Holy Being Human: Dealing With the Incredible Expectations and Pressures of Ministry* (Bloomington, MN: Bethany, 1985).

34. Richard Blackmon, "Good Fences Make Good Pastors," *Leadership* (Spring 1993), 76-78.

35. Jay Kesler, *Being Holy Being Human*.

36. Archibald Hart, *Coping With Depression in the Ministry*, 231.

37. A. W. Carr, "Transference," *The New Dictionary of Pastoral Studies*, ed. A. Wesley Carr (Grand Rapids, MI: Eerdmans, 2002), 377-378.

An Artistic Toolbox for Next Generation Leaders

Rick Bartlett

Gary, Lisa and Samantha are eleventh graders at Washington high school, but attend different churches. Lisa is a straight A student who is friendly, popular and well-liked by her peers. Gary is a good student and an athlete. He's on the football team and runs track. Samantha is quiet and shy. She is a good student, but not a great one. She is often ill at ease in large groups, but she is a loyal friend to Lisa and Gary. She has a deep passion for God and when she isn't with her friends, she can be found off behind her house in the mountains with her Bible and a journal.

Tonight, the three friends have spent several hours at a youth worship event. As they leave the church and walk out into the warm night, Gary turns to the other two.

"Can I ask your advice on something?"

Lisa and Samantha stop walking.

"I've been having some trouble at church. It's getting really frustrating. You know, like both of you I'm a student leader at my church. I signed up because I thought it would give me a chance to have a say in what goes on. But Chad the youth pastor does it all. He never asks us what we want to do or study. He tells us to invite our friends but it's so boring right now I hardly want to go myself."

Gary looks down and kicks at a tuft of grass.

"I can't stand it. I wanted to learn how to be a leader and to be given a chance to do something, but all of us on the leadership committee are just ignored. Is that how it is for you?"

"I'm sorry to hear that," said Lisa. "It's totally different for me. Our student leadership team is considered part of the youth staff. We meet with the adult volunteers, give feedback on events, and help shape future ones. I'm responsible for the welcome team that makes sure that any new person who comes in to our Youth Church on Sundays is welcomed and matched with a "buddy" for the service. I feel like I'm helping our group and getting valuable training for what being in 'big' church is like. Isn't that what church is all about? I can't wait to use my gifts to keep my church going."

"What about you?" Gary asked Samantha.

"My experience is really different from both of you," she said. "You know my church is a lot smaller than both of yours. I don't have a youth pastor who is a superstar, or attend a youth group where we need to divide up into teams. We all help out wherever we're needed. I sometimes teach Sunday school for the third-graders. A few times a bunch of us have served lunch to homeless people. That was fun, actually; it was a couple of families with kids, a single man in his fifties, and me. We got along really well and spent a lot of time praying together afterward. I've really gotten close to one of the families."

"Must be nice," said Gary.

"Yeah, it is," said Samantha. "And the best part is that my pastor's given me chances to participate in the church service. I've read scripture, prayed for the offering, and one time even helped with a baptism. It's like I'm really needed by my church, you know? Like they'll miss me if I'm not there."

"That's pretty unusual," said Lisa.

"I suppose it is," Samantha answered. "I never thought about it much. I thought it was how everyone did church."

How will "everyone do church" in ten or twenty years? The challenge for the church today is to engage the changes taking place in Western culture and find ways to prepare churched mid-adolescents to assume leadership in that new culture.

There are many in youth ministry today who are talking about "student leaders." What do they mean by this title? What training are these students receiving and for what purpose? Many parachurch organizations host large conferences to help churches train student leaders. Are these conferences training leaders to embrace the emerging culture, or are they training for a world that will be obsolete? If the latter is true, how does the training structure need to change?

An Artistic Toolbox for Next Generation Leaders

Leadership is the art of the future. A leader is one in whom the future shines through in support of the present in spite of the past.[1]

Young people are the future. At the same time, they are certainly living in the present with concerns about their looks, current media, the car they drive, and other issues. They are also potentially emerging leaders. If, as Leonard Sweet states, leadership is an art, then what basic skills should young people be learning today to help them become leadership artists in the future?

The First Question

Before discussing these necessary artistic basics, the first question that needs addressing is, "Where are leaders found?" One simple answer would be for churches to be identifying, discerning, developing and training young leaders with leadership gifts from within their congregations. Leonard Sweet states, "To put it bluntly: the whole 'leadership thing' is a demented concept. Leaders are neither born nor made. Leaders are summoned. They are called into existence by circumstances. Those who rise to the occasion are leaders. True, some people are born leaders. But these are few and far between."[2] Walter Wright states, "We begin by following[3] ... and then somewhere along the line, whether we intend it or not, whether we want it or not, whether we realize it or not, people start following us. We become leaders."[4]

Bill Hybels, in his book *Courageous Leadership*, has a different slant on this issue. He argues that leaders emerge out of a corporate vision for leadership development. He states, "Leadership development *never* happens accidentally."[5]

Hybels has found that when calling out new leaders there are three common themes that emerge, and here I believe he agrees with Sweet: it's in the summoning that leaders are found. These three themes are:

1. Someone spotted our potential
2. Someone invested in us
3. Someone trusted us with responsibility[6]

In an interesting twist, Harold Longenecker reverses the order and says leaders are first developed then discovered.[7] This doesn't necessarily agree with the other leadership theories out there, but it does bear further reflection. Longenecker uses the example of Jesus' disciples as men who were developed into their leadership positions. For Longenecker, they weren't already "leaders" but they were potential leaders who by spending time with Jesus emerged into a leadership role.[8] If leaders are called out or discipled out, then it makes sense for churches to be in the "business" of finding and calling young people into ministry.[9]

This leads to another question: can all people be "summoned" into leadership? If Leonard Sweet is correct, anyone could become a leader by being summoned through circumstances into that role. Longenecker agrees that "each believer is a potential leader at one level or another,"[10] if they receive the development he later describes. Hybels would disagree. He identifies specific character qualities necessary in an emerging leader: influence, character, people skills, drive, and intelligence.[11]

Josephine van Linden and Carl Fertman make the case that all teenagers have the potential to lead.[12] They further define this through a discussion on transformational and transactional leadership. Simply defined by van Linden and Fertman, transformational leadership is being (for example leading yourself), and transactional leadership is doing (leading others). With these two definitions of leadership, every young person can be a leader because even if he or she is not a transactional leader, they can always be a transformational one. In fact, transformational leadership is an essential component of any leader. As van Linden and Fertman state, "Originally, people were thought to be either transactional or transformational leaders. Over time, however, the theory has evolved and now reflects the fact that people can be both."[13] Finally, in a statement that summarizes both strands of "summoning" a leader and "developing" a leader, van Linden and Fertman write, "A person does not wake up one day as a leader. Leadership is a personal and developmental process. This development takes place over time, throughout a person's life."[14]

Leaders for Life

Many books have been written on the issue of "student leadership" — that is, training for high schoolers to exercise leadership in their existing arenas such as student government, church youth group, scouts, or sports teams. The focus of this chapter is to concentrate on those students who have already been called out by their church or group, who have been given roles and responsibilities (maybe even given the title of "Student Leader"), but who also sense a larger calling into full-time Christian vocation. Since these students live in the emerging culture and will also be summoned into leadership in the new paradigm, what "artistic tools," as Sweet says, do these students need to help them become leaders in this emerging culture?

The first tool young leaders will need in the emerging culture is "hearing." According to Sweet, the art of hearing in leadership will surpass that of "vision."[15] Vision can be an individual thing. A "visionary leader" need not consult with anyone else in his or her quest for productivity, effective ministry, sales, or whatever the leader is leading people to do. In this paradigm, the person with the vision is seeking to move people based on passion. As Hybels states, "Vision is a picture of the future that produces passion."[16] Hearing, on the other hand, must involve the leader listening to each member of the group being led. An acoustic leader must find out how each person can best be used to help accomplish the overall goals of the leader and project. Sweet compares this to a conductor creating music from a symphony. He writes, "It was the music of leadership and leadership as music that gave meaning to the leadership experience. For the music of the soul to be restored to ourselves and to our organizations, leadership needs to be seen as less a performance art (visionary, manager) than a participation art (conductor, choreographer, impresario)."[17]

In *The Art of Connecting*, Crowne, Muir and Little make the case that "Jesus was a master at listening and revealing and he did it purely out of genuine interest in a person."[18] Leonard Sweet states, "The initial mode of leadership is one of receptivity-hearing, not speaking. Note the choice of the word 'hearing,' not listening. There is a difference. You can listen and not hear. Many people are 'listened to.' Few people are truly 'heard.'"[19] Crowne and Muir write that being listened to creates an openness for others to hear what the leader has to say.[20]

In order to gain skills in hearing, an adolescent may need to begin by being heard. In one of the youth leader training retreats that I led, teenagers asked for opportunities to tell their own story and to hear each others' stories. In one evening the storytelling went on long past the set time to finish. I am convinced this was because there was a strong desire amongst the students to really be heard and this event provided a safe forum for that to occur.

A second artistic tool the future leader will need is to become a self-leader, or in other words, to find their own voice. Socrates' famous quote "know thyself" is an important artistic tool for a young person to grasp. Erik Erikson theorizes that this is especially important for a young person's process of maturity. His developmental theory identifies the task of adolescence as "identity achievement."[21] Having watched young people do this "job" for the past twenty-two years, I've seen that, for many, this is a difficult task. Rahn and Lindhart, reflecting on the writings of James Marcia, state that "His research led him to conclude that adolescents must experience a sense of crisis before they make the commitment necessary for identity achievement."[22] Sometimes the best thing a youth leader can do is provide this experience of crisis in a controlled environment, such as a mission trip, outdoor adventure, or service project.

Furthermore, this search for true identity is becoming increasingly difficult as society and our understanding of "truth" changes. As Kenda Dean writes, "The problem, of course is that the life-task of adolescents, the search for identity, means that youth are desperately seeking something that *does* matter most – for something utterly "true," and therefore worthy of their life commitment."[23] Finding truth on which to stake your life is not an easy task for young people today.

What is interesting is that identity achievement is one thing youth leadership literature takes as a given. For example, Mariam MacGregor, in a list defining "What is a Youth Leader?" has as her first two statements: "believes in themselves" and "stands up for what they believe."[24] These traits imply that the young person knows who they are and what they believe. I agree that this should certainly be the goal of leadership development, but it cannot be assumed that an adolescent comes to a leadership role, position, or "calling out" with that self-awareness intact.

Helping adolescents find their "voice" and become a self-leader is an important component of any leadership development of young people. Sweet says, "To leverage the Power of One, every person needs to find their own Power of Voice – a personal soundtrack that rings true, a soundtrack with a voice-activated aura that can become larger than life. Older treatises on leadership that highlighted 'charisma' were on the right track, but had the wrong concept. It's not the power of the 'charisma' that makes the difference. It's the power of voice."[25] For an adolescent who isn't sure what their "voice" really is, it is critical that they be taught, and given the opportunity, to tell their story.

An Artistic Toolbox for Next Generation Leaders

Sweet identifies four essential issues that need to be considered when helping an emerging leader find their own voice or personal soundtrack:

1. Telling the truth about the best possible future and how to get there
2. Promoting social justice and spiritual vibrancy – leading with deep values and strong virtue
3. Generating original sounds – combining ideas into something new
4. Sounding from experience – developing a wealth of life experiences[26]

These are all essential components for an emerging leader and would make an excellent curriculum for leadership development training and discernment. There are a variety of ways and places where this list could take root in a young person: the local church, youth group, camps, retreats, and other settings where the youth is open to God and to personal growth.

A third essential tool for the leadership artist is a good attitude. John Maxwell is known for saying while a leader can't always control circumstances, he or she can control their reaction to those circumstances. Attitude development is an aspect of self-leadership. Van Linden and Fertman go so far as to say, "A teenager's leadership attitude predisposes him or her to lead."[27] Much has been written lately around the issue of "servant leadership." For Christians, this is often based on a text from Matthew:

> When the ten other disciples heard what James and John had asked, they were indignant. But Jesus called them together and said, "You know that in this world kings are tyrants, and officials lord it over the people beneath them. But among you it should be quite different. Whoever wants to be a leader among you must be your servant, and whoever wants to be first must become your slave. For even I, the Son of Man, came here not to be served but to serve others, and to give my life as a ransom for many (Matt 20:24-28 NLT).

Wright emphasizes this servant leader concept in his book *Relational Leadership*. In a section summarizing the work, he writes, "In these pages we will look at a model of leadership that starts with our relationship with God and moves out from there into relationships of service with those around us. It is a study of the theology and practice of servant leadership..."[28]

A leader sets the tone for the people he or she is leading and also influences the "spirit" of a team. Leonard Sweet calls this "spirit description" and writes, "More important than finding someone to fill a 'job description' is hiring an employee with the right 'spirit description.'"[29] With all the turbulence of adolescence, and the sea of changes young people are going through, one important truth they can be taught is this one: *You can determine your attitude*. In addition to dealing with their own attitude, emerging leaders will need a "spirit detector" to determine the attitudes and make-up of any team they are leading.

In summary, the tools young people need as an artistic emerging leader are: the ability to hear others, finding one's true voice, creating a good attitude, and developing a "spirit detector." This artistic toolbox will be a concept that I can see emerging in future leaders.

In my work, I have observed young people as they intentionally develop their leadership skills. I have seen in these students a passion for theological study and reflection, and openness to new expressions of worship. They have found a desire to study about and respond to a call they sense to full-time Christian service. I have also seen how these young people have flowered in response to being nominated and affirmed by their home congregations to participate in intentional leadership development training. In a sense, these congregations have told these youth, "We believe you've got what it takes to be a godly leader and we affirm God's gifts in you."

As Samantha asked, "Isn't this how everyone does church?"

NOTES

1. Leonard Sweet, *Summoned to Lead* (Grand Rapids, MI: Zondervan, 2004), 11.
2. Sweet, *Summoned to Lead*, 12.
3. Walter C Wright, *Relational Leadership* (Carlisle, Cumbria, UK: Paternoster Publishing, 2000), viii.
4. Wright, *Relational Leadership*, viii.
5. Bill Hybells, *Courageous Leadership* (Grand Rapids, MI: Zondervan, 2002), 122.
6. Hybells, *Courageous Leadership*, 124-126.
7. Harold L Longenecker, *Growing Leaders By Design* (Grand Rapids, MI: Kregel Resources, 1995), 8.
8. Longenecker, *Growing Leaders By Design*, 9.
9. John Neufeld has written an excellent resource for churches to assist them in this discernment process. *Finding leaders for tomorrow's churches* can be acquired from the Canadian Conference of Mennonite Brethren churches at www.mbconf.ca.
10. Longenecker, *Growing Leaders By Design*, 8.
11. Hybells, *Courageous Leadership*, 127-130.
12. Josephine A Van Linden and Carl I Fertman, *Youth Leadership: A Guide to Understanding Leadership Development In Adolescents* (San Francisco: Jossey-Bass, 1998), 6.
13. Van Linden and Fertman, *Youth Leadership*, 9.
14. Van Linden and Fertman, *Youth Leadership*, 11.
15. Sweet, *Summoned to Lead*, 15.
16. Hybells, *Courageous Leadership*, 32.
17. Sweet, *Summoned to Lead*, 19.
18. Roy Crowne, Bill Muir, and Angela Little, *The Art of Connecting: How to Change Your Relationships Forever* (Milton Keynes, Buckshire, UK: Authentic Lifestyle, 2003), 47.
19. Sweet, *Summoned to Lead*, 57.
20. Crowne, Muir and Little, *The Art of Connecting*, 48.

Church Leadership in a New Era

21. Helen Bee, *The Developing Child* (New York: Harper and Row, 1985), 331.

22. Dave Rahn and Terry Linhart, *Contagious Faith* (Loveland, CO: Group, 2000), 110.

23. Kenda Creasy Dean, "X-Files and Unknown Gods: The Search for Truth of Postmodern Adolescents," paper presented at the Third Conference on Youth Ministry (Oxford, UK: International Association for the Study of Youth Ministry, January 1999), White Paper, 4.

24. Mariam G MacGregor, *Designing Student Leadership Programs: Transforming the Leadership Potential of Youth* (Denver, CO: Youthleadership.com, 2001), 9.

25. Sweet, *Summoned to Lead,* 33.

26. Sweet, *Summoned to Lead,* 35-42.

27. Van Linden and Fertman, *Youth Leadership,* 41.

28. Wright, *Relational Leadership,* 1.

29. Sweet, *Summoned to Lead,* 76.

The Church's Place in the World

The Challenge of Being a Community Church in a Commuter Society

Jim Westgate

On the MB Biblical Seminary campus, we recently held a chapel service that featured three churches that have decided to become community churches rather than commuter churches. These three churches represent three very diverse ministries and populations but have one thing in common: they are seeking to be ambassadors of reconciliation to their neighborhoods.

One is a predominately white, middle and upper middle class Mennonite Brethren commuter church that recently began reaching out to the apartment complexes of its neighborhood, which are diverse in class and ethnicity. The second is a predominately middle and lower middle class Black Missionary Baptist church that recently purchased property in Southeast Fresno and intends to reach an Anglo, Hispanic, and African American community. The third church is a multicultural (Latino, Anglo, African American, Khmu, Lao), multi-congregational (four congregations but with one board, one combined budget, operating as one church) and multilingual (Spanish, English and Khmu/Lao) Mennonite Brethren church that decided thirteen years ago not to become a commuter church but to stay in its neighborhood and reach a diverse population, one that is housed in huge apartment and condominium complexes where the transience rate is in the seventy percent range.

These churches are intentionally moving against the flow of our mobile society, which fosters a commuter and consumer mentality, to establish relationships with men and women in the immediate community around their church. The very fact that churches have to intentionally choose to become or remain community churches indicates that some major influences have captured churches and created distance from their communities.

The Church's Place in the World

If we were to ask people in our churches, "How many come to this church from within a one mile radius around the church?" very few hands would go up. It is nothing today for people to spend fifteen minutes to an hour driving to their home church. Along the way they pass ten or twelve other churches, some of which are even from their own denomination. This kind of behavior indicates the tremendous changes that have happened to the church across North America and how it has shifted from being neighborhood-oriented to commuter-oriented.

When I was a child growing up in Peckville, Pennsylvania, churches were naturally associated with neighborhoods. People knew one another and there was a network of healthy and vibrant relationships in the neighborhood. Since my twin brother and I had a tendency to get into trouble, we were very much aware of the dynamics of such a neighborhood network. If we created a disturbance, like starting a fight or taking something that did not belong to us, we were quickly apprehended and reprimanded by a neighbor, who called our parents and then escorted us home, where we were punished all over again for the same crime. This strong neighborhood/community orientation was also reflected in the ministry of the church. The pastor and the church played an important role in the community. The presence of the church building, the congregation and the pastor was recognized by the neighborhood as a place to gather, where relationships were woven together and people cared for each other and the community.

Today, little thought is given to a neighborhood. In Fresno, there are just a few places where the neighborhood concept is still alive. Interestingly, many of these neighborhood communities are in the poor areas of town where people are more dependent on each other. For the most part, rapid expansion of the city and the development of gated communities and huge housing subdivisions have created an isolated and distant population. It is very comfortable to get in our cars and hit the garage door opener, drive to work, finish work and drive back home, hit the garage opener, drive in to the garage, and then go in the house without meeting any one in our neighborhood.

Urbanization

The push/pull factors of urban migration have affected most churches. The expansion of suburban and rural growth has heightened the transitional dynamic within the church. The birth of new shopping malls with the latest trendy stores, large multiplex theaters and other entertainment venues become very attractive to people who are living in neighborhoods where shops and theaters are old and are no longer occupied by a single culture but are invaded by other ethnic groups that make them feel uncomfortable. The development of new housing tracts with new schools, libraries, and infrastructures becomes attractive to people who are living in communities where the schools have become dumping grounds for recent immigrants and lower-income families, and housing and the physical infrastructure of the community are beginning to run down. This creates an environment where the ethnic and class transition of a community creates a push factor and the attractiveness of new housing and commercial developments become a pull factor.

One cannot blame parents of young children, who want the best for their families, for making the decision to move out of the community and into these new developments. Older people feel the same push/pull factors. When communities are in transition, crime tends to escalate and the appearance of the community begins to decline. Older people are afraid of losing the equity they have had in their homes and become fearful of the crime and new ethnic and lower class families that are moving into the community. Therefore they choose to live in newly formed gated communities where safety is guaranteed because of the high walls, security gates and security systems which protect their new house or condominium.

The church that has been in a community for twenty to thirty years begins to face the migration of its constituency and slowly becomes a commuter church. Instead of trying to reach the newcomers who are often different in class and ethnicity, it concentrates on keeping the commuters by putting more energy into the quality of its preaching, worship and programming. This subtle shift in focus is one that moves a church away from Kingdom ministry to consumer ministry. Churches caught in this shift begin to hire more skilled or professional staff in order to heighten the quality of service, and the laity are less and less used or developed for leadership positions. Darrell Guder states:

> Church is conceived in this view as *the place where* a Christianized civilization gathers for worship, and *the place where* the Christian character of society is cultivated. Increasingly, this view of the church as "a place where certain things happen" locates the

church's self-identity in its organizational forms and its professional class, the clergy who perform the church's authoritative activities." Popular grammar captures it well: you go to church much the same way you might go to the store. You attend a church, the way you attend a school or theater. You belong to a church as you would a service club with its programs and activities.[1]

The more a church becomes a commuter church, the less attention it pays to the immediate community surrounding the church. This results in a major spiritual, physical and missional disconnect from the community. The church becomes, with each passing year, more and more distant from the realities of its neighborhood or local community; and the community or neighborhood perceives the church as uncaring and distant. Those in the neighborhood often become cynical about the church and its ability to show the love of Christ in a tangible way. As a community declines and crime increases, the church becomes a target of graffiti and vandalism, which is a sign of disrespect for its presence.

Church Growth Movement

A second major factor that has impacted the church is the church growth movement that was started by Donald McGavaran and Peter Wagner.[2] Through sociological research on the fastest growing churches, they discovered that these churches were growing because they were homogeneous. Sociology proved that the smaller the number of barriers that a person felt, the greater the chance of them not only attending but joining the church. Therefore, churches that focused their attention on people who were of the same class, ethnicity, and race had a greater potential for growth than those that were trying to reach a diverse population. The more the church reduced the barriers that might make a pagan uncomfortable, the greater the chance that they would come to church and hear the gospel. This shift in philosophy of church growth embedded in the church a homogeneous and consumer mentality that has continued to this day.

Most denominational structures adopted this philosophy of church growth. Because they wanted to be good stewards of their resources, it made sense to invest time, energy, personnel and money into reaching people who were similar to each other. Therefore church planting shifted from the city, where diversity was greatest, to the suburbs, where similarity was the greatest. This made perfect sense from an economical and sociological perspective. However, it was not good theology.

2 Corinthians 5:17-21 provides a glimpse of God's work of reconciliation through Christ and our mission/ministry of reconciliation in this world.

> Now all these thing are from God, who reconciled us to himself through Christ, and gave us the ministry of reconciliation, namely, that God was in Christ reconciling the world to himself, not counting their trespasses against them, and He has committed to us the word of reconciliation. Therefore we are ambassadors for Christ, as though God were entreating through us; we beg you on behalf of Christ, be reconciled to God.[3]

As the church in the United States and Canada has bought into the capitalistic ethos of its culture, many decisions are made not on the basis of theology, but on the basis of economic viability and reward. The build-bigger-and-better syndrome evidenced in the catch-phrase "if you build it they will come" has captured the church growth movement. This homogeneous focus, mixed with the rugged individualism that is generated by a capitalistic mindset, has concentrated the efforts of the church on individual reconciliation with God but has grossly neglected reconciliation with one another, especially across barriers of culture, class and ethnicity.

In Ephesians 2:11-3:10 and Galatians 3:26-19 we are reminded that Jesus Christ's death was to bring Jew and gentile, bond and free, male and female together in one body. We are no longer strangers and aliens, but are fellow-citizens with the saints, fellow-heirs, fellow-members of the body, and fellow-partakers of the Promise in Christ so that "the manifold wisdom of God might now be made known through the church to the rulers and authorities in the heavenly places" (Eph 3:10).

The church is the vehicle that is to display the Kingdom of God to the principalities and powers of the world. The church is not the Kingdom but it is to be a reflection of the Kingdom. In the Kingdom of God, the qualities of peace, righteousness, equality, equity, justice and holiness reign. And if a congregation is to reflect the Kingdom of God it must intentionally manifest these qualities through caring and reconciling ministries in its community.

Internationalization

A third major factor is the internationalization of our communities. There is hardly a place in the United States or Canada that has not experienced radical ethnic, class and racial shifts in its schools and communities. Fresno, the fifth largest city in California, now has over a hundred languages spoken in its school system. This is a powerful indicator of the dramatic change in ethnicity, race and class that has occurred over the past fifteen years. Churches in transitional communities are faced with the challenge of whether they are going to reach and receive people to whom we have sent missionaries to for the past hundred years, or whether they are going to go on sending missionaries overseas while ignoring the world at their doorstep.

Shortly after I came to Fresno in the 1990s, I had a conversation with Sharon Stanley, the director of Fresno Interdenominational Refugee Ministry, about the number of churches that were ministering to the 50,000 Southeast Asians who had come to Fresno as a result of the Vietnam War. She explained that the churches of the city had basically overlooked this population and that there were only thirteen Southeast Asian churches – the same number as the major Southeast Asian gangs in the city. In the past ten years this has changed some, but a tremendous amount of work still needs to be done. This is a good example of how deeply the homogeneous church growth principle has impacted our churches.

How can the church begin to change its focus and bring a balance again to becoming a community church? Let me suggest several steps.

Exegete the Church

One of the first steps in helping a church move from a commuter church orientation to a community church orientation is to examine the history of your church. We cannot begin to look at the future until we understand our past. It is important that church leadership takes time to examine why their church was started and what were the goals and objectives of the original group. Often one will find the zeal of the original group was to reach the community where the church was born, but over the years it slipped, because of migration of members, into becoming a commuter church. It is helpful to identify when the shifts occurred, as well as the precipitating factors that caused the shift away from the neighborhood.

A second step in this process is to examine the diversity or lack of diversity in a church. If the church has been a particular ethnic majority for many years, it will have a difficult time embracing newcomers who are different from the majority. Most churches want growth, but they seldom think through the implications. A challenging exercise for churches that desire to become community churches is to play the "implication game." It goes like this: "If the next twenty people to join our church were families with small pre-school children, how would our church have to change? If the next twenty people to join our church were low income whites, or middle class Latinos, or handicapped or African Americans, etc. what would have to change?" This implication exercise will create an atmosphere of positive brain-storming and potential thinking rather than fear of change. It will lead to proactive thinking rather than having a reaction later on that could sabotage the process.

The third step in exegeting a church is examining its culture. Most churches have not given much thought to their unique culture. If a church has a Mennonite heritage then the church will adopt many of the norms of that culture. It will have a common language that is geared for insiders rather than outsiders. The foods served, the music sung, the way people dress, the order of service, the jokes that are told, and the way decisions are made are all are rooted in a cultural context and become the norm for the church. Any outsider will feel these identifiers as soon as they begin to attend the church. Each church has a corporate culture, and it must be able to identify that culture if it is going to intentionally reach out to a community where the culture might be quite different.

The critical question is whether or not the church is culturally flexible or if it is ethnocentric, which means it assumes its culture is best and every other culture is inferior. When the church plays the "implication game" it will quickly become aware of the areas the corporate culture will be challenged. The church must be willing to address the issues of change if it is going to shift from being primarily a commuter church to embracing its community. The exegesis of your church leads to the next step of introducing change, which is "re-formation."[4]

The Church's Place in the World

Exegete Your Community

The church that has become commuter-based has often lost touch with its community. Transition is a constant in urban communities. This means the demographics of a particular community are constantly in a state of flux. Pastoral leaders should visit with the principals of grade schools in their area. Junior and Senior high schools are mostly commuter schools and will not give a good profile of the community around the church. The grade school, on the other hand, has the latest demographic material. I recently served as interim pastor for Butler Mennonite Brethren Church in Southeast Fresno. One of the first things I did when I came to the church was to visit the principal at Greenberg school, which is about four blocks from the church. She was able to quickly call up on her computer all of the latest and most relevant data on families, ethnicity, income, etc. that I would need in order to understand the community around the church. The principal also suggested ways we could engage the students and families in our area to help them do better in school.

The second thing leaders should check is census tracts around the church. For the United States, visit htpp://www.census.gov to look up the census tracts around the church. Click on "American Fact Finder" and it will give you instructions on how to find your census tract or regional information. For Canada, visit www.pcensus.com or http://www.tetrad.com/pricing/can/cn2001.html. Every category imaginable is included in the census material. This information will help you understand the current income level, educational level, racial/ethnic make up, job/profession, home ownership and apartment dwellers, etc. in your geographic area.

However, you can only learn so much from the data. The best way to get to know your community is to explore it on a personal level. Following are three stages of building bridges to your community.

Exploration

In the exploration stage, leaders from the church examine what kinds of changes are happening in the immediate community around the church. Communities change quickly so it is important to know who is leaving and who is coming into your community. It is also important to know what other ministry agencies are working in your community with whom you might network. Think about this stage as though you were a missionary and you were going to a foreign field. You would want to know everything you can about the people, customs, societal structures, etc. If a church does a good job of exploration it will be able to come alongside the community and complement the indigenous ministries and leaders instead of competing with them.

Explore the Community
- Explore the various Ethnic Groups – talk with elementary school principals.
- Explore the economic conditions – talk with social services related to your area.
- Explore the religious background – find out the number of churches and religious groups in your community.
- Explore the agencies already working with groups in your community – this keeps you from reinventing the wheel and allows you to network with other agencies.
- Explore the perceived and felt needs of the group – our understanding of the community as an outsider is very different from the people who live in the community. To discover the felt needs you have to have one-on-one conversations with people and leaders in the community.
- Explore the assets and emerging leaders of the group – If you only study the felt needs, the church will treat the people in the community as clients, which will lead to a superior-to-inferior mentality. There are many assets in the community that can be mobilized to bring transformation to the community. John Kretzman and John McKnight have written an excellent text on "Asset Based Community Development."[5]

Explore the Cultures of the Emerging People Groups
- Explore the history. If we were going to the mission field we would take time to explore and understand the various people groups to which we were going to minister. Somehow, we often neglect this when it comes to reaching people groups in our communities.
- Explore the value systems. Discovering what value is given to family, elderly, children, home, religion, etc. can inform the church in ways to approach the people in the community.
- Explore the customs. A clear understanding of the identifiers that define a people group is extremely important in making sure you build bridges and do not burn bridges to the community.

- Explore the way and pace of life. Every cultural group has a different way and pace of life. In cultures where people are more important than time, the members of that culture will often be late to events because they are in conversation with someone and it would be rude to end that conversation to go to an event.
- Explore the thinking patterns. In Western culture thought is linear; but in Eastern cultures, people think cyclically. This difference often creates confusion in the communication process. Knowing how a person thinks will alleviate a great deal of confusion and frustration.
- Explore the psychological temperaments. Some cultures are very celebrative and other cultures are reserved. These differences in temperaments can lead to clashes.

Explore the Networks in the Community
- Explore the natural gathering places. In poor areas, the laundromat is a great place to meet people, because they have to spend an hour or so doing their laundry.
- Explore the celebration events. Block parties, cultural events, even birthday parties are great ways of meeting a lot of people at one time to begin to build friendship bridges.
- Explore communication patterns. Some cultures prefer that you talk about family and many other subjects before dealing with issues of God, church or religion.
- Explore the relational networks. In Southeast Asian cultures, the clan is a major network of families who are related, and communication flows quickly. If you offend one member of a clan that might include twenty-five to fifty families, you can close the door to most of the other families.
- Explore the educational patterns. Some cultures, such as African American and Latino cultures, are more oral than writing-oriented. This may mean that using brochures or literature to try to introduce your church will be ineffective.
- Explore the service agencies. A church cannot meet all the needs within any given community, but it should know where those needs can be met. Therefore, the church needs to know the other agencies in the community that are providing services and construct a referral list of these agencies.

- Explore the religious groups. It is important to know all of the religious groups in your area and the number of people involved in these groups. This will help you understand the number of people who are not connected to any religious group and allow you to focus on people who do not attend any religious services.

Exchange

The second stage is having an exchange of ideas, agendas and visions with the people and agencies ministering in your community. It is easy to settle for perceived trends, changes or needs in the community and consequently create ministries that are not relevant. By dialoguing with key leadership and ministry agencies in the community, a church can discover both the assets that are embedded in its community as well as the felt and true needs of the community. Through embrace, the church will be seen as an ally instead of an invader of the community. No one church can meet the needs of, or bring complete transformation to, a community. It takes a great variety of ministries and agencies to bring stability and sustainability to a community.

Communication Events
- Visit the community or cultural group in their setting.
- Invite key people to share in your setting.
- Identify "Tree Shakers." These are people who like to agitate or confront the issues and or other groups in the community. They shake things up to see what will happen.
- Identify "Jelly Makers." These are people who know how to build bridges and construct coalitions. They complement the "Tree Shakers" because they know what to do with the fruit when it falls to the ground.
- Small group listening exercises: discover the agenda(s) of the community groups. Do not superimpose your agenda on the community.
- Small encounter groups: discuss and process their agenda(s).

Companionship Events
- Develop personal relationships before you move to group events.
- Create spontaneous personal events: suppers, sporting events, etc.
- Cultivate a small group of change leaders: people willing to take a risk to be a bridging person.

- Invite community or ethnic groups to share in fun events.
- Invite community or ethnic groups to share in worship, and employ joint planning for inclusion.
- Move toward campouts and retreats for bonding time.

Commitment Events
- Develop a regularly-scheduled series of events.
- Join together for agenda sharing and planning for events.
- Lift up and honor indigenous leadership. Cultivate open access to resources.
- Develop a covenant statement of relationship building. Be explicit about expectations of yourself and the other party

Embrace

Once a church has explored the community and had a healthy exchange with leadership and ministry agencies in the community, it is ready for the final stage, which is "embrace." When a church desires to bring transformation to a neighborhood or community, it must be careful to embrace the leadership and agendas of those already working in the community. If this is not done, the entering group will appear arrogant and vitriolic in their ventures, which often leads to rejection and disconnection from the indigenous leadership. A healthy embrace will result in mutual ministry and development of new programs that are owned not just by the church but by the community as well.

Celebration Events
- Mutual Celebration: intentional inclusion of the cultural distinctives of the other group to demonstrate that you appreciate their culture. The mutual that is celebrated should be designed to stretch both ways. It hopefully moves your congregation out of its comfort zone a little bit and also moves the new group out of their comfort zone a little, which creates new ground for dialogue and embrace.
- Small group celebrations.
- Cultural events are a good way to understand the ethos of the culture.
- Worship events will reveal the spiritual ethos of the various cultures and lead to "soul-shaping."

- Holiday events can celebrate the unique traditions around the holidays. People are much more open and receptive during these special times of the year.
- Mutual recognition and appreciation of diversity and unity: this results in the spontaneous embrace of another's cultural uniqueness. It becomes yours to a certain extent.

Projects and Programs
- Mutual design of projects or programs that can serve the community. There needs to be a real partnership developed with community leadership. The asset-based study that was done in the early stages will identify potential leaders and allies with whom you need to partner.
- A philosophy of "workfare instead of welfare" needs to be established early. The church must be careful that it does not assume responsibility for people's problems. The church has to have a posture of coming alongside people and helping them solve their problems. There obviously will be emergencies and certain crises that will demand provision of help without any expectation, but this should not be the norm.
- Leadership of programs that cross cultural barriers should enlist leaders from that racial or ethnic group to become part of the team.
- Church staff must become intentional about its racial and ethic make up if it is going to be effective in building long term bridges to the community.

Re-formation of the Church

Leaders will have to lead a process of "re-formation" to change the culture of the church. The process of change will need missional leaders who can guide the church through this precarious process with keen biblical insight and a strong missional outlook. This is not just about creating some new program but it is creating a new corporate culture or a "new think" for the church. Alan Roxburgh has captured this process of "re-formation" is his book *Crossing the Bridge*.[6] He describes how the church will move through five phases in the process of transformation or reframing the church into a missional community. In my own experience of working as a church consultant with over thirty-five churches that have gone through major transition and revitalization, I have seen these same phases at work.

The first phase of Roxburgh's five-phase process is *stability*, in which most people in the structure desire to maintain the structures that reflect how people perceive things ought to work. In this phase people will tolerate evolutionary change, which occurs in very small increments over a long period of time, and developmental change, which "occurs as improvements are made on the existing systems and practices." The key word in this phase is *continuity*. Anyone challenging the status quo is marginalized quickly.

To stimulate change, leaders will have to introduce into this mix a new language that captures clear biblical values. Leaders will have to discern between "outer language and inner language."[7] Outer language is the more formal explanatory and objective language that is used to describe, discern and dissect issues and problems. Inner language is the intuitive and feeling language that is shared from the heart and is seasoned with a great deal of emotion. The inner language will be critical for transformation because it speaks to the center of a person's life and ignites hopes and dreams. The leader will have to focus on reframing theological constructs in fresh and exciting ways so that they become part of the grapevine conversation. In this process of creating change, leaders will have to engage and embrace traditionalists as well as change agents in the process of transition.

An example of reformation and the stability phase is seen in First Baptist Church in Fresno. When Dr. Willie Nolte was called to First Baptist Church, it was over one hundred years old and filled with older men and women of faith. Willie, who is in his thirties, worked hard at hearing the outer and inner language of his congregation. He found that their original dream was to be a church in the heart of the city. However, as the city changed, members had left the downtown area of Fresno and moved to the north edge of the city. Now, the city has grown way beyond them. As Willie studied city maps he realized that they were a church in the geographic center of the city. So he created a vision statement that stated they were a "Church in the Heart of the City with a Heart for the City." By recapturing the original dream and re-forming it into a new vision, the older people have joined him in the exciting journey of change and re-formation.

The second phase of re-formation is *discontinuity*, in which "internal and external stresses begin to push against the system's habits and practices." It is assumed in this phase that the old ways of doing things will be able to guide the church through this time of instability. There is usually an entrenchment of tried and true traditions and values, and micro-management of details becomes the favorite past time. Those embracing the discontinuity are seen to be traitors and pressure often forces them to leave. Spiritual leaders will have to be reconcilers and engage polarized parties in constructive dialogue. The recapturing and rehearsing of the original vision and mission of the group, which required risk taking and sacrifices in the birth and early growth of the church, will help the church to refocus its attention away from micro-management to re-visioning.

The third phase is *disembedding*, which is a sense of chaos where the systems and structures are no longer able to manage the pressures and changes taking place. "Power struggles emerge and conflict and blaming are common."[8] The church at this point usually moves into a survival mode. Much debating, negotiating, and confrontation are the norm. I find this phase close to the grief syndrome in which people are trying to cope with loss. Some rationalize, others are angry, others negotiate or try to buy time, others withdraw into depression and others begin to adjust to new concepts as a potentially good thing. Roxburgh demonstrates that disembedding is really an outcome of the path that the church has followed during modernity.

The fourth phase is the *in-between world transition*, which is the most difficult phase of the process. It is learning to live without any sense of markers and become comfortable with chaos. The great tendency is to look for some outside source to fix it or bring order to the chaos. However, the outside sources are built on the old paradigm of control and equilibrium. Roxburgh says the "in-between phase is the tension between two options: to recapture what has been lost or risk the discovery of a new future."[9] This is a protracted period of time because a new language and new systems have to be introduced and established. In a world where efficiency is one of the highest values, there is great pressure to look for a quick fix instead of the slow process of internal and external transformation.

Spiritual leaders must keep a Kingdom-focused ecclesiology in view if this transition is going to occur. Otherwise, the system will fall back into an ecclesiocentric mode of operation, where one is trying to manipulate the programs, structures, and ministries of the church to solve the problems. It takes time to cultivate new infrastructures that are oriented toward sending and mobilizing, in place of programs oriented to coming and consuming.

The fifth stage, *re-formation*, is when the system has emerged from transition and constructed a new identity around the old story and the transforming power of the cross. "A new language, a new set of roles, and a new set of rules have emerged to reveal structures, and ways of living out the old story, that will bear little resemblance to the earlier period of stability."

The re-formation of the church will require leaders able to engage the issues, problems, barriers and diversity of viewpoints that are generated through this process. Leaders will also need special skills to embrace the diversity of people, such as the gatekeepers, the traditionalists, the constitutionalists, the radicals and the passive by-standers who emerge throughout this process. It is like guiding a church through a death and rebirth process in which the whole gamut of emotions and reactions will be present in various members of the congregation. The pastoral leadership must be able to embrace the anger, confusion, depression, and frustration, as well as the excitement, visioning and creative strategizing.

The commuter church that intends to become a community church or the church that wants to remain a community church when the community is in transition must be willing to invest major effort in the hard work of research and preparation if it is going to experience "re-formation." My experience has been that many commuter churches want to relate to their community, but do not want to do the hard work of research and preparation before they begin to reach out. Consequently, they experience failure in some of their early efforts and settle back into the patterns of a consumer church, which basically seeks people who like the programming and dominant culture of the church.

Anabaptists, who value community more than many other denominations, should have a much higher commitment to not only experience community but to be a transformational and missional agent to the community in which their church is located.

NOTES

1. Darrell L. Guder, *Missional Church* (Grand Rapids, MI: William B Eerdmans, 1998).

2. Donald Anderson McGavran, *Understanding Church Growth* (Grand Rapids, MI: William B. Eerdmans, 1970).

3. All scripture references in this chapter are from the *New American Standard Version* (The Lockman foundation, 1960) unless noted otherwise.

4. Alan Roxburgh, *Crossing the Bridge* (Costa Mesa, CA: Percept, 2000), 31-44.

5. John McKnight and Jody Kretzman, *Building Communities from the Inside Out* (Chicago, IL: ACTA Publishing, 1993).

6. Ibid.

7. Lovett H. Weems Jr., *Church Leadership: Vision, Team, Culture and Integrity* (Nashville, TN: Abingdon Press, 1993), 103.

8. Alan Roxburgh, *Crossing the Bridge*, 31-44.

9. Ibid.

The Challenge of Dual Citizenship
Pierre Gilbert

Christians normally think of themselves as citizens of the Kingdom of God. As such, they are expected to act and live as Kingdom citizens and to give it their primary allegiance. But Christians are also citizens of nations here on earth and are expected to grant at least some degree of allegiance to their country. In a very real and concrete way, for better or for worse, Christians hold "dual citizenship." To pretend it is not so simply does not reflect reality. What are the implications of such dual citizenship for Christians who live in democratic systems such as those found in the United States and Canada? Since this article is written in the context of the fiftieth anniversary of the Mennonite Brethren Biblical Seminary, I will initially focus this discussion on those who identify with the Mennonite tradition, and then I will expand it to include the broader Christian community.

Traditionally, Mennonites in Canada and the United States have shied away from political involvement. Until the early 1960s, Mennonites generally shunned public service and law in favor of farming, education, and the medical professions. More recently, Mennonites have become much less queasy about politics and political activism. There are at least three reasons behind this trend. First, Mennonites have to a great extent left the rural context and become urban and more mainstream. Second, intellectuals in the Mennonite Church have espoused, mainly throughout the 1960s and early 1970s, an ideology that in fact encourages a much greater degree of political activism. John Howard Yoder[1] has been instrumental in effecting this trend. Third, such political activism is now perceived as essential to help promote the peace and justice agenda that is considered by many

Mennonites as one of the fundamental expressions of the Anabaptist faith.[2]

Like Christians of other traditions in Canada and the United States, the political activism of Mennonites most often tends to reside in one or the other side of the political spectrum. It would be a serious mistake to assume that Mennonites constitute a massive unanimous political block. Mennonites tend to identify with either the liberal left or the conservative right otherwise found in the broader society. I would go so far as to state that the Mennonite community reflects the culture war that has increasingly characterized North American politics since 9/11, and even more acutely since the war in Iraq begun in March 2003.[3] Although the discourse generally remains polite, the tone is unambiguous. Mennonites on either side of the divide cannot fathom how anyone can hold a contrary opinion to their own. The left-wing Mennonites ceaselessly accuse their right-wing counterparts of siding with the evangelicals in confusing their conservative right-wing political agenda with their Christian faith, particularly when it comes to the role of the military, US foreign policy and the place of civil religion in society. On the other hand, lest we think this is a one-sided sin, left-wing Mennonites, in an eerily mirror-image fashion, seem to suffer from the same affliction. Politically engaged Mennonites who do not wish to identify with the conservative American evangelicals usually espouse views that are most consistent with the left-wing political agenda. In fact, I have observed that in some circles, the distinction between the Mennonite/Anabaptist faith and the left-wing political agenda is at best tenuous.

These two groups are similar in one way. At the extreme ends of the spectrum, both are tempted to view their respective stance as the natural default position for good-thinking Christians. It is not something unique to conservative Christians. While the left-wing Mennonites may rant about the evangelicals' confusion of religion and politics, they, in the end, do not fare much better. If Jesus were to appear today, they assume he would sit at their table. He would be a strident supporter of Green Peace. He would be present at all the anti-war manifestations. He would drive an environmentally friendly Honda hybrid.

Liberal left-wing Mennonites usually use the language of "faithfulness" ("Let the Church be the Church")[4] when dealing with the issues of the day and tend to deal with them according to a list of priorities starting with peace and justice, which usually entails a good dose of anti-Americanism or a radical and systematic denunciation of American foreign policy. The recent war against Iraq is an excellent case in point. When it comes to the peace issue, these Mennonites do not hesitate, either individually or through various Mennonite agencies, to publicly express their disapproval. The other issues that get some attention are the so-called social justice agenda (gender issues, aboriginal rights, gay and lesbian rights), the environment and the Israeli-Palestinian conflict.

On other morality issues, left-wing Mennonites tend to be less vocal: abortion, same-sex marriage, the rise of "religious" secularism and the corresponding mounting public dismissal of conservative Christianity receive less attention. Abortion is sometimes addressed, but not nearly as vigorously as some of the other issues I spelled out earlier. A good illustration of this mitigated approach can be found on the Peace and Justice Support Network website of Mennonite Church USA where, after voicing a clear opposition to abortion, in agreement with the Assembly 75 statement, the document then proceeds to qualify that stance. The following excerpt articulates the rationale behind the hesitation to back a forceful anti-abortion stance and is representative of the position held by a significant number of left-wing Mennonite intellectuals across Mennonite denominations.

> The situation in both the Mennonite Church and society has changed, however. Anna Bowman, one of two women on the committee, explained that the 1975 statement was written "prior to the pro-life, pro-choice polarization. We weren't as aware that the members of our churches were in a privileged position." As a social worker, Bowman is aware that many women seeking abortions have not been taught to make responsible choices independent of the men in their lives and do not have support when caught in an unplanned pregnancy. "As a denomination, we still know what we believe, but face a new, different question: Do we have the right to make our beliefs the law of the land, especially when others aren't so privileged?"[5]

The critical question is not so much what the denomination believes, but whether its members have the right to make "our beliefs the law of the land…" In this particular piece, which is fairly characteristic of a broad spectrum of the Mennonite church, to attempt to weigh in on such issues is seen as coercion, domination, and control; "the violent assertion of our rights." While those identifying with conservative evangelicalism would not describe their political activism as some attempt at imposing Christian beliefs, they would tend to be less equivocal on the appropriateness of using political levers to bring about the outcome they seek.

In that respect, left-wing Mennonites often accuse American evangelicals and Mennonites who identify with them of not showing proper concern for peace and social justice and too strident in using their political clout to impose their moral values on the rest of society.

As I pointed out earlier, this great divide amongst Mennonites is not unique. It reflects a much wider and vigorous culture war that is presently being waged in the United States and Canada.

Since the question I identify does not only concern Mennonites, but Christians of all stripes, I will now broaden the discussion to include all Christians. So how do we approach the issue of dual citizenship for Christians? Do we look for a balanced approach between what is perceived as two extremes? In theory, perhaps. In practice, the so-called "balanced" position often turns out to be as elusive as a desert mirage. Rather than attempt to resolve the problem by somehow adding the two and dividing by two, I would like to attempt to provide a framework for Christian social/political activism that I hope will set out a model that reconciles the Christian's twofold identity without necessarily identifying with one side or the other of the political spectrum.

At this point, I need to point out that this article aims at discussing the situation Christians find themselves in democratic countries that uphold individual rights, freedom of speech, and freedom of association. More specifically, it targets the situations of Christians in the United States and Canada. Though it is not my intent to exclude Western Europe, Australia, and other democratic countries, I focus particularly on the US and Canada, because this is the context with which I am most familiar and because there is in fact a significant Christian population that would be concerned by such a discussion. In other words, it is primarily in the United States and, to a lesser extent, in Canada, that the issue is most pertinent and most controversial.

The Search for Universal Values

Though Christians generally believe that the Bible is to be their primary source in the search to develop appropriate models of behavior, they may not be unanimous on where that search should begin. The Old Testament would seem to be a logical place to begin our exploration, but one needs to be careful not to compare oranges and bananas, as the saying goes. Ancient Israel was, to all intents and purposes, a sort of theocracy, a religious state. Though Israel had a king, he was to be Yahweh's representative, and the Sinai covenant, with its laws and stipulations, Israel's basic constitution. The king of Israel, unlike his Egyptian or Mesopotamian counterparts, was no law unto himself; he was responsible to uphold God's law and was, in theory, subject to it. So, when the prophets of Israel condemn the king and the ruling classes, the appeals are based on a failure to observe the basic demands of the law. One of the crispest expressions of that principle is found in Micah 6:8: "He has showed you, O man, what is good. And what does the LORD require of you? To act justly and to love mercy and to walk humbly with your God."[6] Micah summarizes the entire law in three commands: to act justly, to love mercy, to walk humbly with your God. In the context of Israel, those three injunctions make perfect sense. Israel's identity was intimately linked with a particular God. Justice and mercy were not perceived as autonomous concepts; they were the natural expressions of an exclusive allegiance to Yahweh.

While we may completely echo the prophet's call for justice and mercy, it would not be quite appropriate, in a secular state, to call for an unconditional allegiance to Yahweh or Jesus on the part of our government officials. We do, however, believe that all the calls to justice in the prophetic literature, which echo, to a great extent, the core of the Ten Commandments, are valid. There are two reasons why Christians would believe in the legitimacy of extending the prophet's call to their contemporaries. First, it reflects a certain understanding of who God is. Second, we believe that the injunctions to do justice and to show mercy are universally valid concepts regardless of the social or cultural context we may be in. Most Christians would also believe, even if we don't constantly emphasize it, that the only way to sustain these values in any society, is if they are tied to, linked with, or embedded in the belief in a personal and moral God who demands justice and mercy, and holds all men and women accountable. In the end, we may recognize that in a secular and pluralistic society, we can't demand, require or legislate belief in the Christian God. Even then, those of us who work for and promote justice and mercy will recognize deep down in our hearts that we do so because we understand that these values derive from the moral nature of God himself and thus represent universals that should be sought at all times and in all places.

The following example illustrates what I mean. While it is commonplace to vilify the British for their involvement in India in the nineteenth century, it is interesting to note that until British rule, a widow was required to mount the funeral pyre of her husband and be cremated along with him. The rite of sati that had been prevalent in India for thousands of years was finally prohibited when the British put an end to it in 1829. The members of the British parliament who enacted the law and those officers who enforced it in the field did not for one second believe that such a practice could be defended on the basis of the type of post-modern multicultural mush we now find in most Western countries, and which holds every culture, irrespective of practice and belief, in equal esteem. Although the Orthodox Hindus vehemently protested the measure and appealed to the Privy Council in England, fortunately for the widows, the council rejected the appeal. The British knew the practice was wrong and did their best to stamp it out. The issue, here, is not whether the British could or should impose the Christian faith, but whether they would sanction practices they felt went against a moral standard they regarded as absolute and universal.

From the Old Testament, we derive a number of fundamental values that we hold as universal, and consequently as good and appropriate in any context. The intrinsic value of each individual human being as made in the image of God, the notion of human dignity, the defense of the poor and compassion for the weak, the rejection of magic and superstition would rank very high.

In regard to moral behavior, the New Testament presents a contextualization of the most fundamental moral precepts found in the Old Testament. It is commonly advocated that these precepts apply primarily if not exclusively to the Church. In that respect, we interpret the Sermon on the Mount, for example, as the charter for the people of God. I would strongly support the notion that the New Testament precepts are primarily for the community of believers; they are not meant to be law for all. But I would also make the point that if the New Testament moral injunctions in great part reflect the heart of the Old Testament covenant, and if we accept that the most fundamental object of the law is to promote life,[7] it follows then that the most fundamental elements of Old and New Testament moral prescriptions will work for the benefit of the community that adopts them.

In other words, we believe that if a society adopts the most basic moral premises attested to in scripture, it will thrive as a just and compassionate society where individuals enjoy personal freedom and dignity. At least, that is the theory. If, on the other hand, a community does not hold to these beliefs and values we believe are essential to the maintenance of a healthy society, it will decay and people will bear the price of the moral corrosion that will result. This is where the point of the dilemma appears. Does knowing what may be best for our society give us some right to impose our beliefs? While some Christians would balk at the notion of "imposing" beliefs, most would agree that we do have some kind of obligation to intervene in one form or another to shape the community we are part of. The question, of course, is how can we do so with biblical integrity?

Biblical Precedents

There are two passages that I think can provide some direction in regard to Christian political and social involvement. The first one is found in Jeremiah 29:5-28, the second in Romans 13:1.

Jeremiah 29:5-28 is set in the context of the Judean community exiled in Babylon. At that time, the Judeans still entertained some hope that their stay in Babylon would be temporary and that God would soon return them to the Promised Land. Against all expectations, Jeremiah gave them a difficult and expected directive. There would be no immediate return to the land of Israel. Those who had been taken to Babylon would remain in that foreign land for at least seventy years. The Judeans were to embrace the future God was giving to them in their adoptive country and establish themselves in their new surroundings. Moreover, the exiles were to make this new place their home and seek the welfare of the city they lived in. "Also, seek the peace and prosperity of the city to which I have carried you into exile. Pray to the LORD for it, because if it prospers, you too will prosper" (29:7). This text states explicitly that the exiles should seek the "peace and prosperity" of their new home. The reason offered is pragmatic: "if it prospers, you too will prosper."

Inner city pastors and leaders involved in Christian community development often refer to this passage to motivate Christians to get involved in the urban context. In this case, however, the motivation is not quite as self-serving as the Jeremiah text would appear to be. Christian community development leaders sincerely encourage Christians to get involved in the city, not simply to ensure that Christians will have a comfortable place to live in, but because they deeply believe that it is a concrete manifestation of Christ's love.

Christian community development seeks to work within the social structures of a neighborhood in order to bring social healing. While the ultimate goal of Christian community development is to present the person of Jesus Christ, the social and political work done by these people is usually in no way contingent on anyone joining their church. It is important to note here that such work will involve much more than charity, mentoring, or coaching. It often involves aggressive political work on behalf of the community. Even if some might disagree with the underlying evangelistic agenda that is intrinsic to Christian community development, most would affirm this kind of Christian social action.[8]

The second text I wish to draw the reader's attention to is Romans 13:1, which states, "Everyone must submit himself to the governing authorities, for there is no authority except that which God has established. The authorities that exist have been established by God." In this passage, Paul does not primarily intend to provide a basis for Christian social activism. Romans 13:1 is set in the context of a series of injunctions aimed at providing basic instructions for Christian behavior. Paul is basically advocating that Christians live as law-abiding citizens rather than criminals. Paul is being pragmatic. If Christians must suffer persecution, it should not be because of thievery or murder, but because of their witness to Christ.

It is obvious, however, that submission to authorities in the context of first-century Rome and in twenty-first century North America are, to put it mildly, not quite the same thing. In contrast to ancient Rome, where citizens had little say in the politics of the land, residents of the United States and Canada play a crucial role in the creation of their government and the policies it creates. Citizens are called upon to actively shape the society in which they live. Whether Paul could foresee the implications of chapter 13:1 for a society such as ours is certainly open for debate, but at the very least, we can safely assume that the injunction to submit to authorities in the context of a democratic system does imply the obligation for Christians to contribute to shaping the society they live in to the best of their knowledge and abilities, since this is what the political system expects of its citizens. This extrapolation would also be perfectly compatible with the principle of partnership that is an intrinsic component of biblical theology. From the very beginning, God mandated human beings to work in cooperation with God in the accomplishment of his designs for the world (Gen 2:15-17).

What do these two passages mean for Christians today? I would like to propose a preliminary answer to this question by outlining the position of the Canadian sociologist Fernand Dumont in regards to the relationship between the Christian and society.

Fernand Dumont

Fernand Dumont, who passed away in 1997, was one of the most prolific and admired sociologists in Canada. Author of numerous books and articles on topics ranging from epistemology, economics, sociology, history, literature, to philosophy of religions, he was also a committed and vocal Christian. This may seem like a trivial observation, but not in the Quebec context. Although such a personal commitment could conceivably be a liability in some circles in the rest of Canada and the United States, the situation is much worse in Quebec, which has, in the last forty years, experienced both an extremely rapid rate of secularization and nurtured a profound suspicion, if not an outright hostility, toward traditional and conservative Christianity. Most intellectuals in Quebec feel that one cannot simultaneously be a committed Christian and a scientist. Because of this situation, Fernand Dumont spoke and wrote at length in order to reconcile science and the Christian faith.

In a remarkable article in which Dumont discusses how the Christian can relate to the world,[9] he prefaces his main thesis by reminding the reader that the Western world has changed in radical ways in the last century. For example, we no longer live in a conceptual universe where religious and profane categories are mixed and confused; we distinguish, as a matter of course, gospel and clericalism, the state and the church, science and God. Belief in the God of the gaps is obsolete. We no longer live in a world that demands that we revert to God's intervention to explain natural phenomena such as thunder, earthquakes and disease. The scientific method presupposes that natural phenomena can be investigated without ever resorting to God's action to explain their mechanisms. At first sight, such a conceptual model would seem to rele-

The Church's Place in the World

gate the Christian faith to the realm of folklore and popular culture, but Dumont sees it differently. He uses the image of a three-storied house to explain how we can legitimately define the relationship between faith and culture. He emphasizes the fact that though he is referring to three stories, there is still only one house.

The Upper Story: The Rational Organization of the World

The upper story represents the place where scientists live; it is the sphere of rational thought, science, technology and rational organization. Because of the nature of his profession, Dumont mentions that this is where he spends most of his time. "To attempt to explain the coherence of the universe is an ambition without limits," he writes. What cannot be explained is not simply a mystery to leave in the hands of God but an area of further and endless investigation.

The Main Floor: The Human Condition

At this level, Dumont describes a kind of human intervention whose main objective is fundamentally the improvement of the human condition. Dumont is careful to point out that we are not simply referring to the general condition of laborers, women, or the poor. Working at organizing the world according to principles of justice, truth and compassion is valid, because it aims at improving the lives of real individuals. To clarify what Dumont means, we cannot pretend that we are working for the good of humanity and, at the same time, oppress specific groups. If, on the one hand, our society actively seeks the coherence of the universe, it also seeks with the same zeal to enhance the quality of life of humans everywhere. At this level, the believer shares both the concern but also the uncertainty of the solutions needed to improve the condition of men and women in our world. It is not, however, a mere intellectual problem. It is because of our concern for specific individuals that we work to that end.

The Basement: In the Heart of Man

Dumont states that we move from the main floor to the basement, which represents the depths of the human heart itself. It is there, he notes, that we find what he calls the *mal fondamental* (a basic evil, a fundamental flaw), something radically insufficient in human nature: a fundamental "vice in our loves and fidelities," an "evil from which the Christian faith springs and which is common to us all."

Dumont expresses a reality, felt both by believers and non-believers, that something is not right in the very core of the human heart. As if humanity was stuck or paralyzed by a primeval choice – a choice no one is free to erase. There is a "mortgage" we cannot lift. In Christian tradition, it is called original sin, and when we say that, we do not pretend to explain what it is. We observe that it is there, that is all. We clumsily attempt to describe it. We confess its existence. We see it first as a challenge towards God himself. But to have faith is more than simply raising our fist to God; it is to go further. It is to believe in the Christ/God, in his death, in his resurrection, in our redemption. It is to believe that men and women are saved in the deepest recesses of their loves and their fidelities, i.e., in what most profoundly defines them. The Christian message of salvation is most vitally important, specific and relevant in this sphere.

A Model for Us

While I cannot hope to offer, in these few pages, a comprehensive response to the dilemma of Christian "dual citizenship," the following observations are in order. First, Christians have been given, through divine revelation, a set of universal truths that reflect ultimate reality in regard to God, human nature and the essence of the physical universe. Second, because these truths reflect ultimate reality, Christians believe they will ultimately promote life in cultures that adopt them. Third, the community of faith must and should seek the welfare of those around it, not only to ensure its own survival but as an expression of God's love for all human beings.

According to Dumont's model, Christian interaction with the world can occur at three different levels. In the "upper story," the Christian scholar attempts to discover the coherence of the world for its own sake. In that respect, he or she is no different from the non-Christian scientist. Both pursue the same goal and use the same methods. It is interesting to note that the believer and the atheist, the Christian and the non-Christian pursue their profession in the context of a Judeo-Christian cosmological framework that assumes that the universe is an object of investigation and that this object has intrinsic coherence.

On the "main floor," Christians and non-Christians alike pursue objectives that go beyond the mere search for coherence. At this level, human action aims at something deeper and more fundamental: the improvement of human life. Cancer researchers, for instance, do not simply seek the most efficient way to destroy cancer cells; they ultimately seek a cure for a disease that destroys real persons.

In the "basement," there is, however, an area of endeavor that is unique to the Christian. This is what Dumont calls the *mal fondamental*. There is a critical and terminal sickness in the deepest recesses of the human soul, a cancer of the soul. The Bible refers to it as Sin, a fundamental flaw brought about by a primordial act of disobedience committed by the first humans. The cure for this cancer is infinitely beyond modern science, medicine, psychology, or sociology. The only cure for this condition is found in a personal, free and willing encounter with the person of Jesus Christ. The reason as to why Dumont states that this third sphere is specifically and exclusively the realm of the Christian is tied to the fact that the diagnosis of the alleged disease and its cure are derived from special revelation, the biblical text, and not from nature. It is a confessional affirmation and not something that can be verified either through philosophy or empirical science.

The evangelistic and mission enterprise belongs most appropriately and relevantly to this third sphere. This is where individual Christians, churches and para-church organizations operate. It is an exercise in telling the Good News of friendship with God, ultimate healing and eternal salvation. The act of evangelism is by definition a-political. It is non-coercive. One cannot enact laws to force men and women to accept the Gospel. Because choosing to love God and to accept the lordship of Jesus Christ is the greatest act of self-determination, one cannot therefore, by definition, legislate that act; one cannot dictate people into the Kingdom. The evangelistic or missiological enterprise belongs to the realm of loving, even if urgent, persuasion, as when Paul writes: "We implore you on Christ's behalf: Be reconciled to God" (2 Cor 5:20).

The responsibility of sharing the Good News with those around us is clearly an implication of our status as citizens of heaven. It is something Christians must be actively engaged in whether the State approves of it or not. In cases where the State's injunctions conflict with this demand of the Kingdom, our allegiance to the Kingdom of God must supersede our allegiance to the earthly one.

Where Christians most sharply differ is on the character of their intervention in the second sphere of human action: the social sphere (the "main floor"). First, we have a responsibility, both as citizens and

The Challenge of Dual Citizenship

Christians, to participate fully in that sphere of action. For Christians, this involvement may take various forms, and the issues that will be addressed may differ from one denomination to another. But regardless of the ideological differences that may exist between various groups, any action that seeks the improvement of real human beings should be welcomed. At this level, there is no intrinsic conflict between our two citizenships.

It is extremely important to be clear in regards to the legitimacy of Christian action at the second level. Christians may disagree with each other about ideology and strategies, but as long as there is no attempt to use political levers to impose allegiance to a particular religion, I would tend to say that the range of legitimacy is broad. If left-wing Mennonites wish to lobby against military action and US foreign policy, so be it. If conservative evangelicals wish to use their political clout to restrict access to abortion and lobby against same-sex marriage, why not? Morally, philosophically, and theologically, I do not see any problem whatsoever with aggressive political activism, as long as there is a clear distinction between that which is appropriate to the "main floor" and what is appropriate to the "basement." To suggest that the use of generally-accepted political and social levers to promote "Christian" values is tantamount to coercion, abuse of power, or a return to Constantinianism, is sheer nonsense. As "aliens" in the city and "dual citizens," it is both our mandate and responsibility to seek the good of everyone. This involves more than doing charity or taking up some social cause; it also, and perhaps even more importantly, implies the necessity to defend and uphold those values we consider best: for if we fail to promote truth, the foundation on which everything rests will slowly but inexorably erode, leaving in its wake a trail of untold suffering for generations to come.

While all Christians, regardless of religious or political persuasions, will subscribe to the necessity to do good around them, they will not necessarily agree on what constitutes the good, the degree of political activism they should engage in, and the methods that should be used. Some will identify with the liberal left and others with the conservative right. What is most desperately needed is not so much to question each other's right to act in society, but to accept, first of all, the fundamental legitimacy of defending and promoting values that Christians believe are best for our society and the legitimacy of using the most effective methods to do so.

The Church's Place in the World

The approach I advocate is not without its difficulties and its pitfalls, but nothing in this world is clean and risk-free. Every choice or non-choice we make impacts, for good or evil, the world in which we live. For that reason, Christians should enter into vigorous debate with each other on what constitutes the good and how it can be upheld in our world. It may be a naïve wish or an unrealistic aspiration, but it is a challenge that nevertheless deserves serious consideration – if not for our own sake, at least, for the sake of the generations to come.

NOTES

1. John Howard Yoder, *The Politics of Jesus* (Grand Rapids, MI: Eerdmans, 1972).

2. Leo Driedger and Donald B. Kraybill. *Mennonite Peacemaking: From Quietism to Activitism* (Waterloo ON: Herald Press, 1994). See also John H. Redekop, "Mennonites and Politics in Canada and the United States," *Journal of Mennonite Studies I* (1983), 79-105 and John H. Redekop., "Politics," in *The Mennonite Encyclopedia* (Scottdale, PA: Herald Press, 1990), 711-714.

3. George Jonas clearly and succinctly spells out the terms of that culture "war" in his article, "The Culture War's Elected Peacemakers," *National Post* (May 31, 2004).

4. See, for example, Ben C. Ollenburger and Gayle G. Koontz, eds. *A Mind Patient and Untamed: Assessing John Howard Yoder's Contributions to Theology, Ethics, and Peacemaking* (Telford, PA: Cascadia Publishing House, 2004).

5. *Standing Firm*, (n.d.), retrieved August 16, 2004, from http://peace.mennolink.org/articles/abortion.html.

6. All scripture references are taken from *the Holy Bible, New International Version*, Copyright 1973, 1978, 1984 International Bible Society.

7. Here it is important to note that the Ten Commandments are literally, the "ten words." These "ten words" are not given with the intent to make life difficult or to curb individual freedoms, which is what most people tend to associate with laws and commandments. The primary purpose of the Ten Commandments is to order life in the land in such a way as to create the conditions that will permit the continued enjoyment of the new freedom the people have received. Bottom line, the law is not primarily given to judge but to promote life.

8. This mission statement, lifted from a Burundi Christian community development organization, is typical: "Christian Community Development is a Christ-centered organisation [sic] with goals of assisting the poor and the needy of Burundi to know Jesus Christ as their personal Saviour and to overcome poverty" (CCD Burundi, (n.d.), retrieved August July 1, 2004, from http://ccdburundi.org.uk/.

9. See Fernand Dumont, "Après le système chrétien," in L'incroyance au Québec, ed. Gregory Baum, *Héritage et projet*, vol. 7 (Montreal : Fides, 1973), 221-227.

"Remember the days of old; consider the generations long past. Ask your father and he will tell you, your elders, and they will explain to you" (Deut 32:7).

"In the name of the Lord Jesus Christ, we command you, brothers, to keep away from every brother who is idle and does not live according to the teaching [tradition] you received from us" (2 Thes 3:6).

"Tradition, Tradition, Tradition"
(Tevye, in *Fiddler on the Roof*)

Rediscovering the Value of History and Tradition

Bruce L. Guenther

Among many denominations with Protestant and Anabaptist roots, the word "tradition" has accumulated numerous negative associations. The long-standing distrust and suspicion can be traced back to the origins of the sixteenth-century Protestant reformation during which the early reformers emphasized the supreme authority of scripture (*sola scriptura*) as antithetical to the accumulated traditions of the Roman Catholic Church. Tradition was a code-word representing the institutional and sacramental structures that were to be rejected in the attempt to re-establish the purity of the New Testament church; hence, a long history of anti-Catholicism began. Similarly, the early Mennonite Brethren leaders sought to distance themselves from some of the theological emphases and practices (traditions) of the larger Mennonite Church in Russia during the latter part of the nineteenth century.

In North America, where for many decades being part of a Mennonite church included identification with a Russian-German ethnicity, many church leaders came to resonate with the anguish of Tevye in the film *Fiddler on the Roof* as younger generations, who were exposed to a rapidly changing industrialized society, challenged traditional beliefs and practices and leaders witnessed the dissolution of a former way of life. In more recent years, the word tradition has been associated with those who are interested in preserving or reintroducing practices from the past; such individuals are often perceived as being resistant to change, as out-of-touch with contemporary reality, as obstacles to potential growth and progress who will hinder movement towards greater relevance in the future. It is not unusual to encounter such anti-tradition attitudes among seminary students and people within Mennonite Brethren congregations.

A number of scholarly debates concerning the place of tradition and our understanding of the past have recently emerged that have implications for denominational leadership as we enter the twenty-first century. Unfortunately, the ongoing force of accumulated negative associations for the word tradition (and the word history) continues to obscure the value of these debates and their implications for the theological reflection, identity and future direction of denominations with Protestant and Anabaptist roots. Without minimizing legitimate fears and hesitations about the role of tradition, in this short essay I will first introduce the work of several writers who have tried to offer a more nuanced approach towards tradition. This will be followed by a brief survey of three historiographical debates that have emerged during the past two decades of which denominational leaders should have some awareness. Implications of these debates for the Mennonite Brethren church will be included throughout.

The recovery of a more nuanced and wholesome understanding of the importance of tradition is partly due to the work of a growing number of evangelical scholars who have tried to integrate the study of patristics (early Christianity) into the theological reflection of contemporary evangelicals.[1] One of the more provocative contributions is *Retrieving the Tradition and Renewing Evangelicalism* by Daniel H. Williams, a Baptist pastor who, for a time, taught at a Roman Catholic university. He begins by expressing his concern over the growing ahistoricism among evangelical Protestants that has been exacerbated by an excessive concern for pragmatic techniques in ministry and the pursuit of futuristic fads (the heresy of contemporaneity). "While pastors have become more efficient administrators and keepers of the institution, along with being excellent performers, they are losing their ability to act as able interpreters of the historic faith."[2] This has created a condition of amnesia that both robs its victims of memories of the past and threatens their sense of identity.[3] This may be less acute among many Mennonite denominations that tend to be more conscious of their connection to a specific historical movement, but the close association of the Mennonite Brethren with evangelical Protestantism has made them vulnerable to the same tendencies.

Williams' central argument is that "if the aim of contemporary evangelicalism is to be doctrinally orthodox and exegetically faithful to scripture, it cannot be accomplished without recourse to and integration of the foundational Tradition of the early church."[4] He makes a vital distinction between Tradition (capital T), and traditions (small t), which I will follow throughout the remainder of this essay. The former refers to that which Jesus "handed over" to the apostles, and they to the churches; it is not something dead handed down, but rather something living being handed over (see 2 Thes 3:6, 1 Cor 11:23, 15:3, Rom 6:17). It is dynamic, both a noun and a verb; it is the movement by which the Christian faith has been "deposited, preserved and transmitted."[5]

> Tradition denotes the acceptance and the handing over of God's Word, Jesus Christ (*tradere Christum*), and how this took concrete forms in the apostles' preaching (*kerygma*), in the Christ-centered reading of the Old Testament, in the celebration of baptism and the Lord's Supper, and in the doxological, doctrinal, hymnological and creedal forms by which the declaration of the mystery of God Incarnate was revealed for our salvation. In both *act* and *substance*, the Tradition represents a living history which, throughout the earliest centuries, was constituted by the church and also constituted what was the true church.[6]

The doctrinal core of the Tradition eventually came to be known as the rule of faith (*depositum fidei*), which succinctly summarized the main points of apostolic teaching, and was universally accepted within the church by the third century. Tradition (capital T) is differentiated from traditions (small t), which refers to practices and doctrines put forward by the church that are not necessarily prescribed by scripture. Tradition must also be differentiated from traditionalism, which refers to the practice of making tradition itself an authority equal to, or greater than, scripture.[7]

Why Can't We Just Read the Bible?

Williams' work raises two of the historiographical issues I wish to highlight that have particular relevance for Mennonite Brethren. The first has to do with biblical hermeneutics. The denomination has always had a well-deserved reputation for being "people of the book," a group with a strong emphasis on the importance of the Bible. Like many Protestant theologians, Mennonite Brethren leaders claim to uphold the Reformation principle of *sola scriptura*, and understand it to mean that the Bible is the only normative source for Christian faith and practice. A close corollary to affirming the authority of scripture is identifying the essential role of the Holy Spirit in guiding a Christian's interpretation of scripture. Williams, however, suggests that the view that the interpretation of scripture must be guided *only* by the Holy Spirit is simplistic and wrong; it is tantamount to throwing out the baby (Tradition) with the bathwater (tradition), thereby obscuring the rightful place of Tradition in the interpretation of scripture. According to Williams, dividing scripture from Tradition creates an artificial distinction that would have been entirely foreign to the earliest Christians.[8] Scripture and Tradition are complementary and not intrinsically opposed. Tradition, based on the apostolic preaching, was prior to the development of the New Testament; the New Testament documents testify to the way in which Tradition operated in the earliest Christian communities. Moreover, he writes,

> . . . we must recognize that the Bible alone has never functioned as the sole means by which Christians are informed about their faith. It was never meant to. One cannot move simply from the Bible to the chief doctrines of the Christian faith without passing through those critical stages of development that link the past and present together and which make our present interpretation of the Bible intelligible.[9]

Early Christians understood well that one must go outside of the Bible and biblical terms in order to interpret them. The Arians, who represented a significant theological threat during the fourth century, defended their views with appeals to the New Testament documents. This highlighted the importance of using the rule of faith, or Tradition, for interpreting the Bible.

The assurance that it is enough simply to rely on the Holy Spirit's illumination of scripture when reading the Bible is naive and ignores the fact that no one reads scripture in a vacuum. To put it differently, it is not a question of whether a particular tradition or culture shapes our reading of the text, it is only a question of identifying which tradition! Without an intentional alignment with the interpretive Tradition of the early church, it is only a matter of time before other traditions and influences begin to grind the lens through which the Bible is read. Maintaining a clear sense of continuity between the Tradition of the early church and our denomination is an integral part of maintaining a Christian identity: it represents "a bond that defines the way of faithfulness throughout the passing ages of the world."[10] Vigilance in discerning the influences that shape our reading of scripture is particularly crucial amidst the diversity available within a pluralistic, post-modern North American milieu. One ought to be suspicious of those who claim to promote what they consider to be the self-evident meaning of a biblical text. Tradition (large T) serves as a hermeneutical anchor through the storms of cultural change.

Stephen R. Holmes (another Baptist minister who now teaches historical theology) reinforces Williams' work by building a more solid theological foundation for the inclusion of Tradition as an integral facet of biblical interpretation. He begins by acknowledging the pragmatic value of exploring how others in the past might have used the biblical texts, and by offering assurances that he is not endorsing the placement of any non-canonical texts as authoritative alongside scripture. Holmes relies first on the doctrine of creation "to develop a theology of the goodness of historical locatedness," and then posits an ecclesiological argument to suggest that a proper doctrine of the Church requires an acknowledgment of "both the communal nature of theology, and that that community is not limited to the living, but encompasses those who have gone before as well."[11] In short, one cannot claim unmediated access to the Scriptures without acknowledging the place of Tradition and tradition: theology is an irreducibly communal task. Highlighting the importance of community hermeneutics is not unfamiliar language for Mennonite Brethren; Holmes, however, helpfully extends the understanding of community hermeneutics beyond the present into the historical past.

The "Fall" of Constantinianism

A second historiographical debate that ought to be of interest to Mennonite Brethren leaders has to do with questions over the legitimacy of the "fall paradigm" of church history (also referred to as Constantinianism, restitutionism, or the Christendom model). According to this interpretative model of history, the true church of apostles and early martyrs lost its biblical character in the fourth century following the conversion of Constantine and the Christianization of the Roman empire. From this era emerged "an alien charter of faith (usually seen as the Roman Catholic Church, replete with its hierarchical priesthood, creeds and councils, holy days, sacraments, etc.)."[12] The model highlights a remnant of faithful and true believers, usually rejected by the Roman Catholic Church, that can be found in every age, but which bursts forth during the sixteenth century with a fuller restoration of biblical faith. The "true" church is considered essentially discontinuous with the corrupt hierarchy of Christendom. As heirs of an Anabaptist heritage, Mennonite groups have been vigorous proponents of such a view, thereby seeing themselves as among the latest heirs of an ancient, persecuted line of "true believers" that creates a kind of spiritual succession from the apostolic church.[13] The fall of the church has come to be regarded as an essential part of orthodox belief among many evangelicals, and has rarely been questioned by Mennonite Brethren historians.

The legitimacy of this fall paradigm, which has for centuries been an integral part of an Anabaptist theological orientation, is now being challenged from various sides. Historians such as Williams bemoan the way the paradigm has contributed to the ahistoricism within evangelical Protestantism by obscuring the continuity between the reformation movements in the sixteenth century and medieval Christianity.[14] The fall paradigm creates the false impression that Protestants and Anabaptist movements developed independently from the medieval church. The fall paradigm is built upon both a truncated ecclesiology (doctrine of the church) and pneumatology (doctrine of the Holy Spirit): it connects the Day of Pentecost (Acts 2) with the contemporary church, but minimizes the work of the Holy Spirit within the institutional church during the intervening centuries. The ongoing suspicion and even antagonism that continues to exist between some Protestants and Roman Catholics can still be attributed, in part, to the polarization inherent within the fall paradigm. Without denying or minimizing the significant theological differences that exist between Protestants and Roman Catholics, it is important to look beyond the walls created by the fall paradigm, put aside sectarian stereotypes and see that the Holy Spirit has indeed been active throughout history in other denominations. It is also time to affirm the necessity of healing fractured relationships, of greater inter-denominational cooperation, of sharing theological resources, and of building a united front in order to address our post-Christian culture with greater integrity and credibility.[15]

During the past two decades a growing number of Mennonite thinkers have begun moving into the area of systematic theology in an attempt to articulate a distinctly Mennonite theology. These Mennonite theologians are, however, deeply divided in their use and assessment of the fall paradigm.[16] The legitimacy of the model serves as the basis for the work of J. Denny Weaver, who pushes forward the implications of the fall paradigm. For example, he adamantly rejects the historical ecumenical creeds such as the Nicene and Chalcedonian Creeds, on the grounds that they are intrinsically linked to a growing ecclesiastical hierarchy that helped legitimate a major political power. The creedal expressions are, in short, hopelessly tainted by a corrupted religious system, that is, Constantinianism, and are therefore simply theological statements from a particular time and place that are not necessarily applicable to subsequent generations of Christians.[17] According to Weaver, the theological traditions of classic orthodoxy – specifically Nicene-Chalcedonian Christology and an Anselmian understanding of atonement – represent worthy conversation partners, but should not be considered as normative statements. Instead of building upon orthodox theology, which he argues originated in a fusion of church and society, Weaver, like John Howard Yoder before him, sets out to develop a theology that clearly distinguishes the church from the social order. Weaver's theological alternative identifies the way of peace and nonviolence as the central motif within a Believers' church ecclesiology. It is in the rejection of "violence that the reign of God made visible in Jesus is most distinct from the prevailing social order."[18]

Diametrically opposed to Weaver on the matter of Constantinianism is A. James Reimer, who builds a Mennonite theology on classic orthodoxy. He is not uncritical of Constantinianism, but instead of dismissing the claims of orthodox Christian theology, he rejects the unreserved alignment between the church and the political establishment.[19] Reimer argues that "Trinitarian orthodoxy cannot be equated with Constantinianism, but is in fact the best theological defense against all Constantinian-type political theologies (whether of the left, right or centre) that make political and ethical correctness the criterion for good theology."[20] He pushes Mennonites towards grounding an ethic of love not only in the Sermon on the Mount, but also in the reappropriation of classical Trinitarian thought.[21]

It is not difficult to see that the varied approaches of these two theologians raise important issues not the least of which are some fundamental questions about the nature of universal truth. The historiographical debate concerning the fall paradigm has implications for the place given to creeds, for the priority given to "peace" in theological and ethical systems, and for the perceptions and responses on the part of Mennonites to Christians in other traditions (especially the Roman Catholic Church). The position one takes in this debate will invariably shape one's understanding of the relationship between the church and culture in general – and the relationship between church and state in particular.[22] In the decade in which I have been Mennonite Brethren, I have frequently heard the claim that Mennonites are "non-creedal," and yet they have produced more "confessions" than any other Christian tradition; many of these confessions bear some remarkable similarities to the classical creeds. The historiographical debate concerning the fall paradigm needs to shape our understanding of how Mennonites have used confessions. Although Mennonite Brethren leaders have often expressed their methodological preference for " biblical" theology over "systematic," this foray into systematic theology on the part of other Mennonites should not be ignored.[23]

Recovering from the Demise of a Normative (Anabaptist) Vision

The final historiographical debate I wish to introduce looks more specifically at an understanding of the sixteenth-century Anabaptist tradition. A significant influence in the recovery of an Anabaptist identity for many Mennonites in North America during the mid-twentieth century was Harold S. Bender's short address, "The Anabaptist Vision."[24] He outlined three emphases that he considered to be characteristic of original and normative "evangelical Anabaptism:" discipleship, the church as a voluntary and separated brotherhood, and love and nonresistance in all relationships. Underlying Bender's historical interpretation of Anabaptism was the assumption that Anabaptism started in its purest form in 1525 in Switzerland and spread to other parts of Europe where, in some instances at least, minor offshoots deviated from the original expression. The Swiss Brethren served as the source and standard for authentic nonresistant Anabaptism. Bender's work did much to rescue the scholarly study of sixteenth-century Anabaptism from obscurity and historiographical prejudice. Moreover, it helped establish the Anabaptist-Mennonite tradition as a progressive movement that espoused the separation of church and state, freedom of religion, and a communal ecclesiology. Bender's "Anabaptist Vision" gave North American Mennonites a credible past on which to build a proud heritage; it simultaneously served as a kind of theological plumb line for determining what could legitimately be called Anabaptist and Mennonite.[25] Its influence was so widespread that, in the words of historian Paul Toews, it became the "identifying incantation for North American Mennonites."[26] The ubiquitous presence of Bender's understanding of the Anabaptist Vision illustrates well the way Mennonites in North America have used their understanding of the past to define their sense of identity in the present.

The appearance of James Stayer's *Anabaptists and the Sword* in 1972, and a lengthy essay in 1975 entitled, "From Monogenesis to Polygenesis: The Historical Discussion of Anabaptist Origins," signaled a scholarly coup d'etat that marked the end of the historiographical monopoly enjoyed by Bender's "monogenesis" model in North America,[27] and inaugurated in its place a "polygenesis" model.[28] These works, written by a group of social-cultural historians, highlighted the complexity and diversity of Anabaptist origins, ideas and experiences, and specifically called into question Bender's careless generalizations about nonresistance as a central feature of Anabaptism. Greater awareness of the theological diversity among sixteenth-century Anabaptists drew attention to the "confessional partisanship" by which previous Mennonite church historians had selectively endorsed those aspects of the sixteenth-century Anabaptist movement that they considered to be normative, and suppressed information that might challenge their intended version of events.

The seismic historiographical shift created by the polygenesis model not only raised obvious questions about the meaning of Anabaptism and the source(s) of Mennonite identity, but also prompted a more fundamental question: is it even possible to formulate an Anabaptist identity, and if so, on what basis? In the words of Rodney Sawatsky, "What is the hermeneutical key to determine normative Mennonitism?"[29] Many of the proponents of the polygenesis model were social historians who were more interested in the social, economic, religious and political aspects of the movement than they were in theological questions. After wrestling with the additional questions concerning the methodological relationship between history and theology, several Mennonite theologians and historians have tried to use the polygenesis model to work out a response to the questions highlighted above.

Among the more promising proposals is the work of Arnold Snyder.[30] He does not dispute the diversity described by the proponents of the polygenesis model; nor does he ignore or minimize their social and cultural observations. Instead of a focus on origins, he tries to produce a more comprehensive developmental paradigm that takes into account changes in subsequent generations. Instead of emphasizing only diversity and difference, he looks for theological commonality, arguing that the "differences only make sense when they are seen as emerging from a core of shared theological assumptions."[31] Snyder surveys the doctrinal views that the Anabaptists generally shared with other Christian groups (historical Christian doxa or teachings, as summarized in the ecumenical creeds and symbols), the views shared with other Evangelical/Protestant groups (rejection of sacramentalism, anti-clericalism, salvation by grace through faith, and the authority of scripture), and those views that were unique to Anabaptists (pneumatology, soteriology, anthropology, eschatology, and ecclesiology).[32] Snyder's work represents a "church-oriented historiography that believes a theological reading of history is a prerequisite for an adequate understanding of religious movements such as the Anabaptists."[33]

Although the polygenesis historiography has generated considerable discussion among historians and Mennonite theologians, its impact has generally not been felt among the majority of Mennonite church leaders and laity. Explanations for such a lack of awareness and influence vary: Gerald Biesecker-Mast suggests that the new historiography "made it very difficult for church historians to produce a credible narrative that was also accessible and inspiring to laypersons in Mennonite and Brethren churches in search of historical meaning."[34] Expressing a similar frustration is Arnold Snyder:

> It is my impression that polygenesis has been dealt with, in the North American Mennonite Church at least, more by a stubborn refusal to acknowledge its existence than by an effort to reflect upon, incorporate, and assimilate its disturbing findings. Most Mennonite pastors, and the vast majority of Mennonite church members, for example, appear not to be aware of the fact that their Anabaptist parents in the faith disagreed profoundly amongst themselves on crucial theological issues. Instinctively, it seems, we

prefer to imagine a pure past which had all the answers which we then try to emulate as best we can in our time and place.

Of course church history can be used much more easily when the past is idealized, and pure historical examples from a golden age can be held up in the present as models to be emulated. A Mennonite minister preaching a sermon on Peace Sunday, for example, would simply muddy the waters by attempting to explain to the congregation that, as a matter of fact, Anabaptists differed amongst themselves on matters of the sword. Perhaps the mythical image of an Anabaptist consensus concerning non-resistance, for example, has survived the onslaught of polygenesis historiography in Mennonite churches partly because Anabaptist non-resistance remains a useful rhetorical form that meets the prescriptive and sermonic needs of the Mennonite church. Polygenesis does not serve that function nearly so well.[35]

The reasons for the general lack of awareness concerning polygenesis historiography on the part of Mennonite church leaders and laity are likely more complex and numerous than outlined by Biesecker-Mast and Snyder. Nevertheless, their musings are helpful in understanding the lingering success of the less complicated monogenesis-based concept of a singular "Anabaptist Vision."

Several Mennonite groups, including the Mennonite Brethren, have quite intentionally adopted a dual "evangelical-Anabaptist" identity. Unfortunately, knowledge about sixteenth-century Anabaptism among many denominational leaders is often minimal at best; while perfunctory references to an Anabaptist heritage and vision continue, these references seldom reflect the nuances demanded by the polygenesis paradigm.[36] If Mennonite Brethren leaders are interested in giving credibility to their claim to be, among other things, Anabaptist, they will need to wrestle more substantively with the implications of polygenesis historiography.[37] In addition to giving direction and meaning to the internal discussions about an evangelical-Anabaptist identity, particularly in view of the theological diversity that exists within the denomination, a more careful consideration of a polygenesis historiography will also lay a foundation for a more constructive dialogue with other traditions that have descended from the Anabaptist movement.

NOTES

1. See for example Thomas C. Oden, *After Modernity . . . What? Agenda for Theology* (Grand Rapids: Zondervan, 1990); Christopher Hall, *Reading Scripture with the Church Fathers* (Downer's Grove: InterVarsity Press, 1998); Robert Webber, *Ancient-Future Faith: Rethinking Evangelicalism for a Postmodern World* (Grand Rapids: Baker Books, 1999); and the Renovaré series by Richard J. Foster, et al, which includes works such as *Spiritual Classics: Readings for Individuals and Groups on the Twelve Spiritual Disciplines* (San Francisco: Harper, 1993); *Streams of Living Water: Celebrating the Great Traditions of Christian Faith* (San Francisco: Harper, 1998); and *Devotional Classics: Readings for Individuals and Groups on the Twelve Spiritual Disciplines* (San Francisco: Harper, 2000). Note also the Ancient Christian Commentary on Scripture series being published by InterVarsity Press, and the numerous editions of English translations of patristic texts that have recently been published.

2. Daniel H. Williams, *Retrieving the Tradition and Renewing Evangelicalism: A Primer for Suspicious Protestants* (Grand Rapids: Eerdmans, 1999), 10. Williams echoes the earlier indictments made by Mark Noll, *The Scandal of the Evangelical Mind* (Grand Rapids: Eerdmans, 1994); and David Wells, *No Place for Truth, or Whatever Happened to Evangelical Theology?* (Grand Rapids: Eerdmans, 1999).

3. Williams is not alone in voicing such a concern: see for example Jacques Ellul who suggests that "amnesia" is a common condition among those who live in a modern, technological society (*The Technological Society* [New York: Knopf, 1964]).

4. Williams, *Retrieving the Tradition*, 13.

5. Williams, *Retrieving the Tradition*, 35.

6. Williams, *Retrieving the Tradition*, 35.

7. In order to emphasize the point, Jaroslav Pelikan contrasts the two in this way: "Tradition is the living faith of the dead. Traditionalism is the dead faith of the living" (*The Christian Tradition: A History of the Development of Doctrine* [Chicago: University of Chicago Press, 1971], 1:9).

8. D.H. Williams, "The Search for Sola Scriptura in the Early Church," *Interpretation* 52, No. 4 (October 1998): 354-367. Craig Allert makes a similar observation with reference to the sixteenth-century Protestant reformers ("What are We Trying to Conserve? Evangelicalism and Sola Scriptura," *Evangelical Quarterly* (forthcoming)). Both writers make it very clear that they are not questioning the sufficiency of scripture or the principle of *sola scriptura*; they are both trying to help a contemporary evangelical audience recognize the original

intent and limitations of the *sola scriptura* concept.

9. Williams, *Retrieving the Tradition*, 29. The same point is made by Jaroslav Pelikan, *The Vindication of Tradition* (New Haven: Yale University Press, 1984), 31.

10. Williams, *Retrieving the Tradition*, 206, 229-234.

11. Holmes, *Listening to the Past: The Place of Tradition in Theology* (Grand Rapids: Baker Book House, 2002), 5. Holmes does not make the same explicit distinction between Tradition and tradition.

12. Williams, *Retrieving the Tradition*, 102.

13. Menno Simons placed the beginning of the decline of the church "immediately after the demise of the apostles, or perhaps while they were still alive (*Complete Writings*, trans. Leonard Verduin [Scottdale: Herald Press, 1956], 279-280).

14. Williams, *Retrieving the Tradition*, 101-131. See also Daniel H. Williams, "Constantine, Nicea and the 'Fall' of the Church," in *Christian Origins: Theology, Rhetoric and Community*, eds. Lewis Ayres and Gareth Jones (New York: Routledge, 1998), 117-136.

15. Recent examples of constructive dialogues include "Evangelicals and Catholics Together: The Christian Mission in the Third Millennium" (1994); "Evangelicals and Catholics Together: The Gift of Salvation," *Christianity Today* (8 December 1997); and *Called Together to be Peacemakers: Report of the International Dialogue between the Catholic Church and Mennonite World Conference, 1998-2003* (Mennonite World Conference, 2004).

16. The debate was most visibly displayed in the pages of *Conrad Grebel Review* during the 1980s.

17. For a similar view see John Toews, *Jesus Christ the Convener of the Church* (Elkhart: Mennonite Church, 1989).

18. J. Denny Weaver, *Anabaptist Theology in Face of Postmodernity: A Proposal for the Third Millennium* (Telford, PA: Pandora Press, 2000), 27-28. The debate permeates Weaver's work: examples include "Mennonite Theological Self-Understanding: A Response to A. James Reimer," in *Mennonite Identity: Historical and Contemporary Perspectives,* eds. Calvin Wall Redekop and Samuel J. Steiner (New York: University Press of America), 39-62; "Christology in Historical Perspective," in *Jesus Christ and the Mission of the Church: Contemporary Anabaptist Perspectives*, ed. Erland Waltner (Newton, KS: Faith and Life Press, 1990); "Christus Victor, Ecclesiology, and Christology," *Mennonite Quarterly Review* 68, No. 3 (July 1994): 277-290; and *The Nonviolent Atonement* (Grand Rapids: Eerdmans, 2001).

Not surprisingly, one finds Weaver vigorously at odds with D.H. Williams (see especially "Nicaea, Womanist Theology and Anabaptist Particularity," in *Anabaptists and Postmodernity*, eds. Susan Biesecker-Mast and Gerald Biesecker-Mast [Telford, Pennsylvania: Pandora Press, 2000], 255-259).

19. "Christian Theology and the University: Methodological Issues Reconsidered," *Conrad Grebel Review* 9 (Fall 1991): 240-241. Other Mennonite thinkers who would agree that Mennonite theology needs to move within the mainstream of classical, orthodox Christianity include Ronald Sawatsky, Arnold Snyder, and Walter Klaassen. See also Craig A. Carter, *The Politics of the Cross: The Theology and Social Ethics of John Howard Yoder* (Grand Rapids: Brazos Press, 2001), 47-56.

20. "Trinitarian Orthodoxy, Constantinianism, and Radical Protestant Theology," in *Mennonites and Classical Theology: Dogmatic Foundations for Christian Ethics* (Kitchener: Pandora Press, 2001), 248. This essay was first published a decade earlier in *Faith to Creed: Ecumenical Perspective on the Affirmation of the Apostolic Faith in the Fourth Century*, ed. S. Mark Heim (Grand Rapids: Eerdmans, 1991), 129-161. See also "Doctrines: What are They, How Do They Function, and Why Do We Need Them?" *Conrad Grebel Review* 11, No. 1 (Winter 1993): 21-36; *The Dogmatic Imagination: The Dynamics of Christian Belief* (Herald Press, 2003); and Rachel Reesor, "A Mennonite Theological Response to a Canadian Context: A. James Reimer," *Mennonite Quarterly Review* 73, No. 3 (July 1999): 645-654.

21. Another Mennonite scholar who rejects the fall paradigm is Dennis D. Marten, "Nothing New Under the Sun? Mennonites and History?" *Conrad Grebel Review* 5, No. 1 (Winter 1987): 1-27.

22. It is worth noting that a response to "Constantinianism" continues to be the basis for popular theological works such as Stanley Hauerwas and William H. Willimon, *Resident Aliens: Life in the Christian Colony* (Nashville: Abingdon Press, 1989); Rodney Clapp, *A Peculiar People: The Church as Culture in a Post-Christian Society* (Downer's Grove: InterVarsity Press, 1996); and Darrell Guder, et al., *Missional Church: A Vision for the Sending of the Church in North America* (Grand Rapids: Eerdmans, 1998). These authors argue that the trajectory of Constantinanism, that is the alignment of the church with the interests of the state, continues in North America even through some of the very denominations that were part of the sixteenth-century reformation. They are optimistic about the way a pluralistic, postmodern culture has changed the church's relationship to the state thereby forcing the church in North America into a more pre-Constantinian, that is, Biblical posture.

23. The notion that Anabaptists relied only on biblical exegesis and Biblical theology, and not classical dogmatic theology is a myth (see "Introduction," in

Rediscovering the Value of History and Tradition

Balthasar Hubmaier: Theologian of Anabaptism, eds. H. Wayne Pipkin and John H. Yoder [Scottdale: Herald Press, 1989], 15; and John D. Rempel, *The Lord's Supper in Anabaptism: A Study in the Theology of Balthasar Hubmaier, Pilgram Marpeck, and Dirk Philips* [Waterloo: Herald Press, 1993]).

24. "The Anabaptist Vision," *Church History* 13, No. 1 (1944): 3-24; and *Mennonite Quarterly Review* 18, No. 2 (1944): 67-88.

25. For a fuller discussion of Bender's "Anabaptist Vision" see Albert Keim, *Harold S. Bender, 1897-1962* (Scottdale: Herald Press, 1998): 306-331; Albert Keim, "The Anabaptist Vision: The History of a New Paradigm," *Conrad Grebel Review* 12 (Fall 1994): 239-255; and Walter Klaassen, "'There were Giants on Earth in Those Days': *Harold S. Bender and the Anabaptist Vision*," Conrad Grebel Review 12 (Fall 1994): 239-255.

26. *Mennonites in American Society, 1930-1970: Modernity and the Persistence of Religious Community* (Scottdale: Herald Press, 1996), 241.

27. To be fair, there were scholarly voices in North America that occasionally disagreed with aspects of Bender's model (e.g., Robert Friedman, Hans J. Hillerbrand, John Oyer, and Walter Klaassen), but an alternative historiographical framework was not proposed until the 1970s.

28. James Stayer, *Anabaptists and the Sword* (Lawrence, KS: Coronado Press, 1972); and James Stayer, Werner Packull, and Klaus Deppermann, "From Monogenesis to Polygenesis: The Historical Discussion of Anabaptist Origins," *Mennonite Quarterly Review* 49, No. 2 (April 1975): 83-121. See also Werner O. Packull, "Some Reflections on the State of Anabaptist History: The Demise of a Normative Vision," *Studies in Religion* 8, No. 3 (1979): 313-323; James Stayer, "The Easy Demise of a Normative Vision of Anabaptism," in *Mennonite Identity*, 109-116; Werner O. Packull, "Between Paradigms: Anabaptist Studies at the Crossroads," *Conrad Grebel Review* 8 (Winter 1990): 1-22; Rodney Sawatsky, "The One and the Many: The Recovery of Mennonite Pluralism," in *Anabaptism Revisited*, ed. Walter Klaassen (Winnipeg: Herald Press, 1992), 141-154; and Rodney J. Sawatsky, "The Quest for a Mennonite Hermeneutic," *Conrad Grebel Review* 11, No. 1 (Winter 1993): 1-20.

29. Sawatsky, "The Quest for a Mennonite Hermeneutic," 3.

30. A notable alternative is the work of J. Denny Weaver who identifies several "regulative principles" as the basis for an Anabaptist identity and theology: Jesus as norm, the communal nature of the church, and the inherent peacefulness of the community of Jesus followers. These principles separate Mennonite theology from other Christian theologies (see "Mennonite Theological Self-Understanding," 52-61; and *Becoming Anabaptist: The Origins and Significance of Sixteenth-Century Anabaptism* [Scottdale: Herald Press, 1987], 121, 150). Another,

less extensive, theological proposal has been put forward by Levi Miller in "A Reconstruction of Evangelical Anabaptism," *Mennonite Quarterly Review*, 69, No. 3 (July 1995): 295-306. A less theological, and more sociological "taxonomic process" for identifying the "essence" of Anabaptism has been forwarded by Calvin Redekop, "The Community of Scholars and the Essence of Anabaptism," *Mennonite Quarterly Review* 68, No. 4 (October 1993): 429-450.

31. "Beyond Polygenesis: Recovering the Unity and Diversity of Anabaptist Theology," in *Essays in Anabaptist Theology*, ed. H. Wayne Pipkin (Elkhart: Institute of Mennonite Studies, 1994), 10.

32. *Anabaptist History and Theology: An Introduction* (Kitchener: Pandora Press, 1995), 83-99. Snyder's survey of Anabaptist theology is similar to Walter Klaassen's *Anabaptist: Neither Catholic nor Protestant* (Waterloo: Conrad Press, 1973).

33. A. James Reimer, "From Denominational Apologetics to Social History and Systematic Theology: Recent Developments in Early Anabaptist Studies," *Religious Studies Review* 29, No. 3 (July 2003): 238.

34. Gerald Biesecker-Mast, "Anabaptist Separation and Arguments Against the Sword in the Schleitheim Brotherly Union," *Mennonite Quarterly Review* 74, No. 3 (July 2000): 382.

35. Snyder, "Beyond Polygenesis," 6.

36. In working out their evangelical-Anabaptist identity, the Mennonite Brethren also need to give attention to the historical research surrounding the origins of the Mennonite Brethren in Russia during the nineteenth century. Discussions continue regarding the influences that gave rise to the movement.

37. It is ironic (and troubling) to hear pastors and denominational leaders occasionally caricature academics as ivory-tower recluses, dismissing their work as esoteric, too theoretical and irrelevant for practical church leadership and ministry. Yet, the same leaders are often largely ignorant (or at least belatedly aware) of the philosophical and cultural transitions and debates shaping their very sense of identity and self-understanding. The problem highlights the need for a greater degree of mutual respect, and a closer working relationship between denominational leaders and academic scholars in the denomination who work in a wide variety of disciplines. The Mennonite Brethren in North America are fortunate to have a significant number of academic scholars in their pews, but this resource needs to be more intentionally utilized by denominational leaders.

Islands Of Hope
In a Time of Despair

Delores Friesen

Fourteen years ago, a midlife Sunday school class went to the mountains for their annual Sunday school retreat. After the evening session, a couple named Clarence and Martha came up to my room, and were soon pouring out their grief, sorrow and fears. Their youngest son, Loren, seemed to be developing full blown AIDS, but they had told no one, out of deference to his request to keep his illness a secret other than within the immediate family. Furthermore, they were not sure how supportive their church community would be and knew also that their business as funeral directors in a conservative, rural area could be negatively impacted.

At that time, little was known about HIV/AIDS, and many thought it was primarily a concern of the gay community. Some Christians went a step further, stating unequivocally that it was God's punishment for aberrant sexuality. However, despite the risk and pain of care giving, this couple wanted to be near their son and to make his last days as comfortable as possible. They also wanted and needed the love and support of their friends, church, and community.

But keeping Loren's sickness a secret would not be possible for long. When people asked them how Loren was, Clarence and Martha would speak about the fact that he had lost so much weight, and that maybe he had cancer; but they knew and I knew that it would not be good, or even possible, to hide the truth much longer. None of us knew how it would be received. But clearly I lived too far away to be a pastor or counselor to them. When I urged them to come up with someone they could tell before they left the retreat, their faces blanched, and I wondered if I had been too harsh or had rushed in where angels fear to tread. We all agreed it was probably the needed next step – but the questions of who, how, and when left us all exposed in the light of their honesty and confession and the reality of where society and the church were. Soon after, they shared Loren's condition with two couples from their Sunday school class, and later with the whole church.

The assistance of home health care workers and the loyal and ever increasing respect, love and care from their congregation helped Loren through nine long months of increasing disability and pain. Wearing clothing was painful. Standing was almost impossible with his weakened body. The emaciation of advanced AIDS was a shock to all who cared for him and visited him. But when the end came, the family and community were deeply aware that they were all on a journey of faith; and the shared struggle and letting go released them to minister to each other in new and deeper ways.

There was no question about where the funeral services and celebration of Loren's life would be. Pastor Gerbrandt arranged for the worship and welcomed Loren's friends to come. When one of Loren's gay friends wanted to play the organ for the funeral service, the pastor and worship committee agreed. "The crowd which gathered overflowed the 400 seat auditorium. Among those present were more than thirty of his gay friends, about half of whom had been diagnosed with the HIV virus. The family specifically invited them to join in a fellowship meal following the funeral. One member of this group said that of the "many AIDS-related funerals he had attended, this was the first that had left him with some hope."[1] Gay persons from outside the community intermingled with the rural Mennonite community, as they ate, reminisced, and told stories of Loren's life. Many of the guests were touched by the good news spoken both formally and informally by the congregation and the pastor. Some had never worshipped before in a Christian church, and they were touched by the way they were welcomed and received by the congregation. It was also the first time most of the congregation had ever knowingly worshipped together with gay persons. Not much was said or discussed about these barriers, but in the breaking of bread and grieving together, a community of care and compassion deepened.

Meanwhile, at MB Biblical Seminary in Fresno, Calofirnia, Loren's story came to life for the human sexuality class as Clarence and Martha came to tell about their experience, and to share what kinds of counseling and pastoral care a family needs when they walk through this kind of valley of the shadow of death. They made it clear that this disease is devastating to persons infected, as well as to a large circle of friends, family and communities that are *affected* by what the persons living with HIV and AIDS go through.

A Global Perspective

An opportunity to visit HIV/AIDS ministries and projects in Benin, Ghana, Botswana, Zimbabwe, Zambia, South Africa, Tanzania, Kenya, Uganda, and Ethiopia during my sabbatical in 2001 alerted me and the seminary to much more.

All these countries face staggering problems and crises because of the rapid spread of HIV/AIDS. The percentages of their infected populations vary from 3% to 45%. Infrastructures are crumbling under the weight of health care and the loss of the young adults who are their primary workers. "Recent food emergencies in that region have put 14.4 million people at risk of starvation, in part because 7 million agricultural workers have died from AIDS since 1985."[2] The ranks of professional persons, especially nurses and teachers, are also being decimated. Orphans and homeless street children are increasing at astronomical rates as parents die and grandparents and extended family, the traditional safety net, are often unable to care for orphaned relatives in addition to their own children.

One woman we met, for example, had six children of her own and seven children who were survivors of her two sisters' deaths from AIDS. She told us that her orphaned nieces and nephews could go to school because their school fees were waived by the government, but her children had to stay at home because she was struggling daily to find enough food to feed thirteen hungry children, and there was no money to send her children to school, now that she must care for them all. For this courageous woman – who serves the last of their meager two meals a day as late as possible in the evening, so that the children won't wake up crying in the night from hunger – there are few choices.[3]

This threat to life and health on our planet may well become the defining issue of our time.[4] As Nicolson says, "Every now and then something comes along which changes the way we think about everything...We cannot deal with AIDS without taking the spiritual dimension of life into account, and we cannot continue in a spirituality which leaves AIDS off the agenda."[5] Instead of lamenting and analyzing the disastrous loss of life and probable destabilization of the continent (and world) which may follow, this article asks us to consider and celebrate what God's people are doing. How are congregations and individuals responding with courage and compassion in the face of the HIV/AIDS pandemic? What path does faith take in the face of such disaster? What can the North American church learn from the church in Africa? Should every church have an HIV/AIDS response team? How might God want to shape us and our congregations to meet the challenges of the twenty-first century? What are some of the challenges or obstacles that need to be overcome and faced?

"If the church is not able to confess its faith in the eye of this storm, then it will have missed a part of its core calling in these times. On the other hand, if it is able to minister God's presence and to be a prophetic force for change, then it can be a significant part of the answer to the questions posed by the pandemic."[6]

Myths about HIV/AIDS

There are many myths about the HIV/AIDS pandemic that we need to address. Four of these are discussed briefly here.

Myth #1: Nothing Can Be Done; The Problem Is Too Big. The problem is indeed catastrophic. One of the tragedies of 9/11 is that it has so focused the world on the threat of terrorism that we are ignoring the far greater threat of HIV/AIDS. With the attention of the world focused on the Asian tsunami of December 2004 and terrorism, few people are aware of how the devastation caused by the HIV/AIDS pandemic continues to multiply. Yet the death toll from AIDS surpasses that of the tsunami *every single month*. Worldwide, over 1400 children die of AIDS *each day*. "Every year and a half, it claims more human lives than the holocaust, and with the pace accelerating, there will be a new holocaust every year. There is simply nothing left to compare it to, no scale of human suffering and devastation against which this terrible plague can possibly be measured."[7] "AIDS is not a future threat, it is destabilizing our entire planet right now and will have far worse consequences than any event a terrorist could ever invent."[8]

More than 17 million Africans have already died from AIDS and another 25 million are infected with the HIV virus, approximately 1.9 million of whom are children. Every day in Africa wave after wave

Islands of Hope in a Time of Despair

of tidal proportions sweeps across the continent. At its current rate of acceleration, by the year 2010, there will be more orphans in Africa than there are school children in the USA, and life expectancy rates will be half what they were only a decade earlier.[9] Demographic, economic, and governance regression may lead to social collapse. The rates and potential for spread in China, Former Soviet Union and Asia are even greater due to the large populations there.

Myth #2: HIV/AIDS Is A Gay Disease That Happens "Over There." HIV/AIDS is no longer just a "gay disease." It is happening everywhere. Women now make up around half the people living with HIV and globally, women and girls are becoming infected with HIV at a faster rate than men and boys. With over 1400 newborn babies being infected during childbirth or by their mothers' milk every single day in Africa, and women aged fifteen to twenty-four more than three times as likely to be infected as young men, the face of this global pandemic is clearly changing.[10] In many countries around the world, women and girls have little say over when, how, or with whom they have sex.[11] Women know less than men about how HIV/AIDS is transmitted and how to prevent infection, and what little they do know is often rendered useless by the discrimination and violence they face.[12] If the woman becomes pregnant then she may pass the virus on to her unborn child, and two persons are endangered. Some men mistakenly believe that HIV/AIDS can be cured by having sex with a very young girl, and South African newspapers describe girls as young as seven or eight being raped in hopes of a cure. Instead, the young girl becomes another person who is infected through no fault of her own. The vulnerability and lack of entitlement of women and the widespread evils of human trafficking need to be addressed.[13] The "rules and expectations" for male behaviors need to be rewritten so there are other ways of proving masculinity other than the conquest of women. Transforming relations between women and men at all levels of society is one way to change the rates and patterns of infection.

Even though the issues in Africa are somewhat different from those here, many are unaware that in the United States approximately 8,284 children, or 91 per cent of the total 9,074, became infected with HIV because their mothers were HIV-positive.[14] In New York City, HIV/AIDS is the leading cause of death for Hispanic children ages one to four years.[15]

Myth #3: HIV/AIDS Is A Punishment From God. Belinda Anne Maison, 1958-1991, who died of AIDS, wrote, "People still ask me, 'Do you think AIDS is a punishment from God?' I always say that I have no intention of trying to fathom the mind of God. Maybe we can look at AIDS as a test not for the people who are infected, but for the rest of us. I challenge you to consider the notion that AIDS can be less about dying than about choosing how to live. As we enter into this present moment, the thing I remain convinced about, more than any other thing, is that nothing can separate us, ever, from the love of God."[16]

When one walks into hospital corridors and orphan care facilities in Africa, such as the Mother Teresa Home in Ethiopia, and sees more than one hundred tiny babies and children in various stages of the HIV/AIDS infection, many of them dying, it is impossible to stand back and say "This is a punishment from God." Approximately thirty percent of the babies born to HIV-positive mothers will be HIV positive unless a brief, easy and cheap preventive therapy with antiretrovirals is provided.[17] For a few dollars, each mother and baby could be treated, but instead our drug companies' unwillingness to supply the drugs at cost, and our indifference and lack of compassion, continue to create a pathway for more heartache and inestimable loss of innocent lives.

Although some persons who contract AIDS may be reaping the consequences of their behaviors, another reason the pandemic has spun so quickly out of control in much of Africa is related to the poverty that exists due to drought, war, environmental and governance challenges. "When absolute poverty is so extreme that there is no material surplus above that needed for survival . . . people are degraded every day by undernourishment and by the immune suppression that comes with undernourishment."[18] This malnutrition leaves them exceedingly vulnerable to opportunistic diseases and infections. "A significant part of the world's population, perhaps 1-1.5 billion people are in a state of absolute poverty in which the poor are too poor to stay alive. Moreover, they are too poor to achieve economic development, falling into what economists in their formal models, call a poverty trap."[19] For many women, selling their bodies is the only way to feed their children. Poverty also increases the movement of populations, as they seek a means of survival. The ensuing chaos, social disruption, and economic uncertainty create more "perfect conditions" for the spread of diseases and family breakdowns.[20]

Islands of Hope in a Time of Despair

Myth #4: HIV/AIDS Is A Medical Problem; Science Needs to Find A Cure. Two factors that must not be forgotten are that HIV/AIDS is a 100% preventable disease, and there is no known cure. Although the improvement in combination drug therapies has been able to delay progression of the disease, improve immune function and reduce viral load, there is still no cure for HIV/AIDS.[21] The development of HIV vaccines still seems years away, and there is no guarantee they will be effective or within the reach of most of the world. Drugs now available do slow down progression of AIDS, reduce rates of infection, and add years to the lives of those under care. Activist campaigns to encourage the drug companies to make these life-saving antiretroviral drugs available at cost would go a long way towards resolving the orphan problem and slowing down the death rates among those infected.[22] Availability of treatment has a critical part to play in removing stigma, as it means AIDS no longer has to be seen as a death sentence.

However, education and behavioral change are still the primary ways to curtail HIV/AIDS.[23] Prevention and treatment programs work best when interventions are scaled up to reach whole societies and are developed inside the country, rather than imposed from outside. Strong engagement by people living with and affected by HIV is needed. One such program is testing for the presence of HIV: this seems to be one of the best ways to increase healthful behaviors of abstinence and safe sex. Testing also leads to longer life and better opportunities for treatment and prevention. Those who discover they are free of the virus often use this as a motivation to change their lifestyle. Others who find they are HIV positive begin to take better care of their health, join support groups, and seek treatment.[24] Persuading people to be tested requires speaking openly about AIDS – a significant behavioral change in countries and persons given to denial and stigma.

The Role of the Church

Courage and compassion to face a pandemic are not found in the United Nations board rooms, in political rhetoric, or in massive grants of money from governments or Bill Gates, though all of these are needed and valued. Rather, each person's and each congregation's story provides opportunities to grow in compassion and courage.[25] "This pandemic is the acid test of our faithfulness to God's demand that we love our neighbor. How we respond to this plague answers the question of how much

207

value we place on human life."[26] "A crisis on this scale is a crisis for the whole of humanity. Every one of us is implicated in it, whether we like it or not. Everyone has played a part in creating the conditions in which the epidemic spreads. Everyone suffers as the human community loses so many of its young, creative, and productive members. Everyone is at risk of being infected, though the level of risk varies greatly. Everyone faces the questions raised by the onset of the pandemic about what it means to be human."[27]

Florence Ngobeni, counseling coordinator of a South African mother to child transmission prevention program, told us her story. "I can handle most days," she told us, "but when a man old enough to be my father or grandfather cries in my office because his five year old grandson, only child of his deceased daughter, has just been diagnosed with full blown AIDS, I need time to recover before I can go on." She told us of her own university days, the fast living, the unwed pregnancy, her baby who lived less than two years, and what it is like to live with the guilt of passing the HIV/AIDS virus to an unborn child. "In my despair over the death of my child, and my fears and illness, with the specter of death staring me in the face, I sought ways to come back to the faith and the church I had known as a child," she said. "I didn't need judgment and advice, I needed grace, acceptance and love. I already felt condemned and ashamed. I knew what I had done was wrong, and though I too had been a victim of abuse, and had been taken advantage of sexually in my home and by my boyfriends, my innocent child had not had a choice. When I recovered my faith and reconciled with my family, my health improved and I went back to school to become a counselor. Now I am doing all I can to help others who face similar futures of disease, loss, and death."

Instead of being known as an institution that disciplines for sexual sins of unwed pregnancy or promiscuity, the church needs ". . . to be a space to which people come to find forgiveness for their sins and healing for their wounds. Speaking up about HIV and AIDS needs to become part of the vocabulary of the church. Then its worship and witness will signal that those infected or affected by the epidemic are affirmed, accepted, and embraced rather than being judged and excluded."[28] For starters, the whole area of sexual health and fulfillment should be included in congregational worship and education.

The church has traditionally seen its role as caring for the sick and burying the dying. This pandemic begs the church to become involved in advocacy and justice and work with educational, government and social agencies. When there is complicity in silence – not naming the cause of death, for example, or never mentioning HIV/AIDS in our churches – then people do not feel safe to come for the help they need. Furthermore, why would a person get tested, if finding out one's status alienates him or her from family, friends and community or if there is no way to get access to treatment?

In Brazil, where antiretroviral drugs have been made available free of charge, people get tested so that they can be treated and thus extend their life. India has also been producing its own antiretroviral drugs, at a price of $140 per person per year compared to the $12,000 cost for the same drugs in the West. However, "India's government has issued rules that will effectively end the copycat industry for newer drugs. For the world's poor, this will be a double hit – cutting off the supply of affordable medicines and removing the generic competition that drives down the cost of brand-name drugs. . . These rules have little to do with free trade and more to do with the lobbying power of the American and European pharmaceutical industries."[29] Social action is needed to make HIV/AIDS testing, medication and treatments available. The church needs to once again find its voice.[30]

This disease has impacted those who have very few resources to address it. The United Nations Global Health Fund has received less than one third of what it requested from its member countries to fight AIDS, malaria, and tuberculosis, despite Stephen Lewis' description of the lack of funding for the fight against HIV/AIDS as "mass murder by complacency."[31] He became convinced of this after a group of people living with HIV/AIDS in Lusaka told him, "The HIV/AIDS crisis is not a crisis of lack of resources. It is a crisis of lack of conscience. It is the obscene gap between the haves and the have-nots that is driving this holocaust."[32] In many of the affected countries, the health budget per capita is only $10-$12, less than the co-pay many here give for a visit to a health care provider. Our elected officials need to be encouraged to give our full share to this worldwide global health fund. The international community needs to donate some of its great wealth: 25 billion dollars a year could save eight million lives annually.[33]

Furthermore, if countries were liberated from their debts, that money could be used for desperately-needed basic health and educational services. The health infrastructures of many countries need resources and shoring up to provide the needed support for the safe use of antiretroviral medications. We were at one mission hospital in Africa on the day that the last doctor left. This hospital served a wide region of rural villages and towns; it had been established and serviced by Christian missionaries for nearly fifty years. The wards were full of patients, eighty per cent of whom were suffering with AIDS, but there was no doctor and few medications to diagnose, treat or comfort. It is not enough to welcome and bless those who are infected with compassionate care, companion them on their journey to remain healthy as long as possible, and help them face their deaths with dignity and comfort. The church also has to break down the walls of shame, secrecy and stigma that exist in our society, communities and churches and speak out for justice and compassion so that health care, medication and prevention is available to all.

Islands of Hope

How can the church catch the vision of creating islands of hope which in turn create a paradigm for the rest of society? As Rev. Gideon Byamagushi, Anglican priest from Uganda, who himself is HIV-positive, said in a speech on AIDS, "When I meet my maker, instead of my asking God 'Why did you allow it?' I fear God will ask me, 'Why did you allow it?'"[34] Rev. Gideon and others who live with AIDS have asked us to refer to them as PLPWA, Persons living positively with AIDS. This disease that cannot be healed teaches us how to live in the present moment. It shows us how to serve each other in the moments that are given to us. Those who suffer need our help, but even more so we need what they can teach us. "In essence, many say, 'Maybe I don't have that many years to live but I have next week, next month and maybe the week and month after that to live. I have children, I have family, I have friends, I have hope for their future.' Hope remains an individual challenge."[35]

Kenneth Ross tells a moving story of Scottish visitors to Africa who encountered a 13-year-old girl who was solely responsible for her two younger brothers and had given up school to care for them. After the death of their parents, relatives had come and removed everything from the house, even the animals. When visited by a church member, who was moved to tears, the girl said: "Please don't cry for us, because you make us feel hopeless. Even without anything, the Lord is sustaining us. I have seen the hand of the Lord leading us." When asked how she manages, she responded: "God loves and leads us."[36] Ross concludes by saying, "Ultimately, a missiology of presence is about discovering God's presence in the midst of the epidemic."[37]

One of the best examples we saw was a Ugandan medical team of a nurse, chaplain, and driver who go out to the homes of AIDS patients, to administer simple medicines for symptom management and give pastoral care. After seeing Christine risk her own life to insert an IV line into the arm of an emaciated woman who was thrashing about due to high fever, delirium and dementia caused by AIDS, I wrote the following Haiku:

> Christine
> Kneeling at their feet
> A nurse whose patients all die
> She is Christ to them.

The needle could have so easily given a fatal prick to Christine or to the seminary student who, seeing the struggle in the dim light, knelt beside her to help hold the patient's wildly flailing arms. Their courage and compassion were more than a missiology of presence. That day we saw Christ in our midst.

Why Should We Care?

Part of the congregational task is to think and reflect; the other dimension is to be engaged in action. It takes courage and compassion to work in the midst of such a vast pandemic. We were often asked, "Why is the church in North America asleep?" Perhaps more reflection is needed to awaken us to the need to respond. According to Reverend Gideon Byamigushi of Kampala, Uganda, AIDS isn't just a disease. It is a symptom of something deeper which has gone wrong within the global family. It reveals our broken relationships between individuals, communities and nations. It exposes how we treat and support each other, and where we are silent. It shows us flaws in the way we educate each other, and the way we look at each other as communities, races, nations, classes, sexes, and between age groups. AIDS insists that it is time for us to sit down and address all the things we have been quiet about: sexuality, poverty, and the way we handle our relationships from the family level to the global level.[38]

One simple but powerful suggestion is to place a red AIDS ribbon, the universal symbol for AIDS, around the cross in our homes and churches, symbolizing that only through Christ's power, grace, forgiveness, and love can we face the HIV/AIDS pandemic. This also reminds us that we all are in need of Christ's love and forgiveness. As Dr. David Kuhl, palliative care physician, says it, "We all have to come to the foot of the cross in the same way, regardless of whether we have AIDS or not."[39]

The pamphlet goes on to say, "the AIDS crisis is a challenge to the church to model the character of Christ. It is heartening that many Christians today no longer ask why certain people get AIDS but, rather, what God is calling the church to do to help."[40] They suggest that some ways that the church can respond include giving unconditional love, advocating for people with AIDS, offering our distinctive perspective about AIDS to society, giving spiritual direction, assisting families of persons with AIDS, and looking for volunteer opportunities. Government, education and treatment also have major roles to play in creating islands of hope.[41]

Practical Ideas for Congregations

Twelve years after the retreat, the same Mennonite Brethren congregation invited us to come and share about AIDS in Africa. Although their current pastor was not present when the congregation first opened its heart to the family struggling with HIV/AIDS, he regularly addresses AIDS as a crisis that requires a response. One year the congregation raised enough funds to provide approximately 100 relief kits for Mennonite Central Committee.[42] One of their members, who was about ten years old when Loren died from AIDS, is now working with AIDS projects in Botswana. Both he and his congregation have had a life-changing experience.

In Africa, many people courageously offer those dying of AIDS palliative and spiritual care despite a paucity of supplies, including the gloves necessary for protection against infection. African pastors spend much of their time holding funerals and ministering to the bereaved. If every church in the world had an HIV/AIDS response team and responsive leadership, it would go a long way towards bringing the presence and light of Christ into the darkness and despair of this pandemic.

- HIV/AIDS response teams could educate and motivate their congregations to share resources more freely with those in need and make sure that prevention and awareness are a part of every member's commitment.

- World AIDS Sunday worship, liturgy, and mission projects would help awaken and inspire response.
- All Christians could join the African American churches' call to a week of prayer in February for persons with HIV/AIDS.
- Every Christian family could "adopt" a global family that is affected by HIV/AIDS.[43]
- Each Sunday school child could provide school fees for a child of a similar age.[44]
- Teachers and business persons could address the economic and educational challenges. Fostering income-generating projects is an essential strategy.
- Christian universities, seminaries, Bible schools and pastors can inspire and lead a new generation of ministers, missionaries, and volunteers to take up the challenges and opportunities of ministry and evangelism that this pandemic presents.
- Everyone could be encouraged to relate to at least one person who is infected with or affected by HIV/AIDS. These kinds of personal contact evoke far-reaching changes in how the world and this pandemic are viewed.
- HIV/AIDS needs to be kept on our national and denominational agendas – we must lobby for HIV/AIDS decisions and donations that recognize the need for concerted efforts from government and all sectors of society.

Christians and churches in North America and around the world need to be awakened to the tremendous human need and opportunities presented by this pandemic.[45] Our faith in Christ calls us to compassion. We can offer both hope and care by breaking through the denial, ignorance and selfishness that lead to a judgmental or uninformed response.[46] Our resources need to be mobilized and freely given. This pandemic does not have just one solution. It will require "masses of solutions." We must not look away. Nothing we can do will rid the world of this problem, but we must not allow it to destroy our humanity and the values that make life worth living.

May we, like Jesus, go through the towns and villages of our world, healing the sick, casting out demons, and preaching good news to the poor.

NOTES

1. Steve Bowers, "God Will Use This Somehow", *Sharing, Mennonite Mutual Aid* (Winter 1992), 6.

2. Susan Hunter, *Black Death: AIDS in Africa* (New York: Palgrave, 2003), 23.

3. Mennonite Central Committee has a Global Family Program, which assists such families with school fees, uniforms, books, and start-up costs for income generation projects or needed agricultural inputs. About $12.00 USD can provide school fees for one primary child. See www.mcc.org or call 1-800-563-4676.

4. Susan Hunter writes: "According to a recent study released by the Joint United Nations Program on HIV/AIDS and the Asian Development Bank, unless prevention efforts increase, 10 million people in Asia will be infected in the next six years. AIDS will force 5.6 million more people into poverty each year in Cambodia, India, Thailand, and Vietnam. China has only 200 AIDS doctors, and nearly a million people are infected. A vast majority of Asians never hear about AIDS prevention, HIV testing . . . or counseling. The spread of AIDS in Asia is accelerating so quickly that it will soon overtake growth of the disease in Africa. Over the next two decades, the containment of Asia's epidemics will be crucial to global stability because the region is home to 60 percent of the world's population." Susan Hunter, *AIDS In Asia: A Continent In Peril* (New York: Palgrave, 2005), from the dust jacket.

5. Ronald Nicolson, *God in AIDS* (London: SCM, 1996), 1

6. Kenneth R. Ross, "The HIV/AIDS Pandemic: What Is at Stake for Christian Mission?" *Missiology* XXXII, No. 3 (July 2004), 346.

7. Hunter, *Black Death*, 7.

8. Ibid., 7-8.

9. G. Nable in Hunter, *Black Death*, 22.

10. Source: www.data.org/whyafrica/issueaids.php (12/1/2004). Already as early as 1992, WHO was reporting that 90% of the one million persons who contracted HIV between April 1991 and January 1992 did so through heterosexual intercourse.

11. Ross, "The HIV/AIDS Pandemic," 342.

12. Source: http://gbgm-umc.org/health/wad04.

13. Hunter, *AIDS In Asia: A Continent in Peril*.

14. 2001 statistics: Centers for Disease Control & Prevention in Atlanta, Georgia.

15. Therese Rando, *Treatment of Complicated Mourning* (Champaign: Research Press, 1993), 633.

16. "HIV/AIDS: A Christian Response," British Columbia Mennonite Central Committee pamphlet, no date.

17. Hunter, *Black Death*, 24.

18. Kyle D. Kauffman and David L. Lindauer, Editors. *AIDS and South Africa: The Social Expression of a Pandemic* (New York: Palgrave Macmillan, 2004), 6.

19. Ibid., quoting Jeffrey Sachs.

20. "The disease is a pervasive security threat because it leads to growing poverty, food insecurity, economic and social collapse, deaths among the armed forces and police, increased criminal violence, and sudden power imbalances. In 1990, Kenneth Kaunda, then Zambian president, told a visiting U.S. Congressman that he did not know what he would do when the population of street children in that country's capital, Lusaka, reached 500,000 because the roaming bands of uneducated and unsocialized orphans would become uncontrollable." Hunter, *Black Death*, 22.

21. These highly active antiretroviral therapies (HAART) involve a complex protocol of drug dosing that is difficult to adhere to, and can result in drug toxicity and adverse side effects. HAART does not eradicate HIV from latent or silent reservoirs in various bodily tissues or organs, so it is not a cure, despite the fact that its availability has apparently influenced some people to again take risks.

22. The boycott of businesses and companies that invested in South Africa, such as Goodyear, Firestone, General Motors, Kodak, and TIAA/CREF was a big help in dismantling apartheid. Perhaps in much the same way, investments in drug companies could be withdrawn unless they are willing to decide to provide HIV/AIDS medications at minimal or no cost. At the very least, we must provide drugs like Nevirapine (which only costs about $4.00 per pregnant mother and child) and Zidovudine, since they can significantly reduce the incidence of mother-to-child transmission of HIV, if administered to HIV infected pregnant women before and during labor, and to the newborn for the first six weeks of life.

23. In Uganda, public education and prevention campaigns that were supported by the President cut infection rates from 14% of adults in the early 1990s to 5% in 2001. Senegal has a similar story: an active public campaign, person to person throughout the country, has helped them to maintain a 3% infection rate, which is unheard of in the rest of Africa. In Asia, Thailand has also had remarkable success in curbing the spread of HIV/AIDS. In an address at the XV

International AIDS Conference in Bangkok, 11 July, 2004, Secretary-General Kofi Annan states that their recipe for success was "a powerful combination: visionary political leadership at an early stage of the epidemic; allocation of serious resources; strong civil society involvement; along with massive campaigns for public awareness and condom use promotion."

24. If parents who are infected are kept alive through proper medical treatment, they can continue to care for their own children with the added love and wisdom that comes from knowing that your time on earth with your children is limited. If persons could test early and receive treatment, their life span could be increased by ten or possibly even twenty years, enough for many of them to see their children into adulthood. If those infected could stay alive, active, healthy and working, many of the other calamities that are predicted would be reduced or averted.

25. Narrative remains one of the most effective counseling, preaching and teaching tools. All of the stories in this chapter are true; however, some details and names have been changed.

26. Kenneth R. Ross, *Following Jesus and Fighting HIV/AIDS: A Call to Discipleship* (Edinburgh: St. Andre Press, 2002), 4.

27. Ross, "The HIV/AIDS Pandemic," 338.

28. Ibid., 345.

29. "India's Choice" editorial in *New York Times* Jan. 18, 2005.

30. Investments in drug companies could be withdrawn unless they are willing to provide HIV/AIDS medications at reasonable costs. At the very least the drugs that can significantly reduce the incidence of mother-to child transmission of HIV need to be made available. It is unacceptable to have innocent babies infected when the preventive medications cost only $4-6 per infant.

31. Stephen Lewis, "The Lack of Funding for HIV/AIDS is Mass Murder by Complacency" (New York: United Nations, press briefing, 2003)

32. Ibid.

33. Kauffman and Lindauer, *AIDS and South Africa*, 178.

34. Rev. Gideon Byamagushi, "Afterword", in *Gideon Mendel, A Broken Landscape: HIV & AIDS In Africa* (London: Network Photographers, 2001). Address given at Christian Connections in International Health Conference, June, 2001.

35. Kauffman and Lindauer, *AIDS and South Africa*, 177.

36. Ross, *Following Jesus and Fighting HIV/AIDS*, 41; Also in Ross, "The HIV/AIDS Pandemic," 346.

Islands of Hope in a Time of Despair

37. Ross, "The HIV/AIDS Pandemic," 346.

38. Kauffman & Lindauer, *AIDS and South Africa*, 128-129. See also, Byamigushi, "Afterword," 199.

39. "Christians and AIDS: A Call to Compassion" (Akron, PA: Mennonite Central Committee pamphlet, no date).

40. Ibid.

41. Uganda, a country that has had one of the highest rates of infection, has been able to reduce the rate of infection considerably. This turnaround is credited to the increased public awareness and the cooperation and dialogue between churches, government and NGOs. Uganda's Head of State has asked that HIV/AIDS be mentioned at every public gathering. The First Lady has openly campaigned for abstinence, faithfulness and compassionate care. Uganda has made it a priority to break the stigma and secrecy that surround those who are infected, acknowledge the presence and dangers of the virus, teach the importance of prevention and protection of those not yet infected, and care for those infected as well as for those affected by the trauma, illness and death of their loved ones. Churches in Uganda are openly working at all four of these agendas. In one service we attended, pastors read the names of all those who had died that week. Most of them were between the ages of 20 and 40. There were many names. In a group of persons living positively with HIV and AIDS, the opening ritual was naming all those who had died or were homebound since the last monthly meeting. Most of those attending were females, many of them with small children on their backs. In some cases both mother and baby were infected.

42. For details of what kinds of materials are needed, see www.mcc.org. or call 1-800-563-4676.

43. Mennonite Central Committee, Akron, PA, has such a program where a North American family sponsors a global family in Africa, Asia, or Central America. For about $260, an entire family can be helped to educate, feed and clothe their children, including those that have been orphaned due to AIDS. In some cases, it also makes it possible for them to establish a small home business or entrepreneurial endeavor.

44. About $12.00 (USD) can provide school fees for one primary child. For high school students, $100 (USD) will provide uniforms, books, and school fees. By giving up one latte a week, it would be possible to keep one African young person in school.

45. Contact the author at dfriesen@mbseminary.edu for "Questions for Theological and Ethical Dialogue Regarding HIV/AIDS" and other study materials, including a description of the "Time for Action!" conference held at MB

Biblical Seminary in 2002. The syllabus for an HIV/AIDS course is on the MB Biblical Seminary website, www.mbseminary.edu.

46. Desmond M.Tutu, Bishop Emeritus, from Capetown, SouthAfrica, has called HIV/AIDS "the new apartheid." He has said, "It is our new enemy. It is the latest threat to our society and to our humanity. To defeat HIV/AIDS requires the same spirit, the same commitment, the same passion – the same compassion – we summoned in the fight to end apartheid. And just as we realized in our battle against apartheid, we cannot do this alone. We need to summon our own will but we also need the support of the rest of the world." (Tutu, 2003, in *AIDS and South Africa*, p. xi Foreword).

CONTRIBUTORS

Mark D. Baker, Ph.D., is Associate Professor of Mission and Theology at MB Biblical Seminary's Fresno, California campus.

Raymond O. Bystrom, D.Min., is Associate Professor of Pastoral Ministries at MB Biblical Seminary's Fresno, California campus.

Rick Bartlett, D.Min. (candidate), directs the Ministry Quest program, which helps young people discern their call to ministry, and is Student Dean at MB Biblical Seminary's Fresno, California campus.

Chris William Erdman, D.Min., is Senior Pastor at University Presbyterian Church in Fresno, California and an adjunct professor at MB Biblical Seminary's Fresno, California campus.

Delores Friesen, Ph. D., is Associate Professor of Pastoral Counseling at MB Biblical Seminary's Fresno, California campus.

Timothy J. Geddert, Ph.D., is Professor of New Testament at MB Biblical Seminary's Fresno, California campus.

Pierre Gilbert, Ph.D., is Associate Dean and Associate Professor of Biblical Studies and Theology at MB Biblical Seminary's Winnipeg, Manitoba campus.

Bruce L. Guenther, Ph.D., is Associate Professor of Church History and Mennonite-Anabaptist Studies at MB Biblical Seminary's Langley, British Columbia campus.

Jim Holm, D.Min., is President of MB Biblical Seminary.

Jon M. Isaak, Ph.D., is Associate Professor of New Testament at MB Biblical Seminary's Fresno, California campus.

Valerie Rempel, Ph.D., is Assistant Professor of History and Theology at MB Biblical Seminary's Fresno, California campus.

Brad Thiessen is Public Relations Director for MB Biblical Seminary.

Jim Westgate, D.Min., is Associate Professor of Practical Studies at MB Biblical Seminary's Fresno, California campus.